SEOWON

The Architecture of Korea's Private Academies

Korean Culture Series 2

SEOWON

The Architecture of Korea's Private Academies

by
Lee Sang-hae

HOLLYM
Elizabeth, NJ·Seoul

SEOWON
The Architecture of Korea's Private Academies

Text Copyright © 2005 by The Korea Foundation

All rights reserved. No part of this book may be reproduced in any form, except for brief quotations for reviews or in scholarly essays and books, without the prior written permission of the publisher.

Planning, management, and financial support provided by

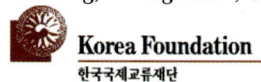

Translated by Sem Vemeersch, Ph.D.

First published in 2005
by Hollym International Corp.
18 Donald Place, Elizabeth, New Jersey 07208, U.S.A.
Phone: (908) 353-1655   Fax: (908) 353-0255
http://www.hollym.com

Published simultaneously in Korea
by Hollym Corporation; Publishers
13-13, Gwancheol-dong, Jongno-gu, Seoul 110-111, Korea
Phone: (82-2) 735-7551~4 Fax: (82-2) 730-5149, 8192
http://www.hollym.co.kr e-mail: info@hollym.co.kr

Hardcover edition ISBN: 1-56591-218-7
Paperback edition ISBN: 1-56591-219-5
Library of Congress Control Number: 2005931468

Printed in Korea

Contents

Foreword ... 1

1. What are *seowon*? ... 6
   Confucian society and private academies of the Joseon period
   1) Background to the emergence of private academies
   2) Function of the private academies
   3) Location of the private academies
   4) History of the private academies

2. Neo-Confucian worldview and *seowon* architecture ... 49
   1) Neo-Confucian worldview and the "Unity of Heaven and Man"
   2) "Unity of Heaven and Man" and the architecture of pavilions and academies

3. Architecture of private academies ... 65
   1) Spatial arrangement and location of buildings
   2) Main buildings and facilities of private academies
   3) Names of private academies and buildings: a reflection of Neo-Confucian ideas

4. Examples of *seowon* architecture ... 98
   1) Sosu seowon
   2) Dosan seowon
   3) Oksan seowon
   4) Namgye seowon
   5) Dodong seowon
   6) Donam seowon
   7) Piram seowon
   8) Byeongsan seowon

5. Hallmarks of *seowon* architecture ... 164

Map of *seowon* sites ... 168

References ... 169

Glossary ... 174

Index ... 184

Foreword

Seowon (private academies) are the crowning glory of Korean Neo-Confucianism, a cultural tradition originating in China but absorbed by Korean literati of the Joseon period and adopted as their ruling ideology. These literati, known as *sarim*, built *seowon* near murmuring brooks and imposing mountains, as retreats where they could steep their minds and bodies in the study and practice of Confucianism, and keep alive the tradition of previous Korean sages by enshrining them as objects of worship.

Amidst the *seowon* buildings, the *sarim* students and scholars could enjoy the cool breeze and moonlight while discussing their study without any constraints, but these buildings also served as schools to study the mandate of Heaven and the order of nature. The *seowon* was the place where the literati came to explore the origin and destiny of all things, and to understand the relationship between human nature and the principle of Heaven. Here they were inculcated with the notion that by constantly renewing one's own heart and mind, not only society but all other things could be reformed as well. They were not just academies of learning; instead of merely picking up knowledge, the students would absorb this knowledge as a catalyst for beauty and goodness, so that they could work to achieve goodness in themselves and in society. The *seowon* educational system imbibed them with a strong sense of justice and trained their spirits so that as officials they would not yield to injustice but face an honorable death or exile rather than relinquish their integrity.

In this sense the *seowon* express the mental universe and views on nature of the Joseon scholar-officials, but they also show how architecture can transform the surrounding landscape through an aesthetic of space and serve as important examples of traditional Korean architecture.

Most *seowon* are wonderful architectural spaces that are completely in tune with nature, that interpret and reinterpret the landscape surrounding them and are actually completely at one with the landscape. They have become an integral part of the natural environment, while this environment has also became part of the *seowon*, or at least one of its important features. This shows that architecture was conceived in relation to its emplacement, its environment.

Moreover, the simple, moderate life pursued by the *sarim* literati and their views on nature are well reflected by the *seowon* architecture. The simple and elegant building style, the management of the architectural space and the layout of the buildings, which are clearly ruled by an intention to embrace the surrounding natural environment and make it part of the Neo-Confucian conceptual universe, all testify to the *sarim*'s pursuit of a Neo-Confucian ideal. These architectural characteristics are based on a restrained and abstract sense of aesthetics, which is fundamentally different from the popular aspects and decorative exuberance of Buddhist temples. In sum, the *seowon* is nothing other than the physical expression of Neo-Confucian values, worldviews, and understanding of nature.

Historically, Korea has always been exposed to the influence of Chinese culture, but at the same time it has also managed to retain its own, distinct culture. Because the *topos*, the natural environment, is different from China's, the character of the Korean *sarim* was also different from that of the Chinese literati. *Seowon* are a good example of this. *Seowon* architecture blends a building style that is suitable to the mountainous Korean peninsula with a Neo-Confucian worldview. The spiritual world of the society that produced them is projected onto the *seowon*, which construct a small universe in which to train the minds and bodies of scholars, provide a place to indulge in nature and celebrate life, provide a framework where student and teacher share the same way of life, and form a spiritual center to reform local society.

I have done my best to produce a book that introduces *seowon* architecture not just to foreign students and scholars of Korean culture, but also to anyone interested in Korean culture, and provides them with a profound understanding of it. Great care has been taken to match the text and the accompanying photographs so that those who want to understand traditional Korean culture and architecture can get the maximum benefit. I hope that by providing a genuine picture of the function and role of Korean *seowon* architecture, readers can obtain a fresh awareness of Korean culture.

I would like to express my gratitude to the Korea Foundation for providing me with this opportunity to introduce Korean culture abroad. Special thanks are also due to the photographer Suh Jae-sik, for vividly capturing the mood of the many private academies. I am also grateful to the translator, Sem Vermeersch, for rendering a text riddled with obscure Neo-Confucian terms into readable English prose, a process which is almost like writing a completely new book. Finally, I would like to acknowledge the assistance of graduate students of the architectural history research team at Sungkyunkwan University, who have joined me on numerous research trips to Korean *seowon* over the past ten years, and many others who helped with compilation of the source materials.

Lee Sang-hae

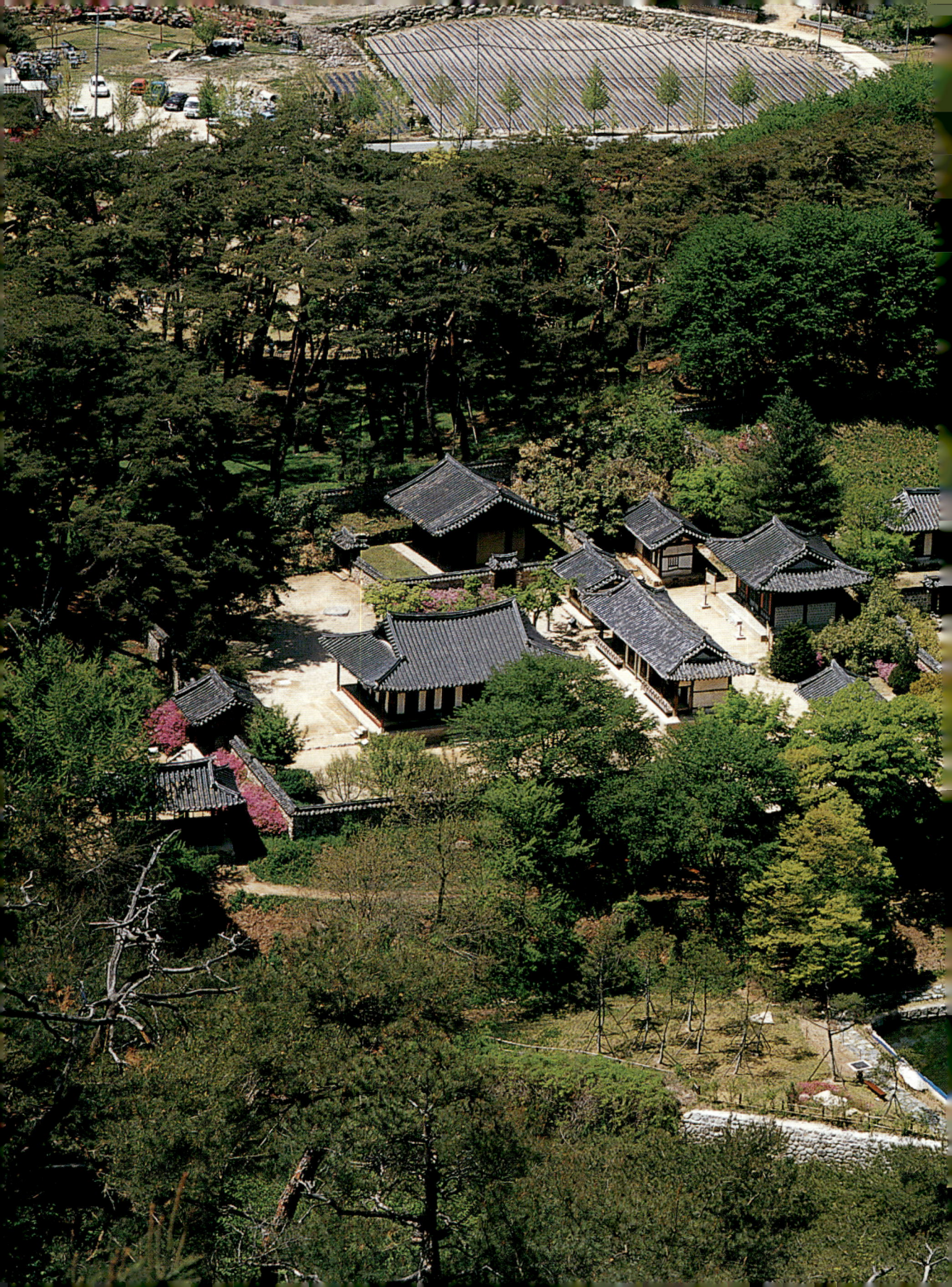

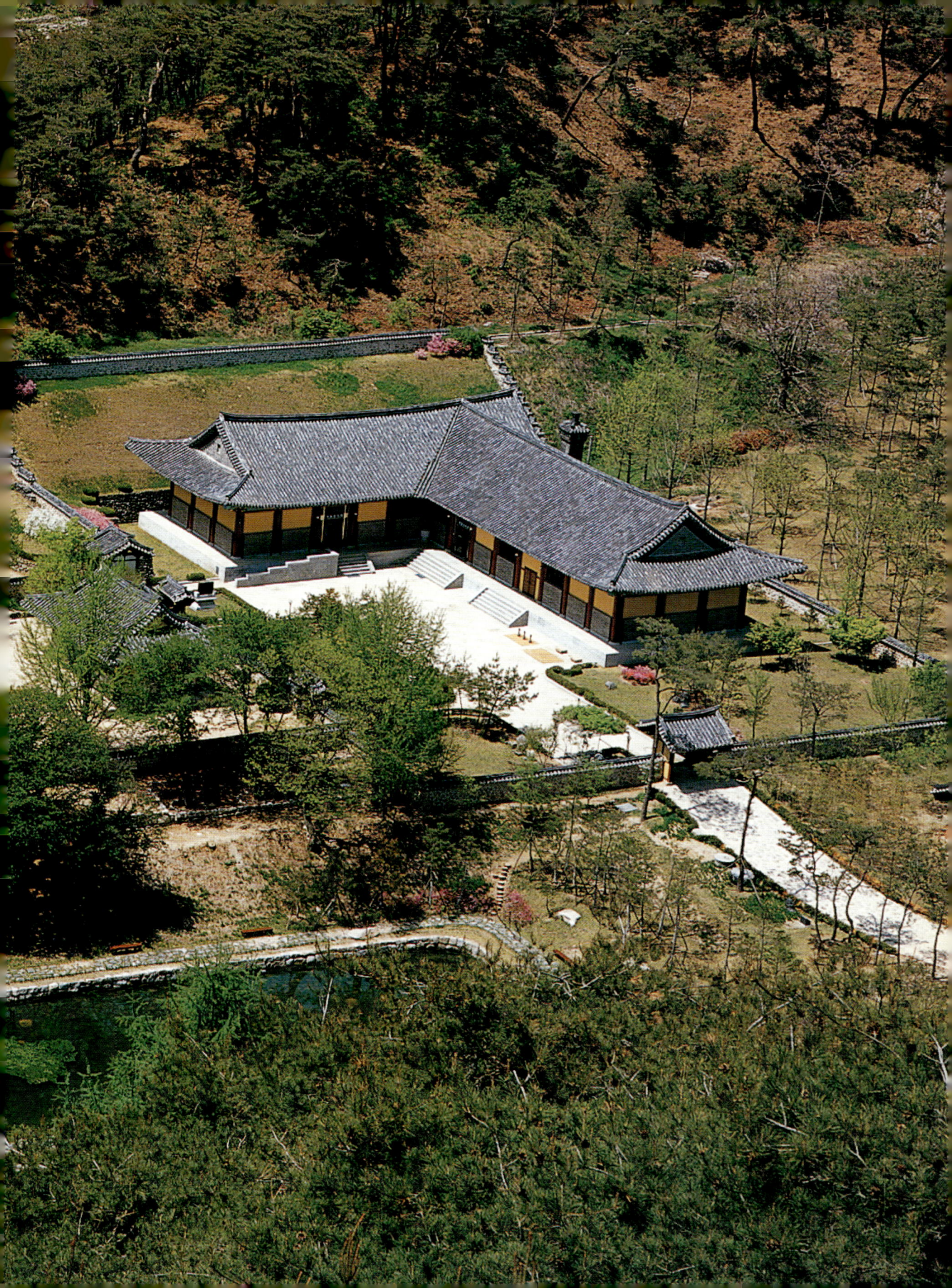

1. What are *seowon*?
   Confucian society and private academies of the Joseon period

1) Background to the emergence of private academies

In many respects the founding of the Joseon dynasty (1392-1910) marked the birth of a new society, which was very different in character from the preceding Goryeo era (918-1392). The new dynasty set out to do things differently in virtually all areas, from politics to economy, society, status ascription, religion, thought, and foreign relations. But its boldest move was to establish Neo-Confucianism as the ruling ideology, eschewing other ideologies such as Taoism and especially Buddhism, which had been the state religion of Goryeo.

Neo-Confucianism, a philosophy systematized into a coherent ideological system by Zhu Xi (1130-1200) of the Chinese Song dynasty (960-1279), provided a metaphysical explanation not just for the fundamental nature of the universe but also for human nature. Neo-Confucianism was adopted by the Mongol Yuan dynasty (1271-1368) after it had overthrown the Song, and it was at the Yuan court that Goryeo officials, who came from a country steeped in Buddhist culture, first absorbed Neo-Confucianism.

The Korean elites who made it the ruling ideology of Joseon envisaged Neo-Confucianism as a system for "cultivating the self and ruling others" (*sugi chiin*): the ruling elites of Joseon, who called themselves *sadaebu*, reasoned that they should perfect themselves morally first before they could consider themselves qualified to rule the people through moral persuasion. "Self-cultivation" encompassed both the perfection of human qualities and the study of texts, while "ruling others" meant to govern the people and serve the public. To realize the ideal of "cultivating the self and ruling others," also called "Learning of the Way" (*dohak*), the *sadaebu* started to build private academies in remote areas of the countryside from the mid-Joseon period onwards.

The private academies, known in Korean as *seowon*, were a new type of private educational institution established by a class of landed scholars known as *sarim*, members of a local elite steeped in Neo-Confucian values. They were self-governing institutions established to perform memorial rites for eminent Confucian scholars deemed worthy of emulation, individuals who displayed exemplary loyalty, and other deceased sages who attracted a following because of their spiritual achievement. They also provided an environment to study the work of

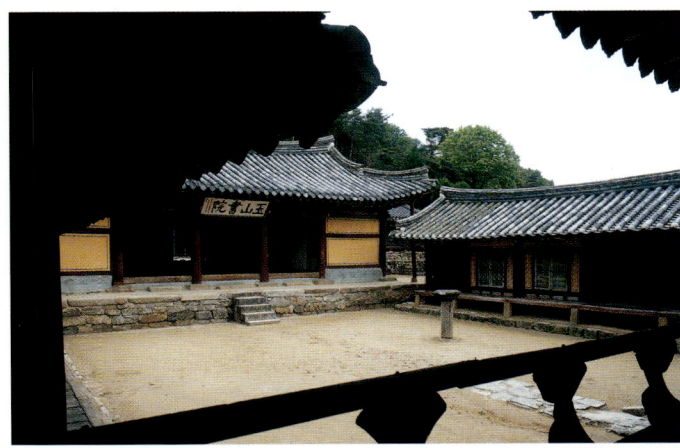

Study compound, Oksan seowon

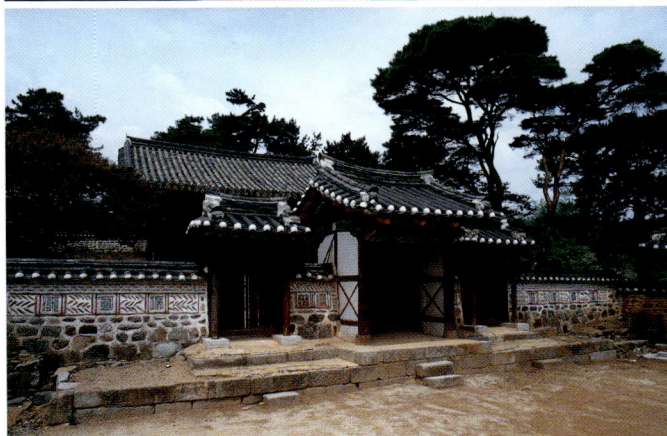

Shrine compound, Donam seowon

these sages, train disciples and spread Confucian moral values in local society. In order to fulfill these core functions, private academies invariably had lecturing facilities where study and instruction in Neo-Confucianism could take place, as well as a shrine where the spirit tablet of the sage was kept and rites performed. Only if both facilities, lecture hall and shrine, are present can we speak of a *seowon*. In cases where there is only a shrine, or only a building for instruction, we definitely cannot use the term *seowon*.

With respect to their dual function as shrines and places of learning, the private academies were very similar to the county schools (*hyanggyo*) established by the state. However, they do show some very important distinctions with these official seats of learning. First of all, the objects of veneration were not Confucius or his disciples as in the county schools, but former sages (*seonhyeon*) of Korea who were in some way or other connected to the private academy's locality; second, they were private rather than public institutions; third, they did not serve to prepare for the civil service examinations but as places for individual learning and cultivation; fourth, they were not located in or near county seats under the direct jurisdiction of the central government but in remote places of outstanding natural beauty.

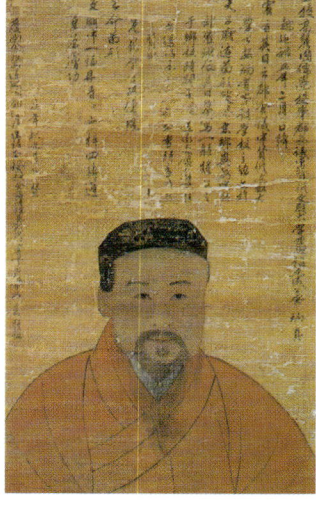

Portrait of An Hyang

The private academies of the Joseon dynasty trace their origin to Baegundong seowon. It was established in 1543 by Ju Se-bung (1495-1554), then serving as magistrate of Punggi county, as a school and shrine in honor of the late Goryeo Neo-Confucian scholar An Hyang (1243-1306) in the latter's hometown of Sunheung, Gyeongsang-do province. After the establishment of Baegundong seowon, further private academies came about when members of the local gentry came to the conclusion that an academy was needed to keep alive the scholarship of a local sage they esteemed, and petitioned the king to receive permission for establishing a private academy. Such chartered academies were private in the sense that they were founded mainly at the behest of local Neo-Confucian literati, though usually with the approval of local officials, but insofar as they received state funding, they also had an official cachet.

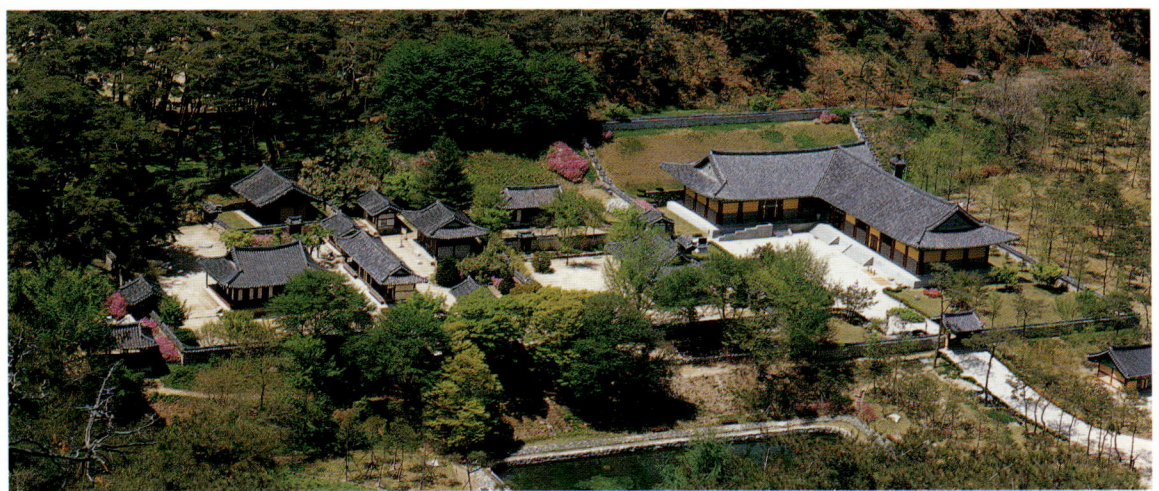

General view of Sosu seowon

From a historical perspective, the *seowon* phenomenon can be regarded as a typical product of mid-Joseon society, when the *sarim* had completely assimilated the Neo-Confucian outlook. After the founding of the Joseon dynasty, those members of the landed elite who had not joined the new dynastic project withdrew to their estates in the country, where they devoted themselves to fostering disciples and educating local people, mainly by instilling elementary Confucian morality. In other words, the *sarim* were members of a gentry class that was very influential in the communities where it was based. Having built themselves a strong power base in these local communities, the *sarim* moved into the central administration when King Seongjong (reign: 1469-1494) started recruiting talented people from local society. But as the *sarim* started carving out a place for themselves in the central administration, they came into conflict with the vested interests of those in power, the so-called "faction of the meritorious and conservative" (*hungupa*), who derived their positions from the hereditary privileges granted to their ancestors as a reward for assistance rendered to the dynasty. The *hungupa* started obstructing and suppressing the *sarim* and eliminated them from power during the first literati purge of 1498 (*Muo sahwa*), carried out under King Yeonsangun (r.1476-1506). With the restoration of King Jungjong (r.1506-1544) in 1506, a new generation of *sarim* moved into offices of power as the administration implemented the policies of the "Learning of the Way" and thus turned to Jo Gwang-jo (1482-1519) and other members of the *sarim* class. However, they met with another serious setback in 1519, when Jo Gwang-jo and many others were either purged or eliminated. As the *sarim* lost out to the conservative faction in the 1519 purge (*Gimyo sahwa*), they retreated to their provincial bases, where they built up an even firmer power base.

Even though the conservative faction carried the day, the momentum of the *sarim*'s rising force could not be stopped. Finally, towards the end of the 16th century they entered the central administration again and established themselves as a mainstream force in politics. From then on, whenever they moved into the central administration, they participated in government, and when they were driven from power they simply retreated to their local bases. It was during this process of power consolidation that the first private academy, Baegundong seowon, emerged in 1543, soon followed by numerous other academies across the country. The process of using the academies as nexuses to which local society gravitated was partly inspired by the similar function of Chinese academies of the Song period, but as they were ostensibly institutions of learning and education, opposing political forces found little pretext to restrain them.

The period that saw the rise of the private academies was in many senses one of transition. Politically, the *sarim* emerged as a new force to be reckoned with, and after clashing with the conservative faction in power, a struggle in which many were martyred, finally gained political power. Philosophically, this was the time when Neo-Confucianism reached its highest sophistication in the debates on the primacy of material force (*gi*) or principle (*i*), and thereby implanted itself firmly in Joseon society. The private academies were thus a product of the times, the result of political and social changes combined with the ascendancy of the *sarim*.

The majority of buildings constructed during the early Joseon dynasty were either palaces or other buildings used for administration, or shrines such as the Royal Ancestral Shrine (Jongmyo) or the Altar for the Earth and Grain Gods (Sajikdan), or else educational facilities such as the National Confucian Academy (Seonggyungwan) or the county schools. The private academies were thus a kind of institution that could emerge only after all these essential state-building structures had been established, after Neo-Confucianism had become firmly implanted and after the *sarim* had started their ascendancy in the political order.

The full-fledged emergence of the private academies can only be understood in view of the political and social structure of the time, as it was intimately connected with the establishment of *sarim* authority in local communities. Because of its importance in fostering talent and educating people, Neo-Confucianism was a core element of the official curriculum at the state schools, but at the same time it also provided the ideological basis that defined the true character of Joseon educational facilities and justified their existence. The county schools were the designated institutions for disseminating this official curriculum, but as the dynasty wore on they became insufficiently funded, making the instructors' posts sinecures. This led to a decline in the standard of the instructors, until finally students refused to attend the county schools anymore. There were other reasons for the decline in educational institutions: King Sejo's (r. 1455-1468) abolition of the Hall of Worthies (Jiphyeonjeon) and King Yeonsangun's deliberate neglect of the National Confucian Academy also played a role. As a result, the county schools gradually declined as they could no longer fulfill their educational role, and the literati instead started to run private schools (*seodang*) in their own residences. As this situation grew more and more common, and as the political and social climate proved suitable, the private academies started to appear. In other words, the emergence of the private academies can be seen as a way of overcoming the limitations of an educational system geared to disseminating an official curriculum, and also as a response to the needs of a society in search of new intellectual vigor and knowledge.

To sum up, the founding of private academies was first of all the logical culmination and combination of two trends that started in late Goryeo-early Joseon: the pursuit of individual learning and the establishment of private shrines. To this should be added the need to evade the pitfalls of political life in the wake of purges triggered by the social and political advance of the *sarim*, together with a desire for learning and a fervor to worship deceased sages. In the course of the early Joseon period, as the *sarim* gained more and more experience in learning and also increased in numbers, they started to transform the order of the local society where they lived; and when finally the institutions of national learning fell into decline, they stepped in to take over this educational role and established private academies in the name of educating the local people.

The landed scholars who were so instrumental in founding the academies were known as *sarim*, a term denoting scholars without office, who sustained themselves economically through small or medium-sized landholdings. During the Goryeo dynasty, this class of small and medium landowners fulfilled the role of village clerks (*hyangni*) and was excluded from positions in the central bureaucracy. However, in the turmoil of the late Goryeo period their status was elevated from village clerk to ranking official, a status which allowed them to join the central government. Moreover, from an intellectual perspective they were eager adherents of the new Neo-Confucian teachings. Although this class of literati with small and medium-sized landholdings was united in its aversion to the late Goryeo order, they were divided over the issue of deposing the Goryeo dynasty and establishing the new Joseon dynasty. Eventually, after the founding of Joseon, those scholars who had opposed the revolution established themselves in local society, where they immersed themselves in individual study and the cultivation of new generations of scholars to carry on their tradition of learning, eventually rising to the fore in the late 15th century. These were the landed scholars, the *sarim*. They were especially active in the Gyeongsang-do provinces, in the southeast of the Korean peninsula. From their strongholds in the provinces, these scholars called for political change, promoting their ideals of moral government and opposing the political monopoly of royal in-laws and merit subjects. Moving into seats of power during the reign of King Seongjong, they tried implementing this moral government, but the royal in-laws and merit subjects felt threatened by this rising force, and triggered the purges that led to the political alienation of the *sarim*. However, the purges failed to break the power of the *sarim*, who had dispersed all over the country, and who now retreated to local communities where they either continued their efforts to advance into central government to implement "moral government" (*dohak jeongchi*), or further strengthened their local power base.

In their strategy for achieving moral government, they promoted previous exemplars of moral learning (Learning of the Way, *dohak*) by calling for the establishment of shrines where they could be venerated. This was both an attempt at consolidating the spiritual and intellectual heritage of an illustrious lineage of Neo-Confucian scholars spanning from Jeong Mong-ju (1337-1392) to Gil Jae (1353-1419), Kim Suk-ja (1389-1456), Kim Jong-jik (1431-1492), Kim Goeng-pil (1454-1504) and Jo Gwang-jo (1482-1519), and a movement to prove the intellectual superiority of the *sarim* and strengthen their political position, all under the guise of educating people at the local level. After debating on what course of action to take to further their doctrines, the *sarim* settled on the idea of venerating famous scholars, and this trend was to prove a fundamental factor leading to the development of private academies.

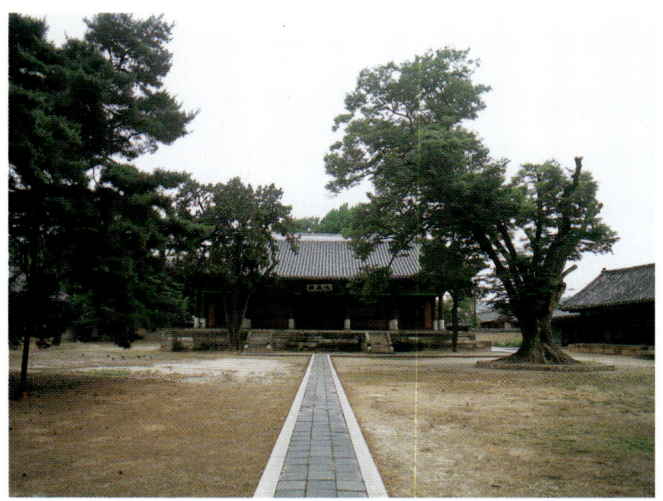

Daeseongjeon, Shrine for Confucius, Seoul

This development started with the induction of Jeong Mong-ju into the Confucian Shrine (Munmyo) in 1517, and culminated in the official recognition of Baegundong seowon, which, thanks to the efforts of Yi Hwang (pen name Toegye, 1501-1570; together with Yulgok Yi I, he is best known under his pen name, a convention followed here) was renamed Sosu seowon in 1550 and given a royal warrant. Building on this momentum, in 1554 Imgo seowon, dedicated to Jeong Mong-ju, was also given a royal warrant, followed in 1566 by Namgye seowon, dedicated to Jeong Yeo-chang (1450-1504). Soon after, private academies were being founded all across the country. And finally, in 1610, the official recognition of the veneration of Neo-Confucian exemplars peaked when five key figures of the *sarim* movement, the so-called five sages of Joseon (*Dongbang ohyeon*), namely Kim Goeng-pil, Jeong Yeo-chang, Jo Gwang-jo, Yi Eon-jeok (1491-1553), and Toegye were inducted into the Confucian Shrine.

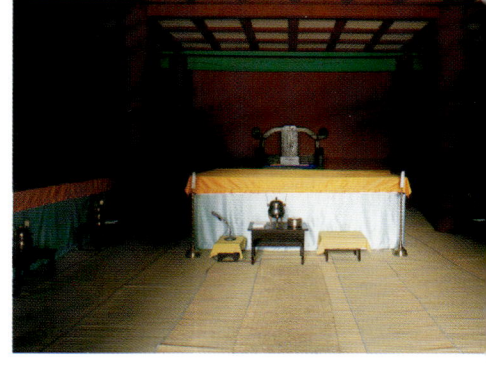

Confucius' spirit tablet inside the Shrine for Confucius, Seoul

While the pioneering private academies thus emerged during the reign of King Myeongjong (r. 1545-1567) in the mid-16th century, as the *sarim* movement entered mainstream politics during the reign of King Seonjo (r. 1567-1608) in the late 16th century, they became an established phenomenon. This momentum continued during the reigns of Kings Gwanghaegun (r. 1608-1623), Injo (r. 1623-1649) and Hyojong (r. 1649-1659), when the private academies spread across the country and grew into independent institutions free from the interference of local officials, while using the support of the central authorities and their economic means as a foothold to reshape Joseon society at the grassroots level. So if we look at the private academies from the perspective of Neo-Confucian politics of the Joseon period, they can be regarded as the product of the conflict between the conservative faction and the landed scholars. But from a broader perspective, they are also the historical products of the shift from Goryeo's Buddhist society to Joseon's Neo-Confucian society.

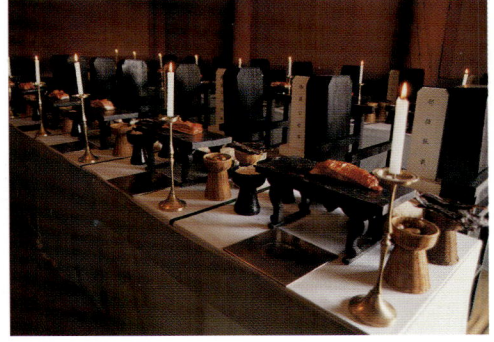

Subordinate spirit tablets inside the Shrine for Confucius, Seoul

2) Function of the *seowon*

(1) Educational role

The *seowon* were established as key instruments in supplanting the educational function of the National Confucian Academy and the county schools during the mid-Joseon period. Unlike the state schools, the academies respected the students' autonomy, and instead of the utilitarianism of preparing for the state examination, they offered the compromise of fostering a broadness of mind and training the students' character. Their education consisted of exploring Neo-Confucianism, the nature of the universe and man's inner mind through the study of the Four Books and Thirteen Classics. An additional outcome of this kind of education and study was that it deepened Korean Neo-Confucianism's indebtedness to Zhu Xi's outlook. Because education at the academies intended to embody the spirit of the *sarim* in the guise of "the way of the scholar-official," it was important for the academies to trace their intellectual lineage to a particular source, in the form of an exemplary scholar-official; thus all the early private academies adhered strictly to the "Learning of the Way" and consistently enshrined the spirit tablets of eminent Korean Neo-Confucian scholars.

Main wood-floored room of the lecture hall, Dosan seowon

Education at the academies was not a one-sided transmission of knowledge from teacher to student through lectures, but emphasized the autonomous learning of students. Through free debates and disquisitions on the classics carried out in their living quarters, students deepened their understanding of these classics. The learning progress of students was then assessed in seminar-style lectures.

During these seminars, held in the great room of the lecture hall, the students would go up to the teacher one by one and recite what they had learned, and were then questioned to make sure that they had interpreted the contents correctly. Instruction was not simply about rote-learning; grasping the meaning of the text was considered more important. If the student passed this seminar test, he proceeded to a higher level, so that education was always in accordance with the student's ability. Lectures were divided into three types: those held every ten days, those held

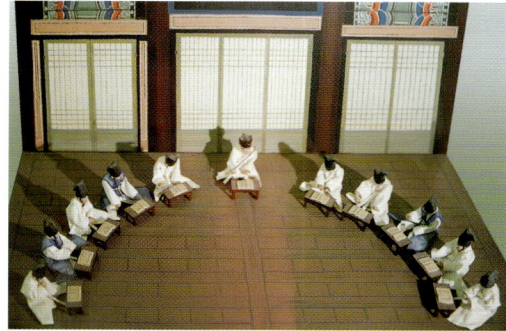

Lecture at Sosu seowon (scale model)

twice a month and finally the monthly lectures. Lectures were usually conducted according the following routine:

- On the lecture days, students on duty placed a desk in front of the teacher's seat.
- The teacher's seat was somewhat behind the middle of the great room of the lecture hall.
- The teaching staff sat on the left and right in front of the teacher, facing either west or east.
- The students sat in the front part of the great room.
- After the roll call of students, one student was called forward, bowed two times before the teacher and then kneeled in front of the teacher's desk.
- The student read the text handed to him and answered questions about it.
- The teacher then conferred with his staff, graded the student and the grade was recorded.
- The student bowed twice and returned to his seat.
- At the end of the lecture, the master of ceremonies came forward and announced that the lecture was over.
- When the teacher got up from his seat, all the students rose simultaneously and bowed twice toward the teacher.
- The teacher nodded in response, signaling the end of the lecture.

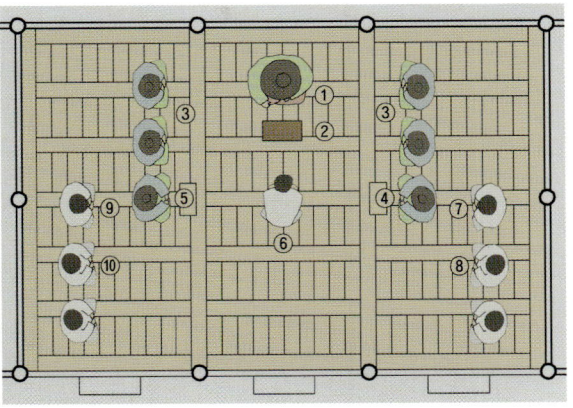

Seating arrangement during a lecture and seminar test held in the great room of the lecture hall

1. president or head instructor
2. teacher's desk
3. teaching staff or resident scholars
4. master of ceremonies
5. steward for the day
6. student on test
7. east dormitory inspector
8. east dormitory students
9. west dormitory inspector
10. west dormitory students

The lecture hall was thus a place where the Confucian ideal of academic training was pursued and where the teacher ensured the transmission of his scholarship by supervising the students' discussion of the classics.

After Confucianism became established as the basic reference point of political culture, the National Confucian Academy in Hanyang (present-day Seoul) became the country's central university, but in the provinces as well, talented people were selected and educated through a network of local county schools. These educational facilities were not only structurally very close to the Chinese system, in their shrines, they also venerated Confucius and his disciples and other Chinese sages. As the curriculum was moreover primarily geared towards preparing for the state examinations, there was no space for the establishment of regional schools of learning or the development of new philosophical trends.

The private academies of the Joseon period on the other hand actively conducted exchanges with other academies of a similar academic persuasion, thus forming solidarity networks and academic factions. They engaged in debates with private academies of other regions and different academic loyalties, a process in which each side's doctrinal position was further strengthened. The most representative of these schools were the Yeongnam school, which formed around the figure of Toegye, and the Giho school centering on Yi I (pen name Yulgok, 1536-1584).

(2) Ritual function

Together with their educational function, the academies also fulfilled a religious function as memorial shrines. Memorial rites were performed inside the academies' shrine. In this shrine (*sadang*), either the spirit tablet (*sinju*) or the portrait of a sage was enshrined, and sacrificial

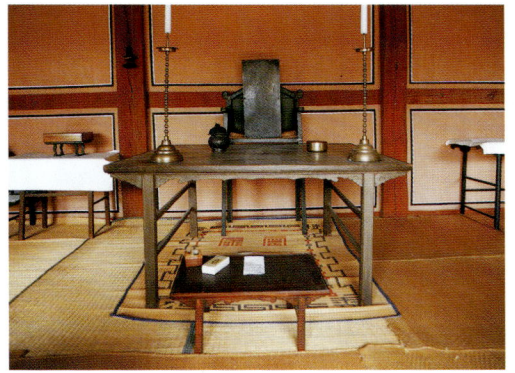

Inside of the shrine, Dosan seowon

rites were performed regularly. Thanks to the patronage and economic support of a state that put heavy emphasis on Confucian policies, the shrines at private academies assisted in transforming the customs and rituals of local society.

Two kinds of rituals were performed to the spirit of the deceased sage: the offering of incense (*bunhyang*), a simple ceremony performed on the first day and day of the full moon of every month, and the sacrificial food offering (*hyangsa*) during the spring and autumn. The sacrificial food offering was usually performed on the middle-*jeong* days (days were counted according to the 60-day cycle of Heavenly Stems and Earthly Branches; *jeong* is the fourth of the 10 Heavenly Stems, thus a *jeong* day is either the fourth, 14th or 24th) of the second and eighth lunar months or of the third and ninth lunar months. Nowadays some private academies perform the food offerings only once a year, either in spring or in autumn.

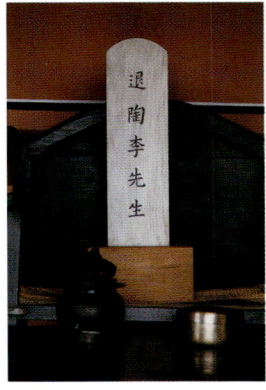

Spirit tablet of Toegye Yi Hwang inside the shrine of Dosan seowon

For the performance of the sacrificial food offering, the ritual officiants purify themselves three days in advance of the rite, so that their body is pure and their mind concentrated. In charge of the ritual proceedings, which are second in complexity only to those at the Confucian shrine, are the main officiants (*heongwan*) and the ceremonial attendants (*jipsa*). Around the time of the ritual, people wearing mourning garb or those without the correct ritual attire are barred from entering the academy's compound. Among the ritual officiants are the ceremonial attendants (*jipsa*), who are in charge of the rites; the hymnodist (*chanja*) who reads from the ceremonial tablet (*holgi*); the eulogist (*chukgwan*) who reads the eulogy (*chuk*); the master of the jar (*sajungwan*), who pours the wine; the attendants (*jipchanja*), who handle the food; the first wine offi-

Memorial rites at Dosan seowon

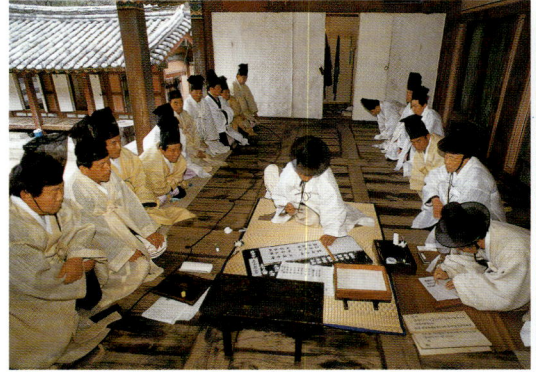 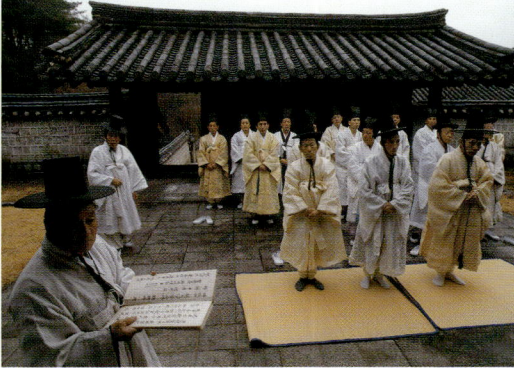

At Dosan seowon, memorial food offerings to Toegye take place twice a year, in the spring and autumn. The administrators who are to perform the ritual arrive at the academy three days before it starts. After paying their respects to each other with formal bows, they retire to the dormitory buildings. Two days before the ritual, they gather in the Jeongyodang lecture hall to discuss the division of tasks, such as who will be the wine officiant or the master of ceremonies, and the composition of the eulogy.

Early in the morning on the day before the ritual, the participating scholars go to the Sangdeoksa for the "coming to the shrine ceremony."

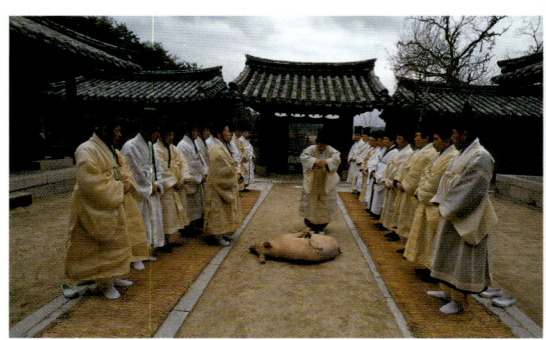 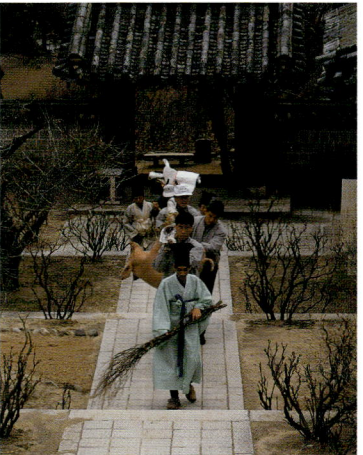

In the afternoon of the day before the ritual, the "ceremonial inspection of the offerings" is held in the yard in front of the lecture hall to assess the quality of the pig to be used in the offering. An administrator wearing a black hemp hood asks whether it is "adequate" (*chung*) to which the main officiant, who wears a horsehair hat, replies that it is "fat" (*dol*), i.e., sufficient for the offering.

Since only raw and unprocessed foods can be used for the offering, cabbage and radishes are used instead of kimchi. After dinner, the Confucian scholars who will perform the ritual go to the Yeoljeong well outside the main gate to draw water for washing the hulled millet and rice, which are rinsed nine times without being touched by hand. The hulled millet and rice are not cooked, but only roasted lightly without water.

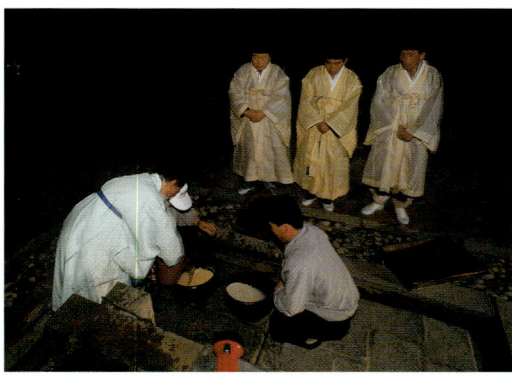 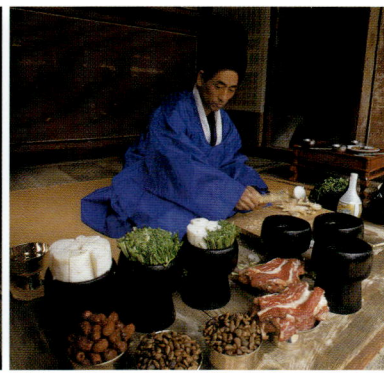

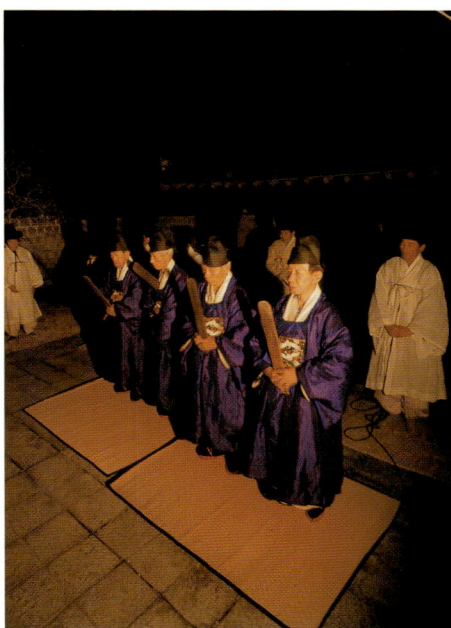
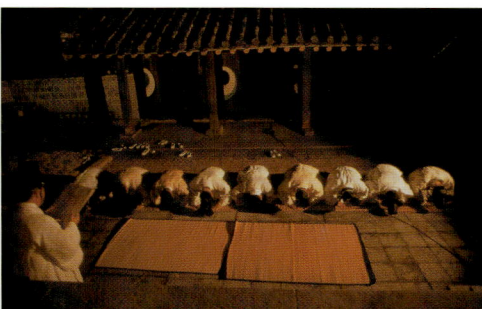
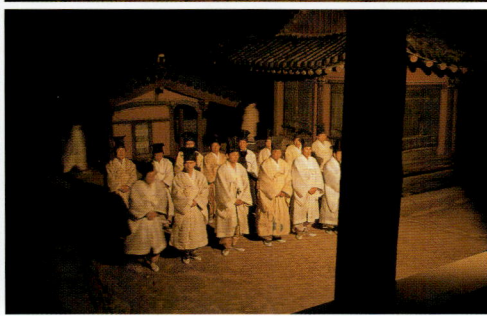

The memorial offering itself is held at two in the morning, the hour of the ox (*chuksi*) in the shrine and lasts for about an hour. All those participating in the ritual wear ceremonial dress, and the master of ceremonies reads the proceedings from the ceremonial tablet in a loud voice; the main officiant and the ceremonial attendants move in accordance with the instructions as they are read out.

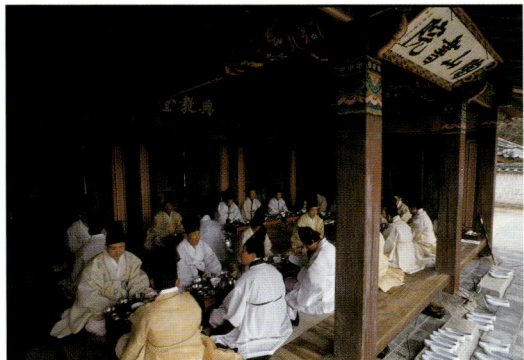
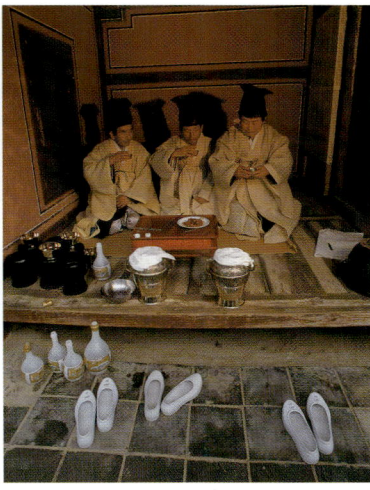

When the ritual offering is over, all the participants take part in the e*umbongnye*, in which they partake of the sacrificial food and drink.

ciant (*choheongwan*), who pours the first libation; the second wine officiant (*aheongwan*), who pours the second libation; and the third wine officiant (*jongheongwan*), who pours the final libation.

In the later Joseon period, as the educational importance of the academies started to decline, their ritual function became more and more prominent, eclipsing the other functions.

(3) Library function

As the academies were established primarily to further scholastic study, they also had to collect and store the books needed for study, which is why they also acted as libraries. This was made possible by the advanced technological level of paper-making and printing in the Joseon period, which ensured that books could be printed in large quantities.

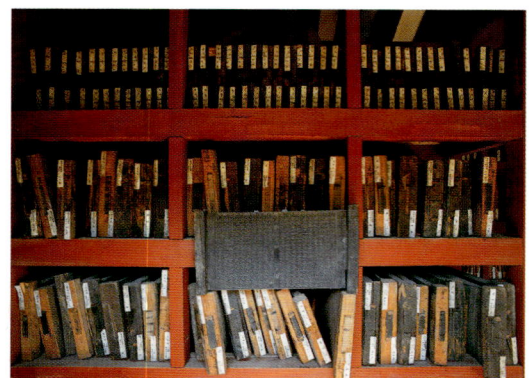

Wooden printing blocks, preserved in the printing-block storehouse of Wolbong seowon

Libraries were important to the private academies from the very beginning, as the first academy, Baegundong seowon, already had one. It came about when the founder, Ju Se-bung, sold 300 *geun* (one *geun* = 600 grams) of copper bowls that had been found during the construction of the academy and used the money to buy a collection of the classics, histories and works of philosophy as well as other Neo-Confucian works. After it was chartered and changed its name to Sosu seowon, it frequently received gifts of books from the state, but it also expanded its collection through purchases and through gifts of works published at other academies or by its former students, so that by 1600 it possessed 107 different titles in

1,678 fascicles (*gwon*, the smallest bound unit of a book and hence a traditional subdivision).

Not only did the academies act as libraries, they were also publishers in their own right, and as the center of publishing culture in their region they helped to enrich local culture and diffuse knowledge. The academies had a publishing workshop, which specialized in producing books used for education and the collected works of the sages revered at the academy. The books were distributed among other academies and former students and were also sent to the royal palace library and some state libraries.

According to the *Study of Publishing Activities (Nupan go)* compiled by Seo Yu-gu (1764-1845) in 1796, by that time 167 different books had been published by 78 different academies.

(4) Management and educational program

Although the academies effectively operated as educational institutions, there was no specific framework according to which matters such as scale and organizational structure, the differentiation between students, entrance requirements and curriculum could be accomplished.

Since education differs according to the students' goals and abilities, in accordance with the ideal of "obtaining an education through one's own efforts" (*jadeuk gyoyuk*) pursued in the orthodox Learning of the Way tradition, students proceeded autonomously in their education. Student life in the academies was theoretically regulated by the same official educational instructions (*hangnyeong*) that governed state schools, namely, the rules drawn up for Zhu Xi's Bailudong (White Deer Hollow) academy, or the academy's own set of rules, but these were implemented in a liberal manner.

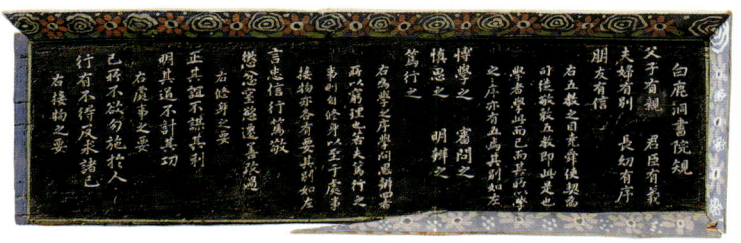

The Bailudong private academy rules

As for the curriculum, a typical example is that of Cheonggye seowon. The students read the following works in sequence: the *Elementary Learning* (*Sohak*), the *Great Learning* (*Daehak*), *Confucius' Analects* (*Noneo*), the work of *Mencius* (*Maengja*), the *Doctrine of* the *Mean* (*Jungyong*), the *Book of Odes* (*Sigyeong*), the *Book of Documents* (*Seogyeong*), and the *Spring and Autumn Annals* (*Chunchu*). On occasion, other parts from the canon, or passages from the histories and philosophic works, were read as needed.

As for the entrance requirements, if we look for example at the people who entered Sosu seowon, then we see that preference was given to Classics Licentiates (*saengwon*) and Literary Licentiates (*jinsa*), both passers of the second-stage civil examination, and those admitted to the National Confucian Academy, followed by those who had passed the preliminary examination (*samasi*). In some cases, with the approval of the Confucian scholars, the administrators could also admit people who had not passed any examinations but showed a great eagerness for learning and exemplary behavior. This shows that some academies did impose conditions for entrance, but in other cases, notably that of Museong seowon and Isan seowon, it was decided that anyone with a strong interest in study could be admitted, regardless of his age or social status. In general, to become a *seowon* student, one had to present strong academic credentials, so that the majority of students belonged to the scholar-official class and were in their twenties and even thirties.

Initially the Sosu academy adopted a quota of about ten students, and most other academies had a similar student intake, but as time went by this quota gradually increased until a student population of about 30 became the norm. During the reign of King Sukjong (r. 1674-1720), chartered academies had about 20 students, while academies dedicated to sages inducted into the Confucian Shrine had about 30 students; unchartered academies usually had about 15 students, although these numbers varied according to the academy's financial situation. By the late Joseon period, when many sought refuge in private academies to avoid corvée services, the most substantial quotas were reached.

The private academies were managed by a president (*wonjang*) and administrators (*yusa*), who reported to the chancellor (*won-im*). As the educational institution of the local *sarim*, the scholars representing the *sarim* in the academy (*wonjung yurim*) elected the chairman. There was no special procedure for appointing the president and administrator, though it was customary to select people of a certain renown who could represent the whole county.

The president was in charge of all the academy's main affairs and was also the person representing the academy and carrying responsibility for it, while the dean managed daily affairs. Among the other officers who helped to run the academy were the vice-president (*won-i*), who assisted the president and replaced him in case something happened to him; the head instructor (*gangjang*) was in charge of lectures; the head tutor (*hunjang*) was in charge of instruction and discipline; the dormitory inspector (*jaejang*) managed the dormitories; the general administrator (*doyusa*) supervised all the academy's affairs, assisted by the vice-administrator (*buyusa*); the drill master (*jipgang*) was responsible for morale; during general meetings of the academy's scholars (*yuhoe*) the steward for the month (*jigwol*) handled all daily affairs, assisted by the steward for the day (*jigil*); the chief council (*jangui*) was responsible for handling all deliberations concerning major and minor affairs; and the amanuensis (*saekjang*) handled various minor affairs.

Major affairs concerning the academy, however, were decided upon in general meetings of the scholars (*yuhoe*), in which local officials could also exert some influence. Toegye, the man who effectively determined the structure and system of the private academies, emphasized their autonomous management, but he also recommended that local officials be put in charge of economic problems, so that the academies could maintain an organic bond with officialdom. He understood that although the academies were private educational institutes, fundamentally they executed the state's educational policies. To facilitate the management of the private academies, rules were drawn up (*wongyu*), which recorded procedures for selecting the dean and students, the educational goals, the curriculum, details on the management of the academy and so on.

The economic basis for running the academies was mainly land and *nobi*, as well as assets. The *nobi* were a class of indentured people, similar to slaves in other societies, but the Korean "slaves" differed insofar as they had property rights and were governed by the same laws as freemen. To obtain official recognition, the academies applied for a royal warrant, and in case they succeeded this resulted in many privileges. Together with the warrant–conferred in the form of a name plaque–the king also bestowed books, land and *nobi*, while local officials provided materials for daily living. Large academies had many estates and *nobi* to work them, while chartered academies received three *gyeol* (one *gyeol* equals approximately one hectare) of land. *Nobi* were needed to perform various essential tasks such as protection and maintenance, the organization of various tasks and the cultivation of land. During the reign of King Sukjong, the quota of *nobi* for chartered academies was set at seven, and at five for unchartered academies. There were also people who indentured themselves to academies to evade corvée duties, but they were employed in much the same way as *nobi*.

(5) Social role

As we have seen, the academies' fundamental role was on the one hand to gather scholars for instruction and study, and on the other hand to enshrine the spirit tablet of former sages and conduct ritual services in their honor. However, their role did not stop at this; by disseminating ethical values in local society and transforming its basic order, they also acted as spiritual beacons to lead the local communities.

As the educational, institutional and ideological mainstay of the *sarim*, the academies could also serve as a stronghold to sway local public opinion: through implementing such strategies as the community compact (*hyangyak*), they could act as the focal point in the indoctrination and integration of local society. The community compact was a kind of voluntary social contract drawn up by Neo-Confucian scholars in consultation with village elders, and which covered everything from ethical behavior and conduct to cooperation and mutual aid. The academies were also places where local officials gathered to discuss current affairs, where the archives of former sages were kept, and where traveling officials could find a place for the night.

Also, as the dynasty wore on and factional strife intensified, the academies led the way in intensifying the divisions between factional ideological positions (*saron*) and the official position (*gongnon*). The latter part of the dynasty saw the proliferation of single-surname villages (*ssijok burak*), and the ensuing entanglement of family lineages with scholarly lineages; in this process the academies became instrumental in maintaining the social position of such family lineages, which meant that their social role became much bigger. But as the academies became more and more embroiled in factional strife and lineage disputes, they were transformed into hotbeds of social unrest, and because they caused so many social problems the state stepped in to take control: this culminated in the destruction of most *seowon* by order of the Daewongun (who acted as regent to King Gojong from 1863 to 1873) between 1865 and 1871.

3) Location of the private academies

Most academies are situated on a gentle incline, facing towards the lower side. This means that the buildings back up on a mountain, usually a rather low one, while they face a flowing brook or a broad field in front. On the other side of the field there is a "front mountain" (*ansan*) facing the academy, so called because in geomantic (*feng shui*) terms it provides shelter and support at the front. The arrangement of the buildings is carefully considered in order to achieve a good panorama and to harmonize with the surrounding landscape. In this respect the academies differ from palaces or the official educational facilities, which are laid out strictly along a north-south axis, with all the main buildings facing south. In some academies, including Dosan seowon,

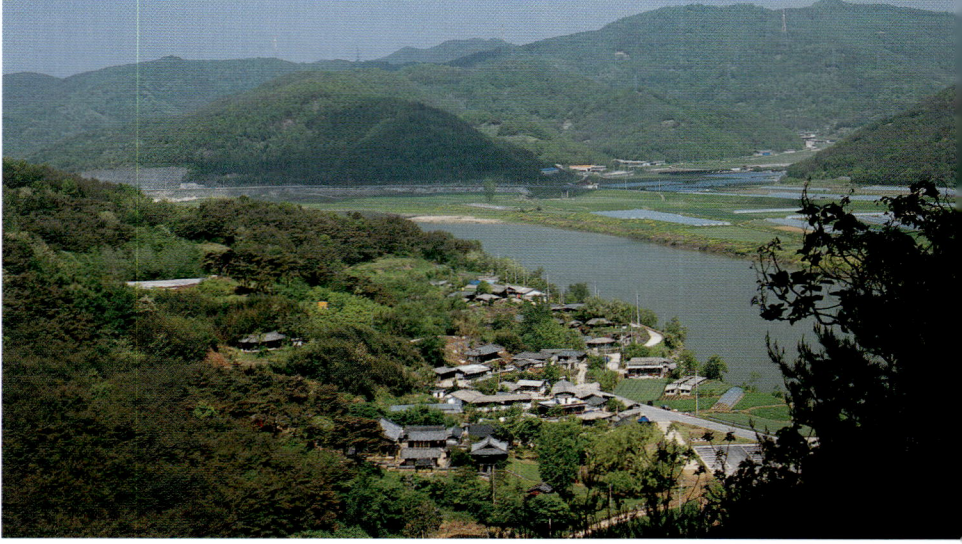

Panorama of Dodong seowon

Piram seowon and Byeongsan seowon, the buildings are also arranged along a south-facing central axis. This was not enforced strictly regardless of the physical environment, but rather because it happened to be the ideal direction in terms of harmonizing with the surrounding landscape and achieving a good view. More representative are the academies where the central axis is not facing southward and the buildings are constructed in harmony with the landscape. This is the case for the Oksan academy, where the central axis faces west, looking out over a brook flowing in front of the academy toward Mt. Muhaksan, thus making the best of its natural setting. Dodong seowon stands on a site looking out over the Nakdonggang river towards the northeast and blends in perfectly with the surrounding landscape. Donam seowon is arranged facing east, looking out over a broad plain in front so that it becomes one with its environment.

While *seowon* were established in accordance with environmental conditions, their locations were also chosen in view of their connections with the sage to whom the academy was dedicated. The locality could be the county where the sage's family originated, his place of birth, the place where he grew up, where he retreated to train his own disciples, where he used to be an official, where he was once exiled, where he displayed his loyalty to the sovereign, or near the site of his grave.

First and foremost among the academies established in the sage's hometown or place of birth is the Sosu seowon, which stands in Punggi, the hometown of An Hyang (1243-1306). Imgo seowon is in Yeongcheon, hometown of Jeong Mong-ju (1337-1392); Namgye seowon in Hamyang, hometown of Jeong Yeo-chang (1450-1504); Ujeo seowon in Gimpo, hometown of Jo Heon (1544-1592); Imcheon seowon in Andong, hometown of Kim Seong-il (1538-1593). Yerim seowon in Miryang, dedicated to Kim Jong-jik (1431-1492), stands next to the village where Kim's birthplace can be found, while Micheon seowon in Naju was founded in the place where Heo Mok (1595-1682) spent his youth.

Geumo seowon in Seonsan was established in the place where Gil Jae (1353-1419) retreated after the demise of the Goryeo dynasty because he "could not serve two sovereigns"; this was also his hometown. Pasan seowon in Paju is the place where Seong Su-chim (1493-1564) re-

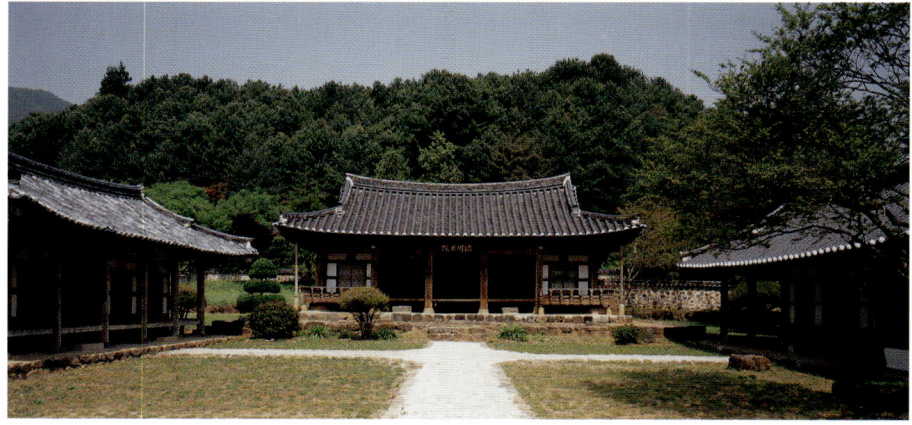

Deokcheon seowon, built in memory of Jo Sik

treated to devote himself to scholarship; Oksan seowon in Gyeongju is where Yi Eon-jeok (1491-1553) sought refuge to study; and Hwayang seowon in Cheongju was founded in the place where Song Si-yeol (1607-1689) retreated. Deokcheon seowon in Sancheong stands near the place where Jo Sik (1501-1572) once established a school called Sancheonjae to spend the last decade of his life transmitting his knowledge and spirit to disciples and instructing them in statesmanship.

Sancheonjae, where Jo Sik used to study and instruct his disciples

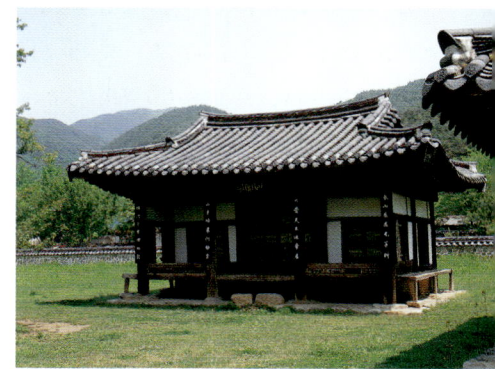

There are also academies that trace their roots to previous educational facilities, notably private schools, which in such cases acted as the academy's precursor. This was the case for Toegye's Dosan seowon in Andong, Kim Jang-saeng's (1548-1631) Donam seowon and Yun Hwang's (1571-1639) Nogang seowon in Nonsan, Kim In-hu's (1510-1560) Piram seowon in Jangseong, and Jeong Gu's (1543-1620) Hoeyeon seowon in Seongju.

Museong seowon in Jeongeup traces its origins to the Taesan shrine, which was erected to commemorate the good government of

Choe Chi-won (857-?) when he served as county magistrate of Taesan. Okcheon seowon in Suncheon was erected on the place where Kim Goeng-pil (1454-1504) was forced to take poison on royal command after he was exiled there following the 1498 purge of literati. Chungnyeol seowon in Yongin, Simgok seowon in Yongin, and Jaun seowon in Paju were all established near the graves of former sages, in these cases Jeong Mong-ju, Jo Gwang-jo and Yi I (1536-1584) respectively. Hwasan seowon in Pocheon was established on a spot from where Mt. Hwasan, where Yi Hang-bok (1556-1618) is buried, can be seen.

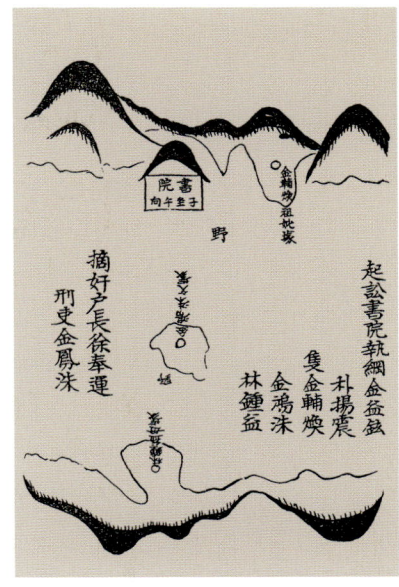

Map of Piram seowon's feng shui conditions

Thus the private academies were habitually established in places associated with former sages, but at the same time they had to serve as retreats where the *sarim* could cultivate themselves and study – in other words, a location of outstanding natural beauty was required. It was none other than Toegye Yi Hwang, who played a leading role in obtaining the royal warrant for the Baegundong academy and who practically launched the movement to found academies, who first formulated these two necessary conditions. To sum up, these consisted of a human factor, namely, the connection with the life of a former sage, and a geographical factor, in that the landscape had to be outstanding. In fact, all the private academies of the Joseon period met these conditions, including the very first one, Baegundong seowon. To select such a spot, the surrounding mountains were closely observed for the features important to *pungsu* (geomancy, the art of choosing auspicious sites), and the buildings were then arranged in accordance with the shape of the mountains and the flow of the water, to achieve harmony with the natural environment.

An important reason for attaching such importance to the scenery surrounding the academies was that the Neo-Confucian literati were looking for places where they could live in seclusion and cultivate their bodies and minds to achieve what they called "Unity of Heaven and Man" (*cheonin habil*). As the most important spiritual idea for the Neo-Confucians, the Unity of Heaven and Man is an ideal for mankind, in which man becomes one with nature and all the creatures of the universe become interconnected. As it was important to realize this ideal through one's personal awakening, the Neo-Confucian literati built their academies close to valleys with flowing streams and beautiful mountains, where they could practice their scholarship and nurture disciples.

Because they could not explicitly reveal the learning they pursued and their inclination toward social revolution, *gasa* (linked verse) literature played an important role in expressing their state of mind. Being without government rank or post, they could only express their feelings and thoughts through poems or *gasa* on nature. Toegye's "Twelve Songs of Dosan" *(Dosan sibi gok)* is a good example of this. Such a disposition was another factor that explains why they preferred to have the academies built in places with beautiful scenery.

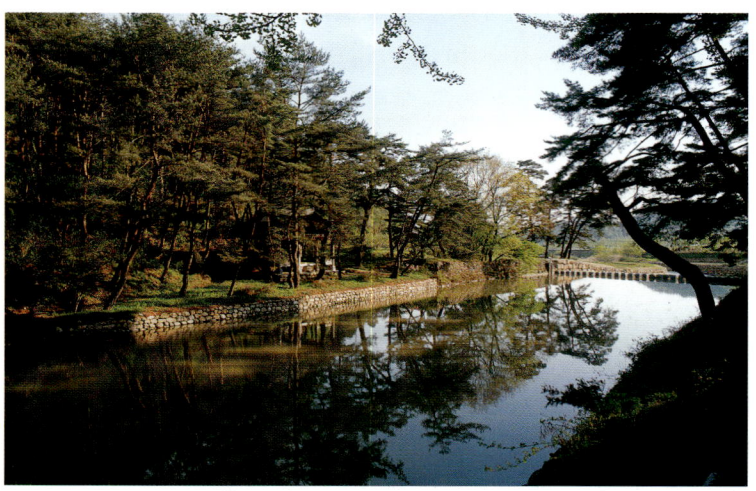

The Jukgyesu stream flowing next to Sosu seowon

Sosu seowon in Sunheung for example is located in a remote and secluded part of the valley where the Jukgyesu stream, originating in the foothills of Mt. Taebaeksan, flows and is surrounded by cloud-covered peaks. When Ju Se-bung chose this place and named it "Baegundong" (White Cloud Hollow), he did so with reference to the Bailudong (White Deer Hollow) academy revived by Zhu Xi: "With its clouds, mountains, hills, rivers and the white clouds perennially enveloping the academy, it is every bit as good as Lushan [where the

Bailudong academy was located]." As Toegye remarked, this is a place fit for scholars to ramble and study. The scenery of the academy, looking out over a path lined with old pine trees and a valley, was chosen not just for the pure enjoyment of the natural landscape, but also because it is a place where it is possible to realize and venerate the Learning of the Way and commemorate former sages. If the private academies were to be a suitable place for literati to retire and cultivate themselves, and for their followers to study and ramble while receiving instruction and training, they had to be far removed from the hustle and bustle of daily life.

Toegye's Dosan seowon is in a place that meets all these conditions. Originally, Toegye established a private school on a spot somewhat lower than and to the south of the present academy. He started building this school in 1557 and it was completed in 1561. After the completion of his school he wrote the *Hymns to Dosan (Dosan jabyeong)*, which offer a glimpse of the surrounding landscape and his state of mind. Summarizing, the description of the landscape in the "Hymns to Dosan" is as follows:

> Looking at the features of Mt. Dosan and its surroundings, the mountain is actually an extension eastward of Mt. Yeongjisan, and is neither very high nor very big, but its valleys are wide and its shape is extraordinary, rising steeply without inclines, and surrounded on all four sides by peaks and valleys that look as if they are holding hands and bowing towards Mt. Dosan. Left of the mountain is Dongchwibyeong (East Emerald Screen) and to its right Seochwibyeong (West Emerald Screen). From Mt. Cheongnyangsan in the east to the mountain's eastern side, and from Mt. Yeongjisan in the west to its western flank, soaring peaks rise up one after the other. These two "screens" stand facing each other, and spiraling down towards the south, the eastern side runs towards the west for eight or nine *li*, while the western side does the same, thus joining forces high above the

wide plain to the south. The stream to the north of the mountain is called Toegye (from which Yi Hwang took his pen name) and the stream to its north is called Nakcheon. The Toegye stream turns around the mountain from the north to join the Nakcheon before flowing eastward, while the Nakcheon, leaving the mountain's eastern side, then flows west before widening and deepening below the foot of the mountain. There you can find a small valley, looking out towards the river and the plain, which is deep and cozy yet offers a wide-open view. The foot of the mountain and the rocks are clear and fresh, and the water drawn from the wells there is sweet and cold; in short, it is an excellent retreat.

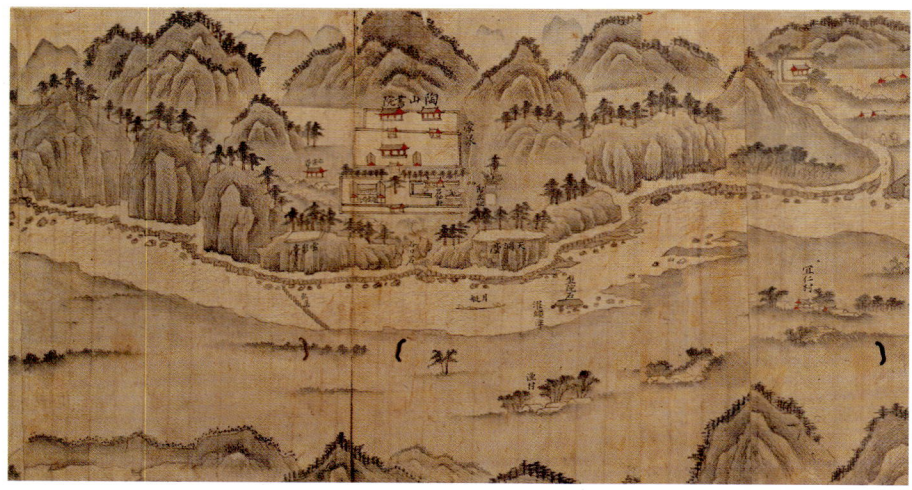

Picture of Dosan seowon drawn by Kim Changseok (1652-1720), Yonsei University library collection

Toegye chose this place for his school by taking into consideration the suitability of all these factors – the mountains, the water and the plain.

Other academies, such as Dodong seowon, Oksan seowon, Namgye seowon, Donam seowon, and Gosan seowon were established on sites with similar conditions, and their buildings were designed to sublimate these locations. But among all the academies, the one that is

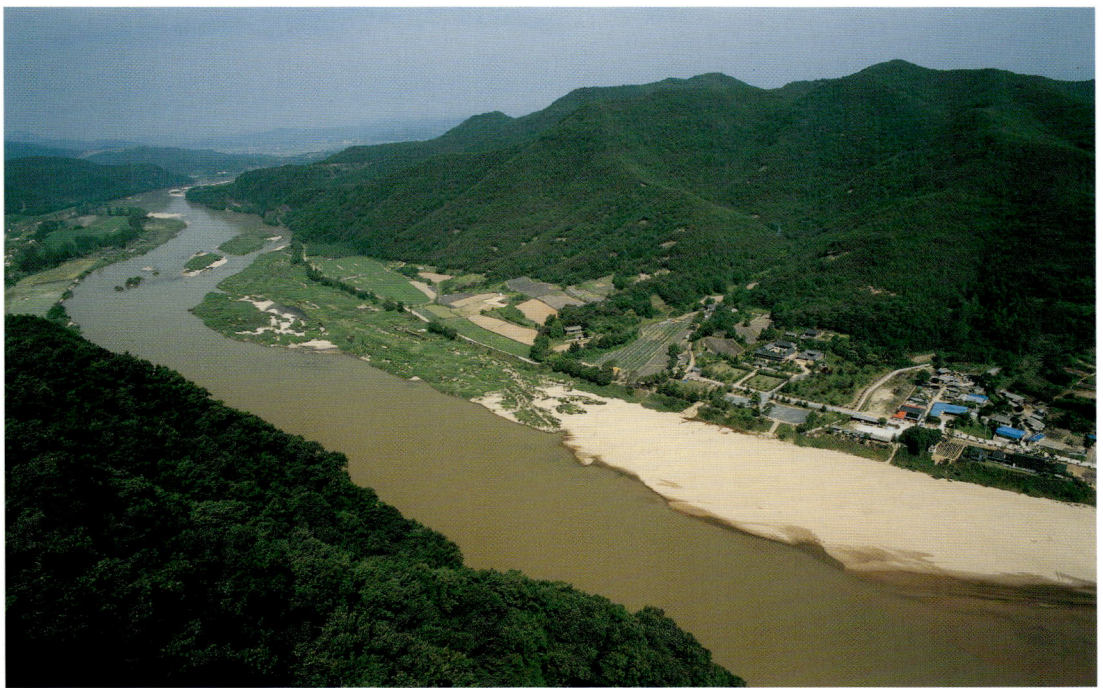

View of the Nakdonggang river flowing in front of Byeongsan seowon and the surrounding landscape

considered the most successful in sublimating its environs through architecture is Byeongsan seowon in Andong, established to commemorate Yu Seong-nyong (1542-1607).

Byeongsan seowon is a magnificent example of how much the Confucian scholars of the Joseon dynasty appreciated the landscape of their country and attests to the spirit and way in which they constructed buildings to be in tune with it. On the shore of the Nakdonggang river, in a place where it spreads wide and its current quickens, and makes a loop in the shape of a jar, stands a mountain that acts like a screen to the river – hence its name, Mt. Byeongsan (Screen Mountain). The mountain's shadow stretches across the river to the other side, where a sandbank spreads out and old gnarled pines stand, and touches the foot of Mt. Hwasan, which stands between the academy and Hahoe village on the other side. Byeongsan seowon is located at the foot of Mt. Hwasan and looks out over the river and Mt. Byeongsan opposite. With the river and the mountain nearby, the academy is laid out very spaciously with its buildings spread out widely. The buildings complement and explain the terrain and the environment, creating a sublime architectural space. This becomes clear especially when standing in the main wood-floored room of the Ipgyodang (lecture hall) and looking out between the pillars at the scenery of the Mandaeru pavilion opposite and the mountain and river beyond: The seven bays of the second-floor loft of Mandaeru divide the scenery into seven screens, so that the landscape seems to be both inside and outside, creating a dramatic effect. The question of how to reshape and recreate the landscape surrounding the constructions through the aesthetics of architectural space is at the very heart of *seowon* architecture.

4) History of the private academies

As mentioned previously, the Baegundong academy established by Ju Se-bung in Sunheung paved the way for the private academies of Joseon. In 1543 Ju Se-bung established the Munseonggongmyo shrine to commemorate the late Goryeo Neo-Confucian scholar An Hyang, but at the same time he also opened a school for Confucian students, thereby defining the format of the private academies as combined commemorative shrines and places of learning. In 1550, thanks to the efforts of Toegye, who had been appointed magistrate of Punggi county in 1548, the academy received a royal warrant renaming it Sosu seowon, thereby making it the first chartered academy (*saaek seowon*) of the Joseon period.

When the king bestowed a warrant on a shrine or academy, it meant that he composed a new name and wrote it on a board, which was then sent to the institution as proof of its new status. Academies that enjoyed this privilege were known as chartered academies, and to enable them to maintain their status and assist in their operations, they were also allocated *nobi*, land and books by the state. As a result, there were considerable differences in status between chartered and unchartered academies.

The granting of a royal warrant to Sosu seowon also implied that the court recognized the private academies as educational institutions on an equal footing with the county schools, and furthermore recognized them as arbiters in determining the orthodox Neo-Confucian Learning of the Way. By acknowledging the academies' social role, the state also recognized their veneration of former sages as well as their educational and edifying role.

After Toegye secured chartered status for Sosu seowon, everyone from the countryside to the capital became aware of the emergence of this new phenomenon, which was further consolidated with the establishment of numerous new academies during the reign of King Myeongjong (r. 1545-1567).

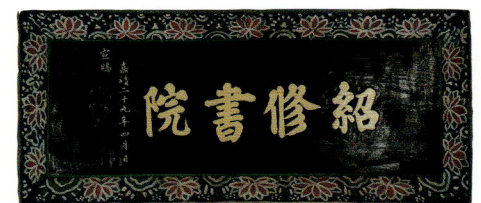

Sosu seowon's name plaque

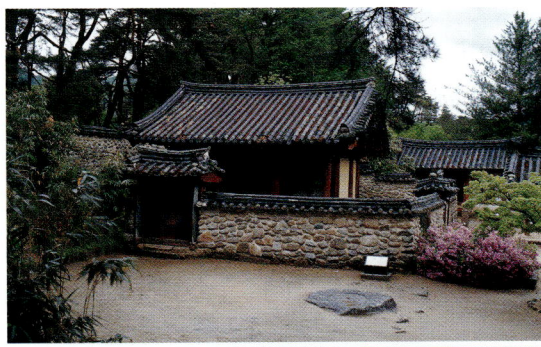

Munseonggongmyo, shrine of Sosu seowon

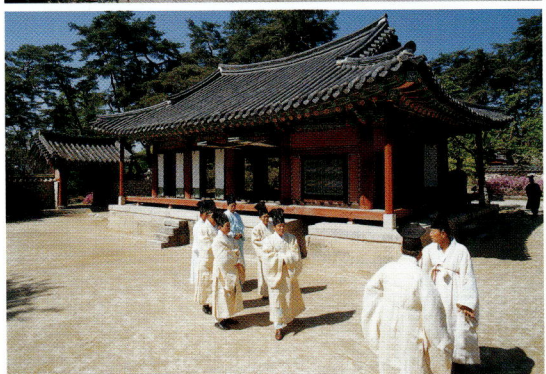

Myeongnyundang, the lecture hall of Sosu seowon

Toegye played a leading role in the movement to establish academies. Concerned about the disorderly state of society in his time, he believed that in order to turn Joseon into a kingdom of truth under Confucianism, it was necessary first of all to educate the people, and he looked to the academies to ensure that the people would be educated correctly. Toegye's views on this are expressed most cogently in a letter he wrote to the Gyeongsang-

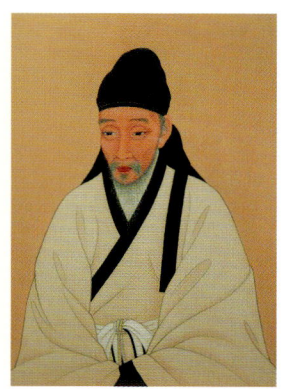

Portrait of Toegye Yi Hwang

do provincial governor Sim Tong-won (1499-?) in 1549, in which he urged him to petition the court to grant a warrant to the Baegundong academy.

In the letter, Toegye argued that the academy could become an educational institution on a par with the county schools, but that it needed official recognition from the state in the form of a warrant, which would also entail practical support in the form of land, *nobi* and books. He believed that the academies should not be tied to any particular county but should operate on a national level; by establishing them in places associated with former sages to elucidate their teachings, the customs and traditions of the literati could be reformed, which would support the king in his government.

The reason academies were so esteemed in China, Toegye asserted, was that "scholars who want to retreat to cultivate their minds and students who want to discuss and learn about the Way dislike the hustle and bustle of ordinary life, so they carry their books and escape to wide-open fields, or the banks of a quiet stream, where they can sing in praise of ancient kings, where they can read quietly about the meaning and principles underlying the world in order to cultivate virtue, become conversant with benevolence, and thus achieve happiness." By contrast, "the institutes of official learning and the county schools are near markets and city walls; while the former are hampered by political instructions, the latter are tied up in all kinds of petty affairs, how can we talk about their public benefit?" As an alternative, he suggests that "the private academies will serve not only as places where scholars can study, they will also be able to foster wise and talented people who can serve the state." For Toegye, "because the school system is the basis for fashioning the Way, and the students are its fountainheads and their prime movers, establishing schools will ensure a good standard for practicing the Way and promoting its ethos."

Toegye made a clear distinction between agents and objects in his edification project, the former role being allocated to the *sarim* and the latter to the ordinary people. He argued that the first task at hand was to rectify the customs of the *sarim* and ensure that their scholarship proceeded on the right basis. He pointed out that an important reason for the existence of private academies in China, which proliferated after the Song period, was that they were charged with the concrete implementation of this edification project. Toegye was convinced that if the private academies were to become firmly established in Joseon society and be able to fulfill this role, they needed official recognition from the court, and for this reason he played a leading role in obtaining a charter for Baegundong seowon.

Toegye's zeal for establishing private academies in Korea was thus based on the realization that in order to form a new humanity the most important thing was to indigenize true Neo-Confucianism, and that the place to achieve this was none other than the place of instruction. In other words, his private academy project was a movement to craft an educational environment that could absorb the rising *sarim* class and instill true learning in them.

Toegye was deeply involved in the foundation and management of private academies, either directly or indirectly through writing "private academy records" (*seowongi*). Thus he can be linked to the founding of Isan seowon in Yeongcheon, Yeongbong seowon in Seongju (known as Cheongok seowon after it was chartered), Yeokdong seowon in Yean, and Yeongyeong seowon in Daegu. By the end of King Myeongjong's reign the number of academies had reached nearly 20, and Toegye had played a role in the establishment of more than half of them. His deep attachment to the academy-building project is clearly expressed in a series of ten poems he wrote about academies in the second month of 1565, including Jukgye seowon in Punggi (another name for Sosu seowon), Imgo seowon in Yeongcheon, Yeongbong seowon in Seongju, Gusan seowon in Gangneung, Namgye seowon in Hamyang, Isan seowon in Yeongcheon, Seoak seowon in Gyeongju, and Hwaam seowon in Daegu.

To establish and consolidate the unique character of the private academies, Toegye composed a set of rules for the Isan academy (known as the *Isan seowon wongyu*), which deal with both the discipline and the character of the academy, covering aspects such as rules on receiving instruction, dormitory rules, the main principles for instruction, study methods etc. These rules formed the basis for all the academy rules of the Joseon period, exerted a great influence on the character of later academies, and helped to determine the ideal model for the academy system.

Although the Isan academy rules emphasize that private academies should have both a lecture hall and a shrine, in terms of importance the lecture hall clearly takes precedence. In the initial period of the implantation of academies in Joseon society, the existence of a shrine was not considered a necessary condition for the foundation of an academy. When Isan seowon was founded by magistrate An Sang on the initiative of Toegye, it did not have a shrine. Similarly, when Yeongyeong seowon was founded in 1563, the lecture hall was constructed first. And at Dosan seowon, where Toegye's own portrait was enshrined after his death, the lecture hall was also built before the shrine.

Toegye's views on the role of the private academies can also be gleaned from his record concerning Yeongbong seowon, written in the seventh month of 1560. In a nutshell, it states that the first role of the academy is to serve as an institution to expound and clarify the Learning of the Way. Second, it is a place where scholars can retreat and cultivate themselves through "learning for oneself" (*wigi jihak*). Third, it should comprise both a lecture hall and a shrine. Fourth, offerings to sages are of secondary importance. Fifth, the person to be commemorated should be someone versed in the Learning of the Way rather than in politics.

As the nature of the academies as envisaged by Toegye, namely, as retreats for instructing the *sarim*, became more evident, they soon came to function as an important basis from which the *sarim* could strengthen their position in local society, leading to a swift growth in the number of academies. Even though the first one, Baegundong seowon, had been founded by a local government official (the magistrate of Punggi county), later academies were all founded on the initiative of local Neo-Confucian literati, who sought to venerate eminent Confucian scholars or loyal subjects and instruct students.

Since the educational function took precedence, this is reflected in the arrangement of the buildings. These early academies, where the buildings are organized around a central lecture hall, became a distinct prototype among the Joseon private academies. Academies of this period were built on natural inclines, with the front part on the lower ground and the back part on the higher ground. The shrine was located towards the back and the lecture hall towards the front, with dormitories (*jaesa*) facing each other on either side of the yard in front of the lecture hall. The area around the shrine and the area around the lecture hall form two very distinct spaces, each surrounded by a wall, and with the difference in rank between the buildings thus expressed, the axis in the architectural plan is made evident. Starting with Dosan seowon, the other academies established in this period – Namgye seowon (1552), Seoak seowon (1561), Yerim seowon (1567), Dodong seowon (1568), Geumo seowon (1570), Yeokdong seowon (1570), and Oksan seowon (1573) – are all based on a similar ground plan, with buildings arranged in the following order: outer gate (*oemun*), dormitories (*jaesa*), lecture hall (*gangdang*), inner gate (*naemun, sinmun*), and shrine (*sadang*).

By the reign of King Seonjo, the number of academies started increasing rapidly. Whereas 18 academies had been established during the reign of his predecessor, Myeongjong, in Seonjo's time alone more than 60 new ones emerged. The representative academies of Myeongjong's reign are Sosu seowon, Munheon seowon, Namgye seowon and Imgo seowon. The representative academies for Seonjo's reign are first of all Deokseong seowon (which later became Yerim seowon), established in Miryang (Gyeongsang-do province) in 1567 to venerate Kim Jong-jik;

Ssanggye seowon in Hyeonpung (Gyeongsang-do province), founded in 1568 and dedicated to Kim Goeng-pil; Geumo seowon, established in 1570 in Seonsan (Gyeongsang-do province) in honor of Gil Jae; Oksan seowon, founded in 1573 in Gyeongju (Gyeongsang-do province) in memory of Yi Eon-jeok; Dosan seowon, founded in 1574 in Yean (Gyeongsang-do province) and dedicated to Toegye; and finally Deokcheon seowon in Sancheong (Gyeongsang-do province), founded in 1576 to commemorate Jo Sik (1501-1572). Since all those venerated at these academies were scholars who had contributed greatly to the development of Neo-Confucianism, it is evident that the academies played a social role as beacons of orthodox Learning of the Way.

Thus as the *sarim* faction gradually captured the political center stage during the reigns of Myeongjong and Seonjo in the mid- and late 16th century, the number of academies increased correspondingly, reaching its apex during Seonjo's reign. This momentum continued during the reigns of Gwanghaegun, Injo and Hyojong. As academies were established in all parts of the country, their power grew to such an extent that local officials could not interfere with them, and with the support of the central government and through their economic power, they played an active role in transforming Joseon society. From the late 16th to the early 17th century, ritual studies (*yehak*) became very important, and with an increasing tendency to make rites and rituals not just something to be practiced individually, but something to sacrifice oneself for, the period of ritual learning had dawned. Thus academies founded during this period thought that their role amounted to more than mere education and secluded training.

Going into the later stages of the Joseon period, the number of academies spiraled out of control. Across the country, no less than 31 academies were dedicated to Toegye, 26 to Song Si-yeol and 21 to Yulgok Yi I. This indicates that the academies gradually lost the spirit of the founding days, and instead of functioning as centers of study and learning, they either gave priority to ritual sacrifices, turned into factional strongholds, or even became the exclusive stronghold of a clan. Thus the academies came to obstruct government politics, and because they enjoyed exemption from tax and corvée labor, they greatly weakened the country's financial and labor basis, giving rise to many political and social abuses. After the 17th century many rulers, especially Sukjong (r. 1674-1720) and Yeongjo (r. 1724-1776), tried to curb these abuses, but largely to little effect. Finally, the Daewongun (Yi Ha-eung, 1820-1898), who acted as regent to King Gojong (r. 1863-1907) between 1863 and 1873, managed to abolish many private academies with four abolition edicts issued between 1864 and 1871, leading to the destruction of many academies.

Number of private academies and shrines

(based on Han Yeong-u, *Dasi channeun uri yeoksa*, p. 298)

Reign	Number
Jungjong (1506-1544)	16
Myeongjong (1545-1567)	19
Seonjo (1567-1608)	85
Gwanghaegun (1608-1623)	38
Injo (1623-1649)	53
Hyojong (1649-1659)	37
Hyeonjong (1659-1674)	69
Sukjong (1674-1720)	340
Gyeongjong (1720-1724)	28
Yeongjo (1724-1776)	163
Jeongjo (1776-1800)	8
Sunjo (1800-1834)	1
Heonjong (1834-1849)	1
Cheoljong (1849-1863)	1
unknown	50
Total	909

First of all, the Daewongun set an example by destroying the Mandongmyo shrine, the stronghold of the Noron faction in Cheongju, Chungcheong-do province, in the third month of 1865. Then he gradually pushed back the stubborn resistance of the local Confucian literati by abolishing academies all over the peninsula. He was especially keen to reduce the overbearing power of the Noron faction and thereby revive the authority of the royal court.

Founding - chartering of private academies and shrines

(based on *Hanguk minjok munhwa daebaekgwa sajeon*)

Reign	Founded (incl. warrant)			Royal Warrant		
	Academy	Shrine	Total	Academy	Shrine	Total
Jungjong (1506-1544)	4	12	16	-	1	1
Injong (1544-1545)	-	-	-	-	-	-
Myeongjong (1545-1567)	18	1	19	4	-	4
Seonjo (1567-1608)	63	22	85	16	4	20
Gwanghaegun (1608-1623)	29	9	38	12	2	14
Injo (1623-1649)	28	25	53	4	-	4
Hyojong (1649-1659)	27	10	37	7	4	11
Hyeonjong (1659-1674)	46	23	69	31	11	42
Sukjong (1674-1720)	166	174	340	105	27	132
Gyeongjong (1720-1724)	8	20	28	9	2	11
Yeongjo (1724-1776)	18	145	163	7	8	15
Jeongjo (1776-1800)	2	6	8	3	9	12
Sunjo (1800-1834)	1	-	1	1	-	1
Heonjong (1834-1849)	-	1	1	-	1	1
Cheoljong (1849-1863)	-	1	1	1	1	2
Gojong (1864-1907)	-	-	-	-	-	-
Unknown	7	43	50	-	-	-
Total	417	492	909	200	70	270

Mandongmyo was a shrine founded in 1703 by Gwon Sang-ha (1641-1721) on the instructions of his teacher Song Si-yeol to perform sacrifices to two Ming emperors: Shenzong (r. 1573-1620), who sent troops to Korea to repel the Japanese invasions ordered by Hideyoshi, and Yizong (r. 1628-1644), the last Ming emperor. The shrine faced north, in deference to the south-facing imperial court of China, and in 1704 the first sacrifices were offered to the deceased emperors; in 1776 it received a royal warrant. In front of Mandongmyo was Hwayang seowon, founded in 1696 in honor of Song Si-yeol. It is located in Hwayang-dong, where Song retreated during a period of intense factional wrangling. Among the many academies devoted to Song, this became the most representative stronghold of the Noron faction in its struggle for power. Originally, it was located outside Hwayang-dong on the Mangyeongdae terrace, but later it was relocated to a place in front of Mandongmyo and to its right. Its buildings face north and are arranged in an L shape as if to encircle it.

The academy that is most often mentioned in discussions of the destabilizing effect of the academies in late Joseon is Hwayang seowon, and with it Mandongmyo. As Song Si-yeol was revered as the symbol of the Noron group, this became their headquarters, and as it gradually expanded its landholdings, it changed into a hotbed for all kinds of misconduct. The rapaciousness of Hwayang seowon reached its climax with the issue of written notices with an imprint, known as the Hwayang ink plaques (*Hwayang mukpae*). Anyone receiving this plaque, regardless of whether he was a commoner or an official, had to offer up goods or sacrificial money needed for the maintenance and construction of the academy; those who refused were arrested and either intimidated or given the death penalty.

On the ninth day of the third lunar month, 1865, the Daewongun issued a royal order on behalf of the king and queen, stipulating that the warrant and plaque of Mandongmyo should be moved to Gyeongbonggak in Changdeokgung palace in Seoul, and that the shrine itself

Engraved printing of Hwayang seowon and Mandongmyo

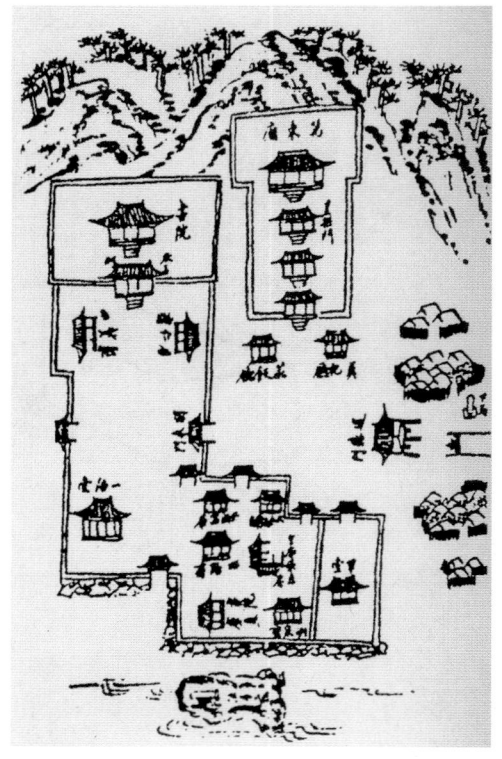

should be abolished. In 1871, despite the fierce resistance of literati of the Noron faction, Hwayang academy was also abolished. All that remains today is its foundations.

After demolishing Mandongmyo, in 1868 the Daewongun abolished a further 1,000 unchartered academies, and in 1871, on the principle of "one person, one *seowon*," no more than one chartered academy was to be devoted to the same person, meaning that only 47 academies were allowed to exist – all the rest were to be demolished. Among the private academies and shrines that survived this clampdown, 36 are located in South Korea and 11 in North Korea.

The abolition of the private academies carried out by the Daewongun provoked a very strong reaction from the main victims of this policy, the local Confucian literati, who protested vehemently and sent petitions urging the court to retract it. In 1871 the literati of Gyeongsang-do province rose up in opposition and sent several vituperative petitions. In 1873 Choe Ik-hyeon (1833-1906), famous for his role in the debate on "defending orthodoxy and rejecting heterodoxy" (*wijeong cheoksa ron*) in defense of orthodox Zhu Xi thought, criticized the Daewongun for abolishing the private academies and impeached him, a move that helped to force the Daewongun out of power later the same year.

When the Daewongun ordered the abolition of the private academies, many tried desperately to maintain their existence by fulfilling the order only partially: Some removed the lecture hall but retained the shrine, some removed the shrine and turned the lecture hall into a private school, and others separated the shrine and the lecture hall by moving the lecture hall to another place; thus the appearance of the academies was fundamentally transformed. From 1874 on, the new political and social situation permitted a minor revival of the academies, which continues to this day. However, these reconstructed academies usually forfeit their educational role, only continuing the veneration of the sage to whom they were originally dedicated.

Until the middle of the 17th century, the private academies thus functioned as bastions for selecting outstanding Confucian scholars and arming them ideologically through study and cultivation. Centering on the cultivation of the individual to foster people of outstanding morality, the educational and scholarly function of the academies played a leading role in transforming Korean society after the mid-Joseon period. However, after this flourishing period of "cultural government," by the latter half of the 17th century the *seowon* started showing signs of corruption. It reached the stage where "scholars of a community vied to emulate one of their seniors and establish an academy for him, even if

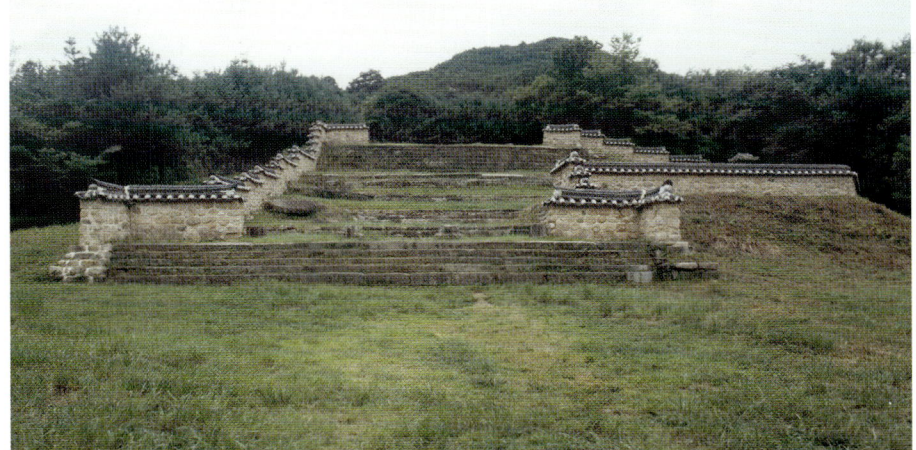

Mandongmyo site

he was only slightly more enlightened than the others, and venerated him without even reflecting on what he did. ... They wielded absolute authority in their community and used their power with such impudence that even the local officials could not impede them." Thus the private academies of the Joseon period flourished or languished according to the political and social situation, and as such their social influence also swung between positive and negative.

Concerning their positive influence on society, however, we can mention their promotion and development of cultural education, the fostering of talented people needed by the state and society, the development of Neo-Confucian studies and the expansion of the field, the consolidation of a superior Confucian tradition, and the supporting and strengthening of values and education at the local level.

2. Neo-Confucian worldview and *seowon* architecture

1) Neo-Confucian worldview and the "Unity of Heaven and Man"

Confucianism is the doctrine that forms the mainstream of Chinese thought. When Confucianism was established in pre-imperial China (before the Qin dynasty, 221-206 B.C.) it was a discipline seeking to achieve virtue and morality on the basis of ritual propriety (*ye*). During the Song dynasty (960-1279), it was reformed and revitalized as Neo-Confucianism, which added a metaphysical and cosmological dimension to Confucianism.

Although the content of the Confucian classics had previously been interpreted mainly in terms of virtue and morality, Song scholars went one step further by interpreting them in a metaphysical sense, thus reconstructing the Confucian theoretical framework to include cosmological speculation and a theory of human nature.

The main exponents for developing this trend were Shao Yong (1011-1077), Zhou Dunyi (1017-1073), Zhang Zai (1020-1077), the Cheng brothers Cheng Hao (1032-1085) and Cheng Yi (1033-1107), and finally the main systematizer, Zhu Xi (1130-1200).

The architecture of private academies, which acted as centers for Neo-Confucian scholarship and the training of students, was intimately connected with the cosmological epistemology and theory of human nature pursued by Neo-Confucianism. Thus to understand the architecture of the academies, it is necessary to understand the ideal of "Unity of Heaven and Man" (*cheonin habil*) that the Neo-Confucians pursued with such zeal.

The concept of "Unity of Heaven and Man" is essentially a philosophy that seeks to adapt to nature and the Mandate of Heaven. Heaven as conceived by the Neo-Confucians encompasses many meanings, ranging from the physical conception of visible reality or a symbolic idea embracing all natural phenomena to a conceptual and abstract idea of natural principles, destiny, the basis of virtue, or the main subject matter of the universe.

The conceptual meaning of Heaven is already apparent in ancient Chinese discourses about the Heavenly Mandate. By the Eastern Han dynasty (206 B.C. - A.D. 8), Dong Zhongshu (179-104 B.C.), who virtually ensured that Confucianism became the state ideology of the Han, argued that Heaven and Man are connected (*cheonin sanggwan seol*), meaning that human affairs are scrutinized by Heaven, so that if man committed a wrong, Heaven would send a warning by producing natural calamities.

In the Heavenly Mandate doctrine, Heaven like man is seen as an entity with real needs, desires and feelings, and while listening to and watching man it manifests its will. In the realm of politics, the Heavenly Mandate is given to the person with the utmost virtue to rule the people in lieu of Heaven. On the personal level, it is explained as the person's duty to manifest the original virtuous nature bestowed by Heaven, and developed into an ethical concept emphasizing the need to accumulate and cultivate virtue.

The theory that man and Heaven are connected is also called the theory of "man and Heaven affecting and responding to each other" (*cheonin gameung seol*) and holds that natural phenomena and human affairs coexist in a mutually corresponding relationship. Heaven interferes in the world of human politics and society by warning and encouraging people through calamities and portents, while man also models his ethical and political order on Heaven. In other words, it is a kind of mysticism in which the natural world and human society are mutually interconnected. Dong Zhongshu describes the relatedness of man and Heaven as follows: although Heaven created the myriad things and beings, man is a small universe patterned on Heaven.

After the Han period, the Heavenly Mandate theory and the theory that man and Heaven are connected were combined with mystical prognostication, which was thought to predict fortune and human affairs, and during the period of North-South division in China (420-589), further accretions and adaptations. Because it was especially the mystical and magical properties and the instigation to seize power that caught people's imagination, by the Tang period (618-907) the government frequently banned these manifestations of the Heavenly Mandate and the interconnectedness of man and Heaven doctrines.

However, in the course of the Tang and Song dynasties these theories evolved further, turning the cosmological interpretation into a full-fledged philosophic discourse, eventually to be integrated into the "Unity of Heaven and Man" doctrine by Song Neo-Confucians. The "Unity of Heaven and Man" is the fundamental theory of Neo-Confucianism, illuminating the innate identity of man and Heaven and thus man's practical destiny.

In a sense, Dong Zhongshu's theory of the interconnectedness of man and Heaven, holding that Heaven and man are of the same nature, can be regarded as similar to the "Unity of Heaven and Man" theory. However, in the metaphysical systematization of this theory by Song Neo-Confucians, the similarities between Heaven and man are turned into a much more systematic theory.

The theory of the similarity between man and Heaven was based on the understanding that the fundamental virtue of Heaven was implanted in man's heart-mind (unlike Western thought, East Asian philosophy does not distinguish between the heart as the seat of passions and the mind as the seat of reason), so that the Way of Heaven (*cheondo*) and the Way of Man (*indo*) were integrated. In the words of the Neo-Confucian scholar Cheng Yi, "originally there is no distinction in the Way of Heaven or of Man, but being in heaven it is called the Way of Heaven, being on earth it is called the Way of Earth, and applied to man it is called Way of Man." Thus Heaven and man are unified through the Way.

According to Zhu Xi, the nature emphasized by Cheng Yi when he talked about the unity of Heaven and man is nothing but principle (*seong jeuk i*). Zhu Xi reasoned that "what Heaven bestows on man and the myriad beings is the mandate, what man and the myriad beings receive is nature." By distinguishing between "Heavenly Mandate" and "human nature" and equating human nature with principle, he wanted to avoid the error of identifying it with human desire and used the term "Heavenly principle" (*cheolli*) to emphasize the originally virtuous nature of man. This explanation became the main current in Neo-Confucian metaphysics. On this basis Neo-Confucianism is often referred to as the learning of nature-mandate (*seongmyeong*) and principle-material force (*igi*).

From the Neo-Confucian perspective, the human substance man is born with is pure virtue (*deok*). In other words, the heart-mind of human beings is innately good. The original form of this virtue is luminous, and the task of people of learning is to keep polishing this virtue so that it shines as in its innate state. The Neo-Confucians especially emphasized the idea that "Heaven and man unite in virtue" (*cheonin hapdeok*): based on his need for virtue, man receives a virtuous nature from Heaven itself. The great virtue of nature has to be expressed in human life through man's creation and creative potential, so that man can be elevated to become the perfect completion of nature.

Neo-Confucians did not recognize Heaven as just simply a part of nature. They regarded a state of unity between Heaven and man as the highest ideal, and recognized that the basis for providing the principal meaning of existence to all beings was bringing down to earth the principle that Heaven produced harmony and order by internalizing the Way of Heaven in the self (*jagi naejaehwa*).

Neo-Confucian epistemology was based on the premise that the principle governing Heaven and the principle governing life on earth were ultimately not different, and held that following this principle was the ideal for man. Although Neo-Confucian philosophers saw nature as being imbued with the "principle of heaven" (*cheolli*), their cosmology is not concerned with theories of the creation of the universe, but rather with the relationship between the universe and reality, and especially the problem of values contained there.

Therefore Neo-Confucians sought this ultimate principle in all living things in nature. That is why they made the "investigation of things to establish knowledge" (*gyeongmul chiji*, from the *Great Learning*) their basic method of scholarship. "Investigating things" means that when you investigate the principle thoroughly, you can see through the inside and outside, roughness and fineness of things to know it as it is; "establishing knowledge" means to pursue your knowledge to the end to eliminate the things you do not know.

For Neo-Confucians, the "Unity of Heaven and Man" is not simply knowledge in itself, but the attainment of an intuitive communion through realization. Reaching this stage was likened to attaining the highest state of spiritual freedom. What made the union of Heaven and man possible was reaching the state where nature and man become one. This is the key point in explaining what the pursuit of the "Unity of Heaven and Man" meant in the organic mental system of the Neo-Confucians; it also clarifies why human architecture was not conceived as being different from nature, and why man and society cannot exist as isolated entities separate from nature.

That is why Neo-Confucians sought out places of outstanding natural beauty where they could admire nature and foster people. The representative structures built by these scholars were pavilions (*nujeong*), cloisters (*jeongsa*), cottages (*byeolseo*) and academies (*seowon*). These structures provided leisurely repose and communion with nature, but they were also places where the Neo-Confucians sought to realize their ideal of scholarship and life.

Using nature as a medium, the Neo-Confucians made structures to realize the cosmic harmony and order that is the key point in the "Unity of Heaven and Man." In a place where architecture and nature can become one, they built structures that made the natural object and the self into one principle, as a means for comprehending Heaven and man as one. As places for harmonizing with nature, pavilions, cloisters, cottages and academies played an important role in realizing the ideology of "Unity of Heaven and Man." The technical solution to achieve this in architecture is manifested in the selection of place, the location and the arrangement of the buildings.

2) "Unity of Heaven and Man" and the architecture of pavilions and academies

The "Unity of Heaven and Man" ideology exerted great influence on the selection of a site to construct a building, and this is especially evident in the location of pavilions (*nujeong*) and private academies, the representative architectural products of a mature and flourishing Neo-Confucian culture. The *sarim* founded pavilions or private academies in the depths of nature, in valleys near flowing water and mountains, where they could retreat for study and self-cultivation. As Toegye put it, by staying in places of great beauty and tranquility, where you can study without the distractions of a worldly environment, the educational outcomes are greatest.

The pavilion, open on all sides and planted directly into nature, was especially conceived as an architectural space onto which the self

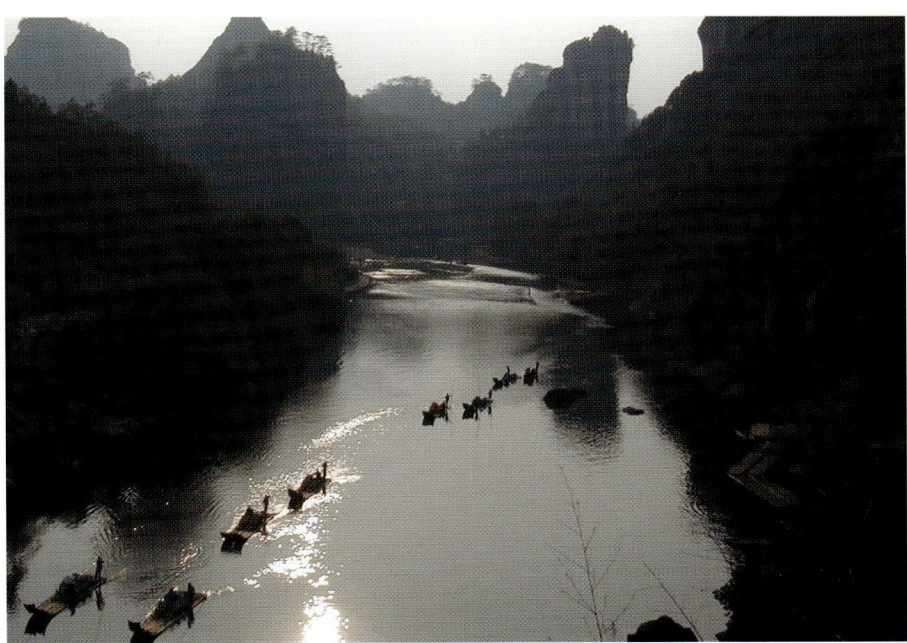

One of the Nine Bends of Wuyishan

could be projected and from which the world could be contemplated. Such a structure is not made to be admired from the outside, but is rather intended to allow the person inside it to admire nature by looking outside. Moreover, the Neo-Confucians tended to give names to the surrounding trees, stones, water and mountains to incorporate them into the Neo-Confucian mental universe and grant them existential value, so that people could have a varied encounter with nature. The purpose of architectural space was thus to bring Heaven and man together by allowing the individual to confirm his value in the world through the personification of nature; this quality is an important characteristic of Korean architecture. Pavilions, in other words, functioned as a kind of landscape support from where distant mountains, or hills and streams could be viewed. They are places through which wind and light pass unimpeded, and where man can open his heart to the surrounding nature.

From the above, it is clear that the location and layout of pavilions and private academies was determined by a mentality in which the

"Unity of Heaven and Man" and an organic relationship with nature were prominent.

The mid-16th century was a defining point in the Confucianization of Joseon society, as Neo-Confucian scholars started to pursue their ideal of unity of Heaven and man in earnest by constructing cloisters and cottages in the midst of nature to cultivate themselves and find the principle unifying them with Heaven and nature. They especially identified with the example set by Zhu Xi when he settled down near the nine bends of the river near Wuyishan mountain in Chungan county, Fujian, and built the Wuyi cloister (*Wuyi jingshe*) nearby to break free from the fetters of official life, develop his scholarship and lead a life in unison with nature. To realize the ideal pointed at by Zhu Xi, they also sought out places similar to the nine bends (*gugok*, Ch. *jiuqu*) of Wuyi to incorporate them into their conception of nature and build an infrastructure for retreats.

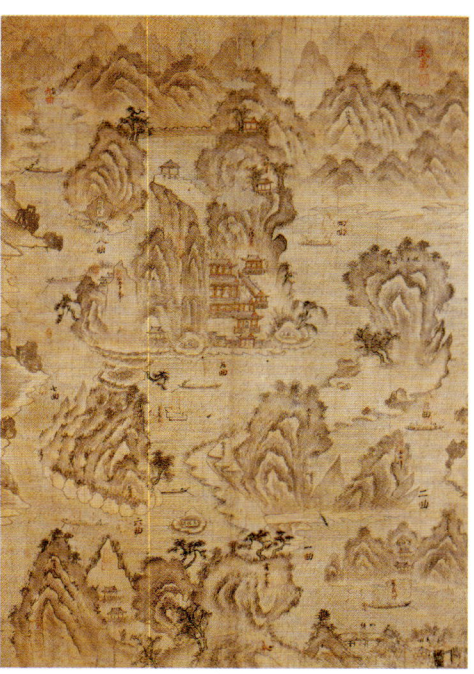

Painting of the Nine Bends of Wuyishan

For the Korean literati, who were infatuated with Zhu Xi's scholarship, Wuyishan, where Zhu Xi retreated to study and lecture, represented the ideal landscape. It was nothing less than a real-life utopia, a sacred and beautiful place they longed for. They deeply regretted that they could not go and see Wuyishan for themselves, so they avidly read the "Record of Mt. Wuyishan" (*Wuyishan zhi*) and recited the poems (accompanied by pictures) extolling the place, even painting pictures on the theme of Wuyi's nine bends (*Wuyi jiuqu*). After Toegye's death, the "Nine bends paintings" (*gugok do*) became an established genre and a means to penetrate Zhu Xi's scholarship.

Zhu Xi chose the nine bends near Wuyishan to admire the beautiful natural landscape and pursue his own learning, and built several cloisters for retreat there (*Hanquan*, *Wuyi* and *Zhulin jingshe*), composing his "Paddle song of Wuyi" (*Wuyi zhaoge*) in retreat. He also repaired the Bailudong and Yuelu private academies so that they could be used for training students. Korean Neo-Confucian literati deeply admired Zhu Xi's lofty academic world, and sought to emulate his life by building similar constructions.

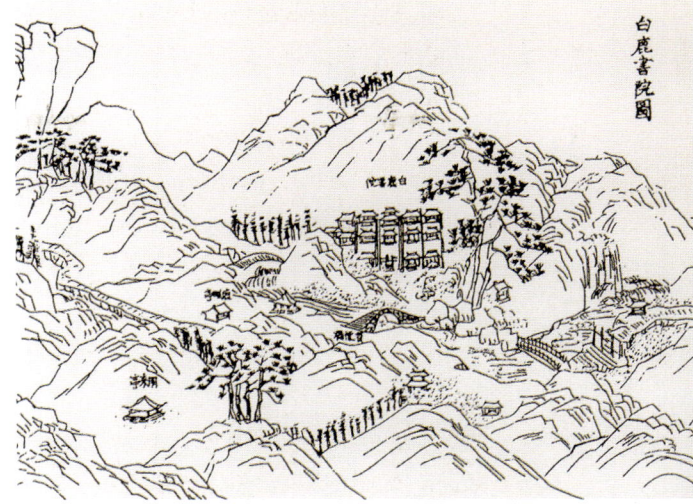

Engraved printing of the Bailudong private academy restored by Zhu Xi

In fact, the cloisters built by Zhu Xi are known as vihāra (*jingshe*, *jeongsa* in Korean), which is originally a Buddhist term meaning "a quiet and peaceful place where monks can practice and live." It was adopted by Neo-Confucians in the sense of "a place to cultivate scholarship or study," and the Korean literati held up Zhu Xi's construction of cloisters as retreats as an ideal, building their own cloisters for study and the cultivation of scholarship.

For the Neo-Confucians of Joseon, Mt. Wuyishan was not just a natural landscape, but a symbolic expression embodying Zhu Xi's scholarly world. Because they revered and followed Zhu Xi's synthesis of Neo-Confucianism, they were also keen to implement his ideas and plans. For them Mt. Wuyishan was not just a place with beautiful scenery; as they regarded the place where Zhu Xi had studied as a setting without equal in the universe, which simply had to be revered. Thus they sought out landscapes in Korea that were similar to those depicted in paintings of the nine bends of Wuyi and imbued these sites with elements of Zhu Xi's '*gugok*' (Nine Bends), sometimes building cloisters there for retreats and the training of followers.

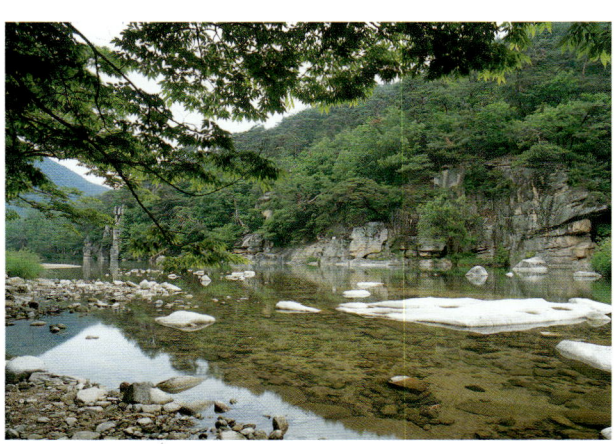

One of the Nine Bends of Hwayang, where Song Si-yeol retreated for study

For example, just as Zhu Xi built the Wuyi cloister and composed the "Hymn on leaving Wuyi cloister, with introduction" (*Wuyi jingshe zayong bingji*), Toegye built the Dosan private school near Andong and composed the "Hymns on Dosan, with introduction" (*Dosan jabyeong byeonggi*) and the "Twelve songs of Dosan" (*Dosan sibi gok*). Yi I (1536-1584), also known as Yulgok, built the Eunbyeong cloister in Haeju (Hwanghae-do province) and wrote the "Songs of the nine bends of Gosan" (*Gosan gugok ga*). Song Si-yeol (1607-1689) and Kim Su-jeung (1624-1701), influenced by Yi I's "Songs of the nine bends of Gosan" built a cloister and sought out the Hwayang and Gogun Gugok near Cheongju and Hwacheon, respectively.

Toegye wrote his "Twelve songs of Dosan" after retiring from official duties and building the Dosan private school to educate his followers, giving expression to his ideal of retreating in nature and achieving unity of Heaven and man. The first song starts as follows:

> Everything seems to go awry, but what to do?
> An ignorant scholar buried in the countryside, where did he go wrong?
> His love of nature turned into a chronic disease, what use its cure?

His earnest desire to live in nature and his love of nature is expressed literally by the phrase "a heart for sources and stones" (*cheonseok gohwang*) and life in the countryside as "a foolish student in the wilderness" (*choya usaeng*). Toegye is here asking: What does it matter if I leave fame behind, bury myself in the countryside without wanting anything, and live as one with nature? This feeling is expressed in many passages of the "Twelve songs of Dosan", but the following passage is the most representative:

> Why is the green mountain always green?
> Why does the flowing brook never stop day or night?
> Let us also try to be as constant as the mountain and the brook.

This passage conveys an educational message, pledging to overcome the fickleness of life by making integrity and personality the means to achieve a consistency and permanence akin to nature, evoked by the images of "green mountain" and "flowing brook." Rather than a life of emptiness and doubt, the author urges us to train mentally and academically with unflagging effort to achieve an "eternal greenness" in our life. In a straight and unadorned style, Toegye here evokes the life of a dedicated scholar, who turns away from ordinary society to immerse himself in nature, train the next generation of scholars and engage in profound contemplation.

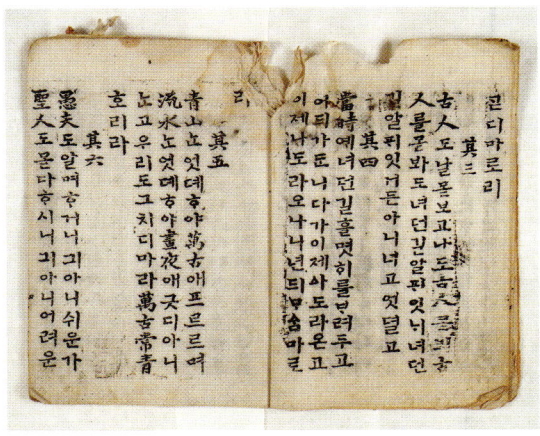

Part of the "Twelve songs of Dosan"

This ideal of retreating into nature and seeking a life in which Heaven and man are one is also found in the construction of *byeolseo*, or cottages. These were small houses built in a natural landscape for study and self-cultiva-

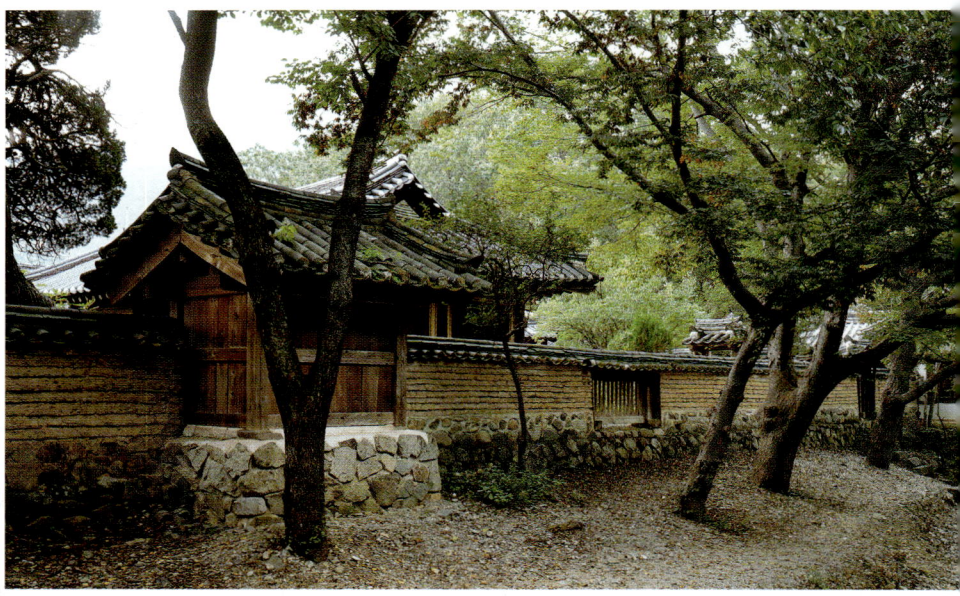

Dongnakdang, seen from the bank of the brook that flows in front of it

tion by literati who wanted to retreat and focus on study and education. Thus the architectural space of these *byeolseo* was also determined by the mental universe and values of the Neo-Confucian literati.

Byeolseo were simple and convenient constructions, consisting of a room and a wooden veranda. However, their architectural space was not limited to the construction itself, but extended to its exterior to draw the surrounding natural environment into the building. The simple structure of the *byeolseo* architecture, integrated with nature, is conducive to the literati's method of study and training, with the ideal of "residing in reverence to attain the utmost principle" (*geogyeong gungni*) and "investigating things to achieve knowledge" (*gyeongmul chiji*).

The choice of location for a *byeolseo* was guided by the criterion that the natural environment should be well suited to academic training and the cultivation of personality. The *byeolseo*'s architectural space was defined by the relationship and interaction between nature and architecture. The choice of a natural environment that accords with the need to study and educate, and the concern about the relation between nature and architecture reflect the "Unity of Heaven and Man" doctrine of the Neo-Confucian literati who built the *byeolseo*, that is to say, the specific way in which they imagined and personified nature.

Among the representative scholars who built *byeolseo* are Yi Eon-jeok and Toegye. Yi Eon-jeok built the Dongnakdang in Angang, near Gyeongju, and Toegye built the Gyesang and Dosan private schools in Yean, the buildings of which are good examples of the characteristics of *byeolseo*.

After retiring from official life, Yi Eon-jeok built a private dwelling at a place where he could retreat and study, constructing his Dongnakdang in a valley near a flowing stream. Whereas the Dongnakdang itself is surrounded by a wall in which lattice windows were installed, thus adopting a somewhat distant and negative relationship with the brook, the Gyejeong (brookside pavilion), on the other hand, stands facing the brook directly in a positive, open way. This is explained by the different character of these two structures: Gyejeong stands in a private space, while Dongnakdang was open to visitors who came and went. "Dongnak" literally means "solitary joy," an appropriate name for a self-contained living space in which to pursue principle with a reverential mind, and thus reveals Yi Eon-jeok's purpose in building this cottage.

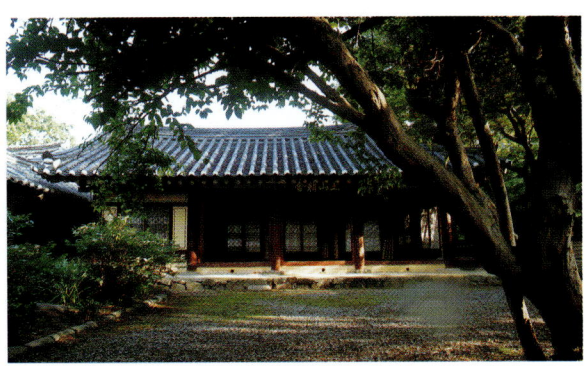
View of Dongnakdang, where Yi Eon-jeok retreated to study

Toegye built the Gyesang private school as a place where he could retreat into nature and teach students. Thanks to the painting of this school by Jeong Seon (pen name Gyeomjae, 1676-1759), we can see that it was surrounded by mountains and that there was a brook flowing in front of it. Thus it was very similar to Dosan seodang, which in Toegye's own words was "embraced by mountains and valleys on all sides."

Both Gyesang seodang and Dosan seodang are good examples of the location of *byeolseo*. Looking at the *Dosan seowon do* painted by Jeong Seon, we see that it stands in the middle of mountain ranges and streams that surround it completely.

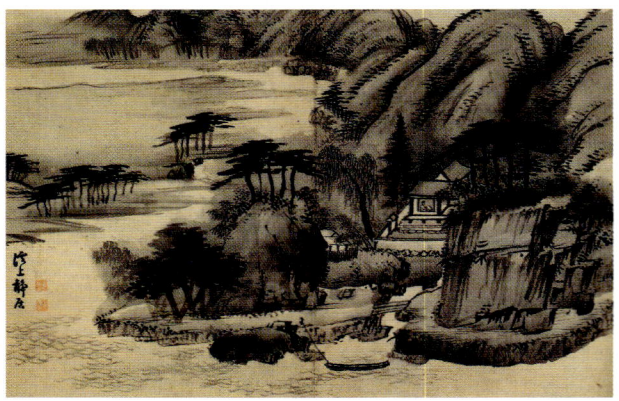

Gyesang jeonggeo do (Quiet repose in Gyesang, by Jeong Seon)

Thus the Neo-Confucian literati conceived of the cloister (*jeongsa*) and the *byeolseo*, which can be seen as being derived from the cloister, as spaces from where they could project their ideas about the meaning of nature onto nature itself, and where they could realize their ideal of learning. In contrast with the high and splendid architecture used for seats of power, cloisters are spaces that achieve more through their emptiness than through any majestic display. The architectural space of the cloisters is not limited to the buildings, and by extending this space to embrace the surrounding nature, it becomes a construction that through its emptiness becomes richer, as it is open to everything.

A *jeongsa* consists basically of a room and a wood-floored veranda (*maru*), amounting to an average floor space of no more than three *kan* (bays, the rectangular space delineated by four columns, a traditional unit for measuring the size of houses). A characteristic feature of *jeongsa* architecture is that while the room and the veranda both communicate with the surrounding landscape, they still coexist within the same building.

Although pavilion architecture, to which the cloisters and *byeol-seo* belong, originally does not have enclosed rooms but only open, wood-floored verandas, in the course of time *ondol*-heated rooms were inserted in the cloisters. This was the result of a shift in the attitude of Neo-Confucian literati towards this type of building. For them the cloister was no longer merely a building from which to enjoy the landscape and relax, but had changed into a residential space that furthermore served to pursue scholarship in harmony with nature, cultivate the mind and foster disciples.

An example of this is Amseojae, located in Hwayang-dong, Cheongju (Chungcheongbuk-do province). This was the place Song Si-yeol retreated to after retiring from government to pursue his scholarship and educate students, and is a cloister located on the fourth bend of the Hwayang nine bends by the Geumsadam cliff. Song Si-yeol, who was captivated by Zhu Xi's scholarship, tried to replicate the nine bends of Wuyi in the Hwayang nine bends, and thus the Amseojae was modeled after Zhu Xi's Yungu cloister.

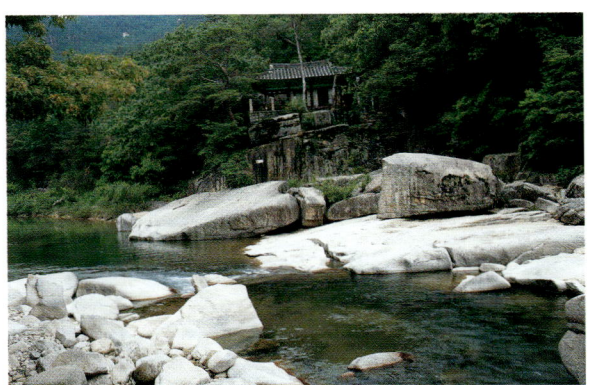

Amseojae

The floor space of Amseojae measures two by three *kan*, with the three *kan* on the southern side occupied by a wooden veranda. Two *kan* on the eastern side have heated *ondol* floors, while the sixth and last *kan* is an elevated veranda open on three sides (*numaru*) situated on the western side, and looking out over a stream. A poem composed and sung by Song Si-yeol at this place reflects his thoughts well:

Neo-Confucian worldview and *seowon* architecture

> The stream has opened up the boulders,
> And in that space a cottage was built.
> Sitting quietly in search of the classics, the students
> Exert their utmost to follow just an inch of the teaching.

This way of achieving harmony between architecture and nature as reflected in the cloisters, built as a retreat in nature, is one method of creating a human living environment in harmony with nature. This environment shows that the true appreciation of beautiful scenery is the highest plane of understanding attainable by man, the plane where the unity of Heaven and man can be achieved. The planning of this Neo-Confucian architecture reveals the intention of personifying nature and making man part of nature. In a nutshell, the "Unity of Heaven and Man" doctrine can be explained as a system of thought that does not segregate culture and nature. Cultural phenomena are also natural phenomena, and natural phenomena also express a cultural meaning: This concept is clearly expressed in the pavilion architecture of the private academies.

3. Architecture of private academies

1) Spatial arrangement and location of buildings

According to Confucian ethical norms, the concept of propriety (*ye*, also embracing ritual actions) is very important. It is not only a conceptual basis for ruling the country, it also circumscribes the actions of people. In a Confucian society, architecture too is seen to function within the framework of propriety. In particular, the formal rules regarding architecture are an important part of the ritual codes (*yeje*) of Confucianism. Moreover, there is also a special ritual architecture (*yeje geonchuk*), which came into existence in response to the requirements of *ye*.

As its name indicates, ritual architecture mainly comprises constructions where rituals are performed or where the Board of Rites (*yebu*) is housed. Among these are sacrificial buildings such as the Suburban Altar to Heaven and Earth (Gyogu), the Royal Ancestral Shrine (Jongmyo), and the Altar for the Earth and Grain Gods (Sajikdan); buildings for cultural edification, such as the bright hall (*myeongdang*), and the *byeogong*, structures described in the *Book of Rites* that expressed the ruler's civilizing power; and also educational buildings. But the most important architecture is undoubtedly that of the sacrificial institutions and shrines. From the perspective of Confucian ethical norms, it is therefore compulsory that educational buildings such as the National Confucian Academy, the county schools, and the private academies should have a shrine to perform sacrificial rites.

Also, in Confucian thinking the concept of correct lineage occupies a very important place. This refers to the correct transmission of teachings, in other words to the orthodox teaching transmitted from teacher to student. In Neo-Confucianism, the teacher-student lineages (*dotong*) that determined much of intellectual and official life, and the prestigious caretaking roles in the Shrine for Confucius (Munmyo) are all based on this concept. Debates on how to display the main line of royal descent in the Royal Ancestral Shrine, where the spirit tablets of deceased members of the royal lineage are worshiped, and the *pungsu* specialist's calculation of hierarchies in mountain ranges, are all grounded in this concept of correct lineage.

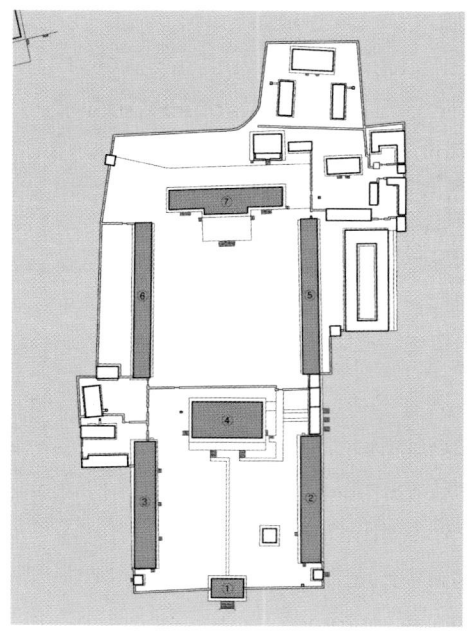

Building arrangement of the National Confucian Academy, Seonggyungwan

Shrine compound
1. spirit gate
2. eastern chamber
3. western chamber
4. shrine

Study compound
5. eastern dormitory
6. western dormitory
7. lecture hall

For the Joseon court, which had adopted Neo-Confucianism as its governing ideology, the ritual codes and the concept of orthodox lineage were equally important. The royal palaces, the Royal Ancestral Shrine, the Altar for Earth and Grain Gods, and the National Confucian Academy were all important buildings and facilities to implement the dynasty's ritual program. Just as the Shrine for Confucius symbolizes the main Confucian lineage starting with Confucius himself, the shrines of private academies symbolized the main lineage starting with the Korean sage worshiped there. Since the first private academy, Baegundong, was established in memory of An Hyang, the first to introduce Zhu Xi's teachings, it came to symbolize the orthodox Neo-Confucian lineage of Korea.

The official school system of the Joseon dynasty comprised the "Four schools" (*sahak*) in the four districts of the capital and the county schools in the provinces, with the National Confucian Academy acting as the highest educational institution, ranking above all the others. In the main, these institutions were composed of the Shrine for Confucius, in which offerings to Confucius and his disciples took place in the Daeseongjeon main shrine and its east (*dongmu*) and west (*seomu*) detached wings; the Hall of Bright Ethics (Myeongnyundang), used for lectures; and the *dongjae* and *seojae*, the eastern and western dormitory buildings.

Insofar as they comprised both areas for instruction and for worship, the private academies followed the model of the official schools in their implementation of the Neo-Confucian ritual program. Like the official schools, the academies were needed by the *sarim* literati for education and the performance of sacrifices. But whereas in the case of the Shrine for Confucius the objects of veneration were determined by the state, in the case of the academies they were selected by private groups.

A typical private academy can be divided into several important areas, among which the sacrificial or shrine area, where previous sages are enshrined and rites performed in their honor, comes first; furthermore, there is the study area, where the students study and cultivate themselves; the pavilion-gate area (*numun*), where everyone comes for repose; the administrative area, which oversees the lecture facilities and shrine; and finally the area surrounding the academy.

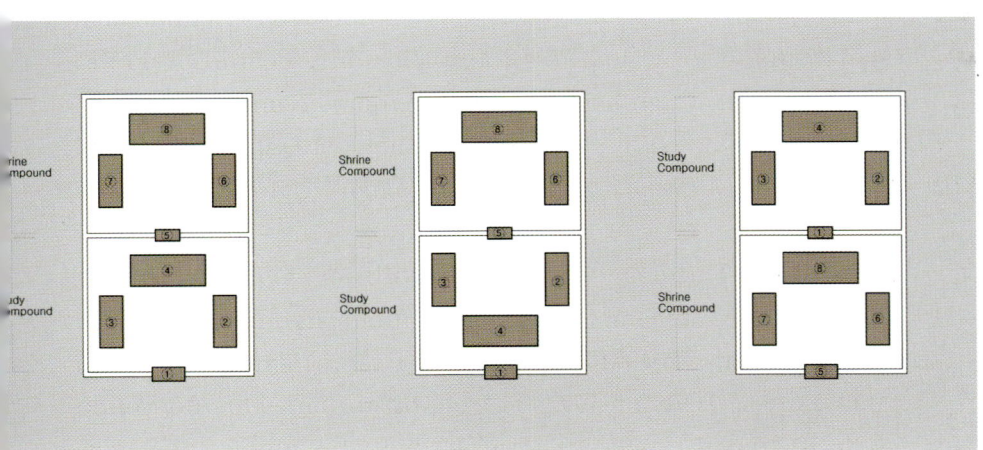

Building arrangement of a typical county school

Study compound
1. gate
2. eastern dormitory
3. western dormitory
4. lecture hall

Shrine compound
5. spirit gate
6. eastern chamber
7. western chamber
8. shrine

Architecture of private academies

In general, the pavilion-gate area is at the front of the private academy; it is after passing through this area that you enter the study area, and then finally the shrine area. Each of these three sections is enclosed by a wall, while the landscape around the academy constitutes the surrounding area. The lecture hall is at the heart of the study compound, while the *dongjae* and *seojae*, where the students study and sleep, are located either in front of or behind the lecture hall. The study and pavilion-gate areas were built so as to allow people to move in and out freely, creating a vibrant and open atmosphere. Access to the shrine compound on the other hand was always restricted, and its construction emphasized a solemn and peaceful mood.

The Baegundong academy was established at a time when shrines and lecture halls were still regarded as separate entities. This sets it apart from *seowon* founded in later years, when it was generally recognized that private academies consisted of both a shrine and a lecture hall. From the arrangement of buildings in the Sosu (i.e. Baegundong) academy it is clear that it dates from a period when the typical *seowon* layout had not yet been established. Although the shrine and study areas of the Sosu academy are clearly differentiated, there is almost no indication of their mutual relationship in the arrangement of their buildings. Also, the relationship between the lecture hall

Main gate, Sosu seowon

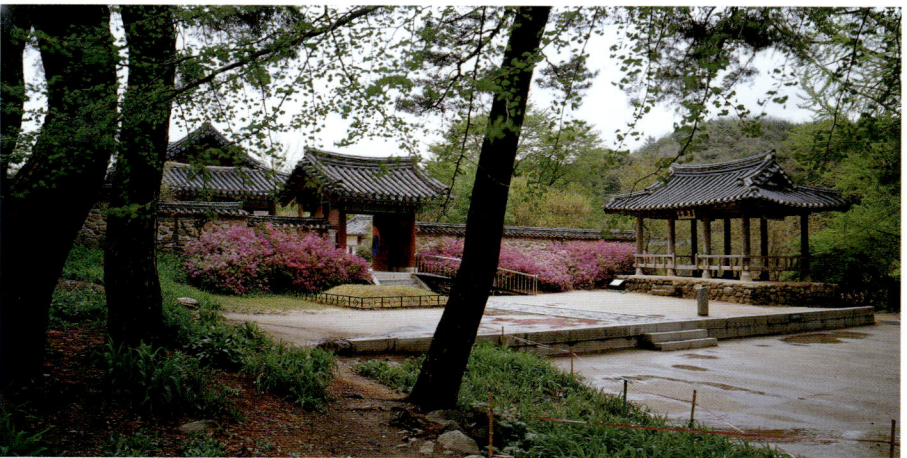

(Myeongnyundang) as the center of the study compound and the surrounding dormitory and study buildings is not at all evident; the front gate is a simple one-*kan* gate, and there are no separate gates for the different compounds (the so-called triple gate (*sammun*) pattern) as in later academies. In other words, the architectural layout of Sosu seowon reveals neither the character, function, nor the mutual relationship between the buildings.

Although private academies served both educational and religious roles, Toegye's efforts ensured that the educational role took precedence. In most of the academies erected in the century or so spanning the later years of Myeongjong's reign, the reign of King Seonjo (1568-1608), and the reign of King Hyeonjong (1660-1674), the lecture hall is at the heart of the academy's layout. This is the period when the *sarim* literati started entering the political arena, and when the private academy's architectural arrangement was consolidated. As the academies' scholastic function was paramount in this period, a logical outcome of this trend was that the representative architectural *seowon* type established in this period placed the lecture hall at its center.

If we take a look at the location and building arrangement of academies founded in this period, it becomes apparent that they were built on sloping ground, with the front located on the lowest ground, and that the shrine is located at the back, the lecture hall in the middle and the dormitories facing each other in front of the lecture hall. The shrine area and the study area are each located in separate compounds surrounded by walls, and from their relative position and design it is immediately evident that the study area was considered more important. The representative private academies built on this plan during this period are Namgye seowon (1552), Seoak seowon (1561), Yerim seowon (1567), Dodong seowon (1568), Geumo seowon (1570), Oksan seowon (1573), Dosan seowon (1574), Deokcheon seowon (1576), Seogye seowon (1606), Byeongsan seowon (1614), and Nogang seowon (1675, in Nonsan).

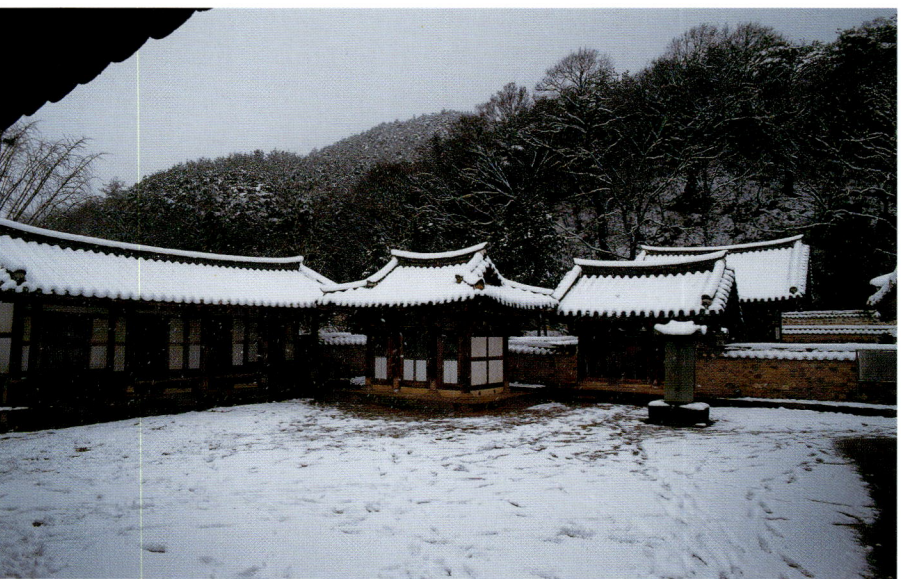

View of Piram seowon, where the dormitories are placed behind the lecture hall

By contrast, the layout of *seowon* established in the 70-year period from Sukjong's reign (1675-1720) to the beginning of Yeongjo's reign (1724-1776), a period when *seowon* construction proliferated, centers on the shrine. The proliferation of *seowon* was halted only during Yeongjo's reign: in 1741 alone 173 *seowon* were demolished, with the total number destroyed during his reign reaching 300. With the construction of so many new academies, their educational function started to decline, while the shrine came more to the foreground. As a result, the distinction between main areas and subordinate areas became more

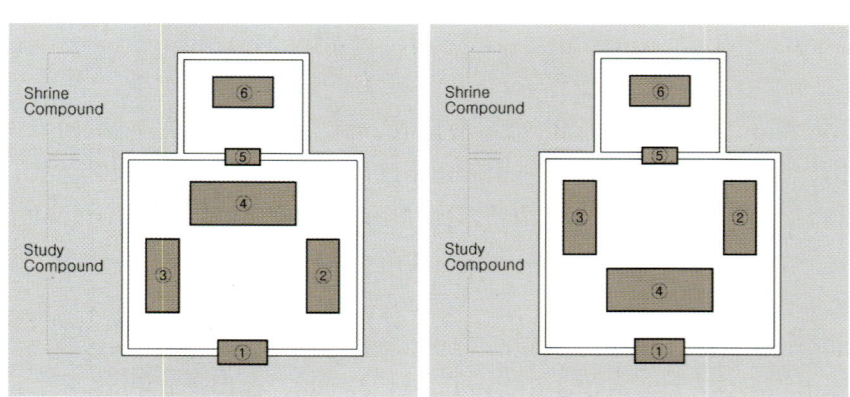

Building arrangements of private academies where the dormitories are located in front of the lecture hall (left), and behind the lecture hall (right)

Study compound
1. gate
2. eastern dormitory
3. western dormitory
4. lecture hall

Shrine compound
5. spirit gate
6. shrine

70 THE ARCHITECTURE OF KOREA'S PRIVATE ACADEMIES

and more blurred. Especially the role of subordinate buildings such as the building where ritual offerings were prepared (*jeonsacheong*) and the library (*jangseogak*) was no longer evident in the architectural arrangement of the buildings.

This shift in emphasis from the educational to the ritual role is reflected in the architectural layout of these new academies. In this new arrangement, the lecture hall loses some of its prominence, and the dormitories are moved towards the back of the lecture hall: They are now located between the lecture hall and the shrine. Also, the buildings that assist the lecture hall's educational role start to decrease, while those assisting the shrine in its functioning show an increase. The representative academies of this period are Piram seowon (moved to its present location in 1672), Simgok seowon (1650), Deokbong seowon (1695), Bongam seowon (1697) and Heungam seowon (1702).

2) Main buildings and facilities of private academies

(1) Entrance

Hongsalmun gate (red gate with spiked top)

The private academy's grounds start at the gate Hongsalmun. As a symbolic structure emphasizing the solemn and sacral character of the academy, this gate is the first structure one encounters on the way to the academy's entrance. In fact, there are no actual doors in the Hongsalmun, and it has no roof. It only consists of two poles on either side of the road, connected with each other at the top by two horizontal bars, on which are planted a row of wooden arrows. Because it is painted red and studded with arrows, it is called Hongsalmun, which literally means "red arrow gate." Such gates,

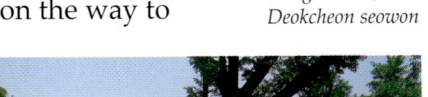
Hongsalmun, Deokcheon seowon

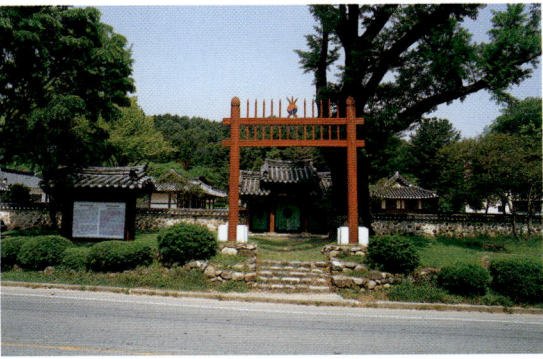

which are also erected at the entrance of royal tombs and county schools, serve as markers to signal that you are approaching a hallowed area where the spirit tablet of a king or former sage is kept, or another important place worthy of respect.

Dismounting stone (*hamaseok*)

Since private academies contain shrines where the spirit tablet of a deceased sage is enshrined, as a mark of respect for the deceased's soul everyone regardless of rank and status had to descend from his horse or get out of the palanquin when reaching this stone marker. The stone, which is also referred to as a *hamabi*, or dismounting stele, is usually erected near Hongsalmun. A *hamaseok* was also erected in front of other important places that were deemed worthy of reverence, including the palaces, the royal memorial shrine, the National Confucian Academy, and the county schools. In present-day Korea the custom of getting off your bike or stopping your car and getting out to greet an important person can still occasionally be observed, and may well be a remainder of the custom of dismounting before the *hamaseok*.

One or two gingko trees were often planted in front of the

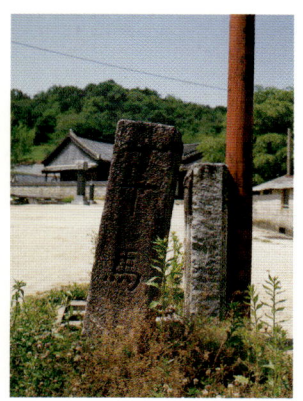
Dismounting stone, Donam seowon

Outer gate with even ridgeline, Oksan seowon

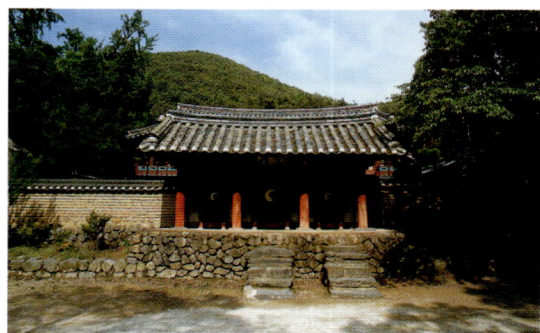

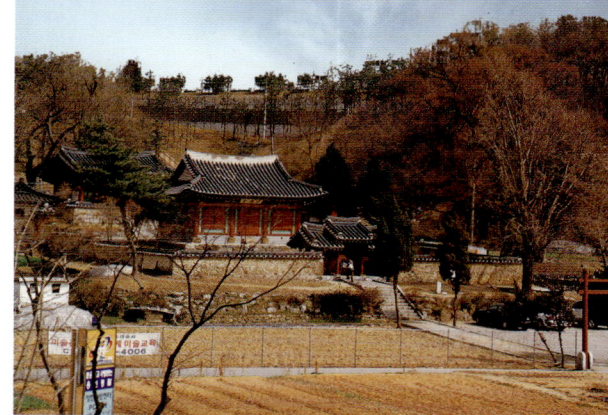
Outer gate with elevated middle ridge, located between Hongsalmun and the lecture hall of Simgok seowon

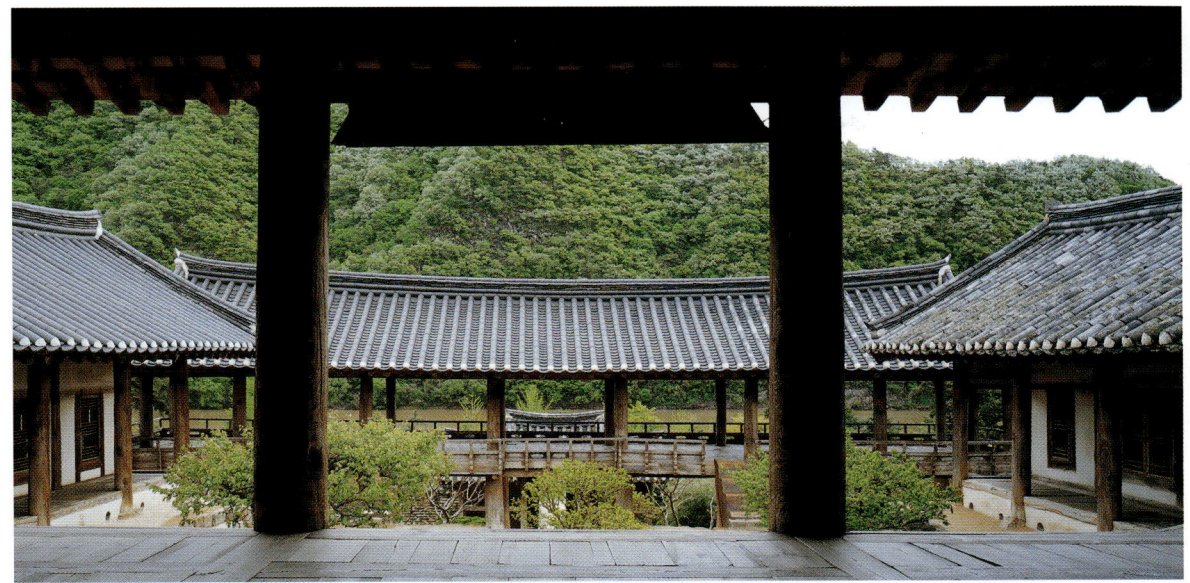

Mandaeru, Byeongsan seowon

academy or near Hongsalmun or the *hamaseok* to indicate that this was also a place of education. Because the gingko tree shoots up straight and fast towards Heaven, it came to symbolize the fostering of many upright and high-minded officials. Also, the many fruits borne by this tree expressed the wish that the academy too might produce many scholars year on year.

The outer gate, pavilion and gate pavilion

The outer gate (*oemun*) is the academy's main gate. Because it usually occupies a surface of three *kan*, it is also referred to as the "outer triple-gate" (*oesammun*). In some cases the middle section of the gate's tiled roof is elevated over the two side sections, but it is also common to have gates with one straight ridgeline.

The private academies were located amidst beautiful natural scenery, as this allowed the scholars to retreat and cultivate their hearts and minds to achieve the ideal of unity of Heaven and man. Now the most appopriate form of architecture in this regard is the pavilion,

Hyeongaru, the pavilion gate of Museong seowon

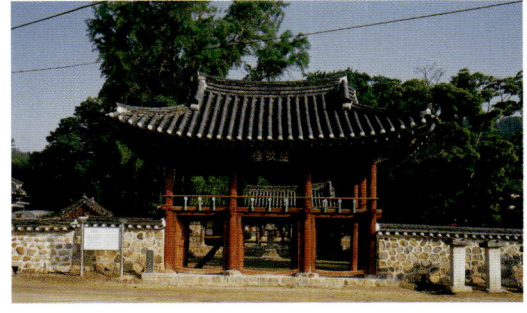

which is open on all sides. On the open wooden floor of the pavilion, scholars could engage in debates, have poetry meetings, or just relax and absorb the scenery. Thus the pavilions were often used by students to take a break from their arduous study and lift their spirits by contemplating nature. For this reason, pavilions were often located at the entrance of the academy, the place where nature and human construction meet.

A pavilion (*nu*) is a two-story building with a loft (*darak*), which is open on all sides. Depending on the academy, some have no outer gate but instead use the pavilion as an entrance gate, some have established the pavilion just inside the outer gate, and some academies simply have no pavilion. Among the pavilions that function simultaneously as the outer gate (therefore called pavilion gate, *numun*) are Pungyeongnu of Namgye seowon, Suwollu of Dodong seowon, Hwagyeollu of Piram seowon, and Hyeongaru of Museong seowon. Examples of pavilions that are established inside the academy's perimeter behind the outer gate are Mubyeollu of Oksan seowon and Mandaeru of Byeongsan seowon.

(2) Study compound

Passing through the outer gate or pavilion gate you step into the study compound. As the area where students receive training and cultivate their minds, it consists of a lecture hall and student dormitories. As for the arrangement of these buildings, generally the lecture hall (*gangdang*) is in the middle of the compound with the dormitories (*dongjae* and *seojae*) in front of it, although in some academies of the later Joseon

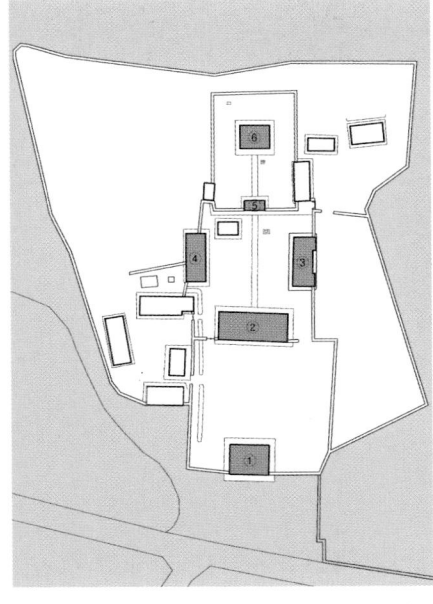
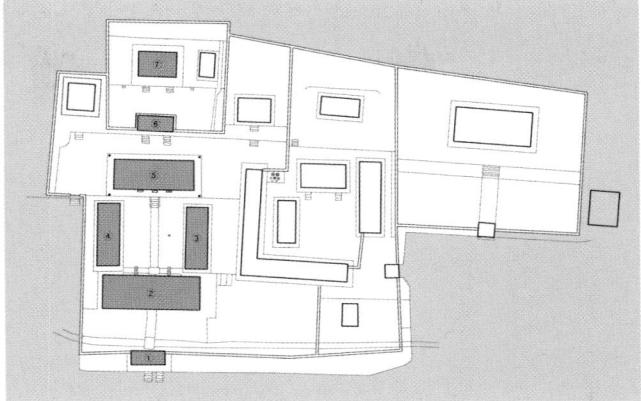

Building arrangement, Piram seowon; an example of a private academy where the dormitories are situated behind the lecture hall

Study compound
1. gate-pavilion
2. lecture hall
3. eastern dormitory
4. western dormitory

Shrine compound
5. spirit gate
6. shrine

Building arrangement, Oksan seowon; here the dormitories are situated in front of the lecture hall

Study compound
1. gate
2. pavilion
3. eastern dormitory
4. western dormitory
5. lecture hall

Shrine compound
6. spirit gate
7. shrine

period the lecture hall is located towards the front of the compound and the dormitories behind it. Representative of the former arrangement are Namgye seowon, Oksan seowon, Dosan seowon, Yerim seowon and Byeongsan seowon, while many academies in the southwest are representative of the latter arrangement, including Piram seowon, Heungam seowon and Bongam seowon.

Lecture hall

The lecture hall is the place where students learn the Confucian classics, though it also acted as a residence for the president and vice-president. This is where the president gave seminars, which would invariably start by intoning the Bailudong rules and the Community Compact (*hyangyak*). It was also used as a general meeting place for the academy's scholars and a gathering place during sacrificial rites.

Lecture hall, Dodong seowon

Most of the lecture halls measure five bays lengthwise, although this varies somewhat from one academy to another. In cases where the lecture building measures five *kan*, the three bays in the middle make up the main wood-floored room, while the one-*kan* rooms on each side are *ondol*-heated rooms. Looking towards the lecture hall from the yard in front, the room on the right is used by the president, and the one on the left by the vice-president. The main floored hall is the central area in the scholars' pursuit of learning and inner cultivation, and is used for lectures and discussions between teachers and students but also to perform rituals.

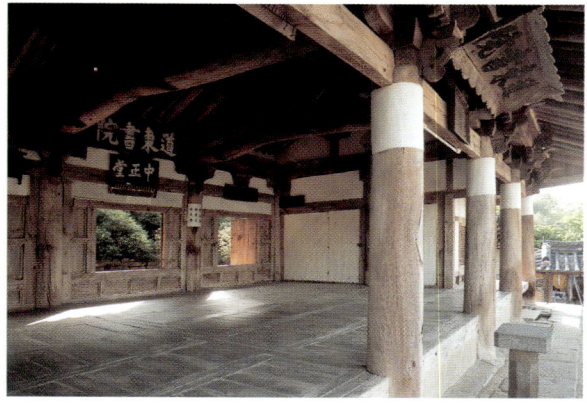

Main wood-floored room of the lecture hall, Dodong seowon

The lecture halls are usually given names that end in the suffix *-dang* (hall), as in Myeongseongdang of Namgye seowon, Guindang of Oksan seowon, and Cheongjeoldang of Piram seowon. Below the eaves on the front side of the lecture hall hangs a board inscribed with the academy's name, while the name of the lecture hall itself is inscribed on a board that is usually hung on the back wall of the lecture hall. Above the entrance to the *ondol* rooms boards are hung with the names of these rooms. Furthermore, the Bailudong academy rules are hung on the walls and ceiling of the main floored hall, together with the academy's record (*wongi*) as well as exhortations and epitaphs. There are usually two flights of stairs leading up the foundation platform on which the lecture hall sits, one on the east for scholars and students, and one on the west for servants and other people of lower status. Reflecting the Confucian worldview and values, the lecture hall is not very impressive in size but rather elegant in a restrained way.

Lecture halls are found not only in private academies, but also in the National Confucian Academy, county schools and Buddhist temples. In the case of the National Confucian Academy and the county schools, the lecture hall is invariably known as Myeongnyundang. In Buddhist temples, the place where sūtras are read or the Buddha's dharma explained is also called a lecture hall (*gangdang*). During the Three Kingdoms and Unified Silla periods the lecture hall was located behind the "Golden Hall" (*geumdang*), the main worship hall housing the Buddha statues. In the course of the Goryeo period, however, the Golden Hall was transformed into a Dharma hall (*beopdang*), which also served as a worship hall. In some cases, a building called *gangwon* (lecture institute) was erected on the left or right side of the yard in front of the Dharma hall and used as a lecture hall.

Dormitory

The dormitory (*jaesa*), as a place where students slept and studied, was usually equipped with both a wood-floored room and one or more *ondol* rooms. There are usually two dormitory buildings called *dongjae* (eastern dormitory) and *seojae* (western dormitory), facing each other on the western and eastern sides of the yard in front of or at the back of the lecture hall. If they are located in front of the lecture hall, when looking out from the lecture hall the eastern dormitory would be on the left and the western dormitory on the right. The eastern dormitory housed the more senior students.

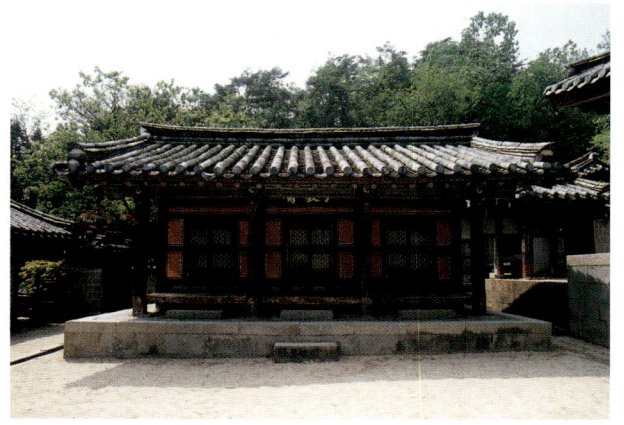

Honguijae, the western dormitory of Dosan seowon

The scale of the dormitory buildings varied from two to five *kan* lengthwise and from one to three *kan* on the sides. The buildings' foundation platform was one tier lower than the lecture hall, the buildings themselves were smaller than the lecture hall, and the roof styles were also different: While the lecture hall had a hipped and gabled roof, the dormitories had a lower, simpler pitched roof. This distinction in building styles served to express the difference in rank between these buildings.

Printing-block storehouse, library

Insofar as it functioned as an educational facility, the collection, storing, management and printing of books formed an important part of the private academy's activities. During the Joseon period, books were produced by movable type printing, woodblock printing, copying, and carving on stone. Academies that had the financial means printed their own books, which were mostly the collected works of former sages printed with woodblocks. The wooden slates used for woodblock printing were stored in the printing-block storehouse (*jangpangak*), while printed books and documents were stored in the library

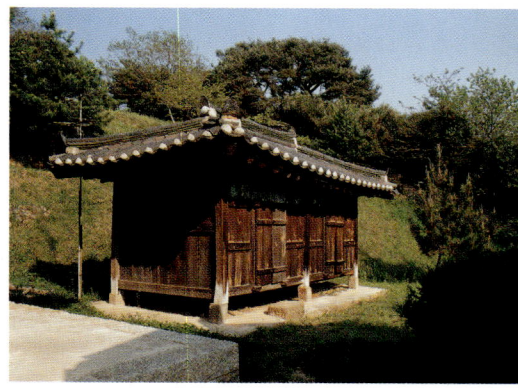

Printing-block storehouse, Namgye seowon

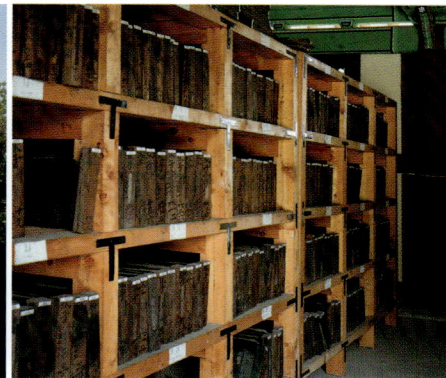

Inside view of the printing-block storehouse of Munheon seowon: printing blocks and rack for storing them

(*jangseogak*), both buildings that formed part of the study compound. Only big academies had separate buildings to store printing blocks and books. Although these buildings belonged to the study compound, they were usually at some distance from the lecture hall and the dormitories so that if a fire broke out it would not spread. Books and documents were guarded jealously, and they were not allowed to be taken out of the academy; the entrance to the library was also closely monitored.

The printing-block storehouse and the library usually had a pitched roof, and in the middle bay at the front, or in all bays, there was a door made of wooden planks; the floor was also made of wood. Because moisture can damage printing blocks and paper, the circulation of air was encouraged by making ventilation holes in the walls or installing lattice windows. For the walls, wooden planks were used rather than earth, as these let in more wind. The wooden boards of the floor were installed somewhat above the ground, to protect against moisture seepage.

The libraries made a major cultural contribution at a time when books were not widely available, and so the publication, spread, collection and conservation of books at academies during the Joseon dynasty played a role that was at least as important as that of modern libraries and university publishers today.

(3) Shrine compound

Behind the study compound, encircled by a wall is the compound with the shrine at its center. This compound usually consists of the spirit gate, the shrine and an auxiliary building for the preparation of ritual offerings (*jeonsacheong*).

Spirit gate

As the main gate leading to the shrine compound, the spirit gate (*sinmun*) functions as a barrier between the study and the shrine com-

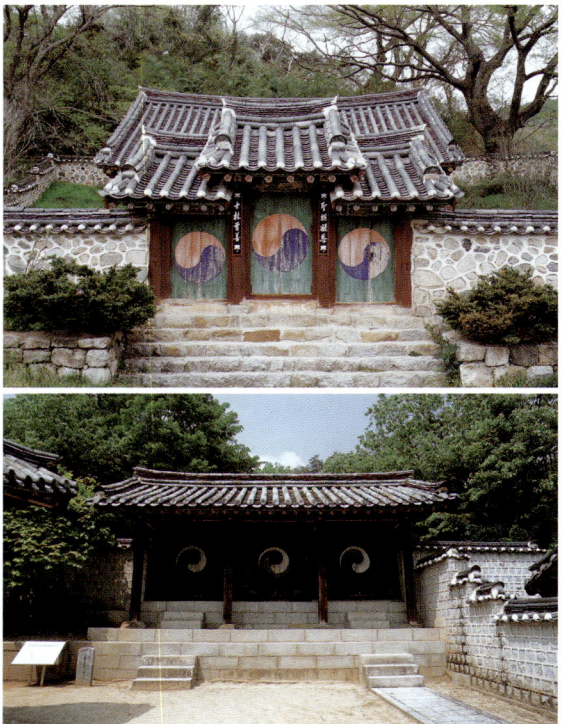

The spirit gate in Museong seowon with an elevated middle ridge

The spirit gate of Dosan seowon with an even ridge line

pounds. As it is the last gate within the private academy's perimeter, it is also called the inner gate (*naemun*), in contrast to the outer gate, the main entry to the academy. Furthermore, as it usually consists of three *kan*, it is also referred to as the "inner triple gate" (*naesammun*). In cases where there are three bays, with a gate door in every bay, the middle gate door is usually kept closed, only being opened for the ritual officiants at sacrifices. Otherwise only the western gate may be used to enter the shrine.

Shrine

The shrine (*sadang*) was at the heart of the shrine compound, and as it housed the spirit tablet of the academy's spiritual mainstay, to whom offerings were made twice a year in spring and autumn, this was the innermost sanctum of the academy, and as such commanded the most respect. Whereas the National Confucian Academy and the county schools had a shrine dedicated to

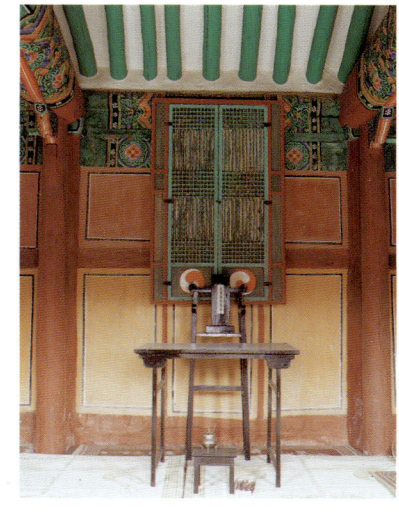

Interior of the Taesansa shrine at Museong seowon

80 THE ARCHITECTURE OF KOREA'S PRIVATE ACADEMIES

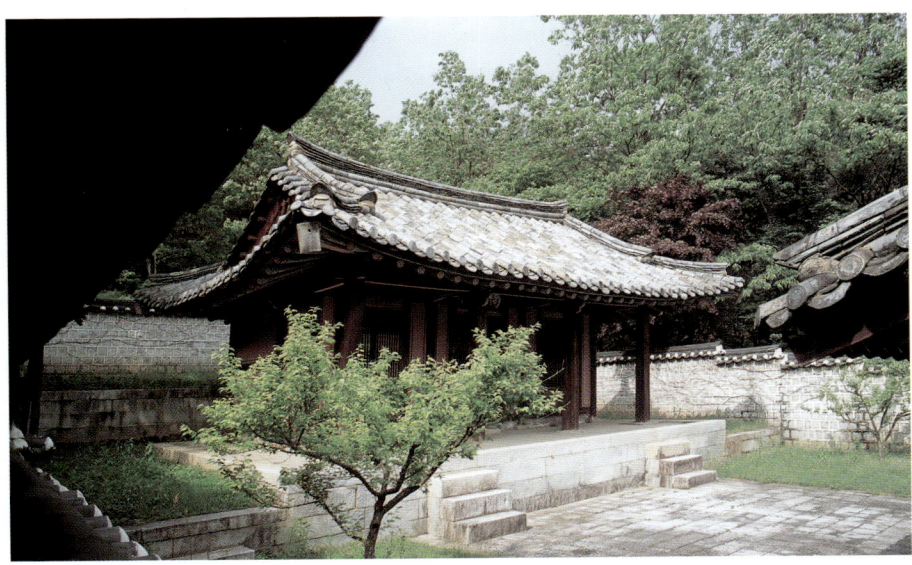

Sangdeoksa shrine, Dosan seowon

Confucius and his disciples, the academy shrines were dedicated to Korean sages such as An Hyang, Jeong Mong-ju and Toegye. These sages were venerated for varying reasons: Some were upheld as paragons of loyalty, others, especially in the later part of the Joseon period, were respected teachers whose disciples wanted to show their reverence. Depending on the background of the person venerated at the shrine, academies can thus be divided into those putting the Learning of the Way first, then into those honoring loyalty, and finally those founded by a particular clan or lineage.

Originally only one person was enshrined as the main object of veneration and offerings in a shrine, but later on, for various reasons additional people were enshrined as objects of worship. In principle the shrine consisted of just one building, but in some cases additional shrines (*byeolsa*) were established, as in Namgye seowon and Dodong seowon, although these were

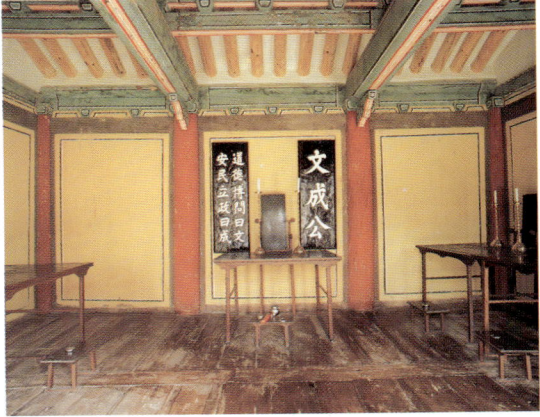

Interior of the shrine at Sosu seowon

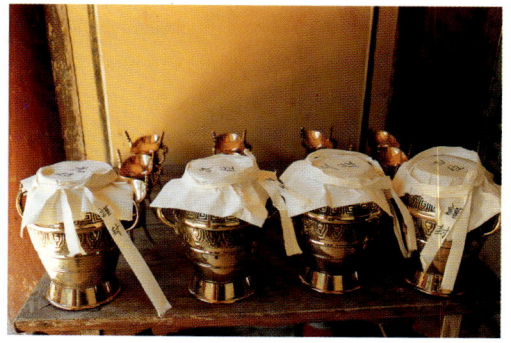

Ritual implements at Sosu seowon

demolished during the reign of King Gojong (1863-1907). In some private academies, such as Obong seowon in Gangneung and Jaedong seowon in Goheung, two shrines were established. In the latter half of the 18th century an important shift took place; as the educational function of the academies was neglected in favor of its ritual role, the shrines were regarded as more important.

Most of the shrines measure three *kan* in length and two *kan* in width. At the front of the building, two flights of stairs lead up the foundation platform, where an extra *kan* of floor space (*toetkan*) outside

Ritual implements

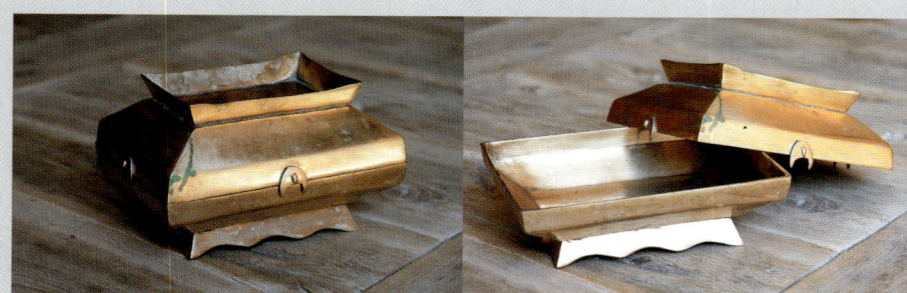

Bo, a brass container for rice and millet

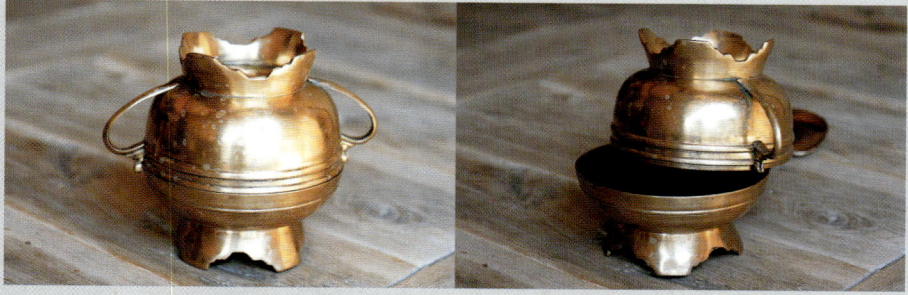

Gwe, a brass container for Chinese millet

the building proper is provided for the performance of rituals; this ritual space is covered by a roof supported by pillars, but is otherwise open to the elements. Most shrines have a pitched roof. Because it is used to enshrine a spirit tablet, which is usually placed against the back wall, the only entrance is at the front of the building; the walls are thick and inside it is dark, creating a melancholy and reverential atmosphere. The spirit tablet of the main person to whom the academy is dedicated is placed on a table standing against the central part of the back wall; sometimes subordinate people are also worshiped to the left and right, in which case they are arranged from the right-hand side (west) of the back wall to the left-hand side according to their rank.

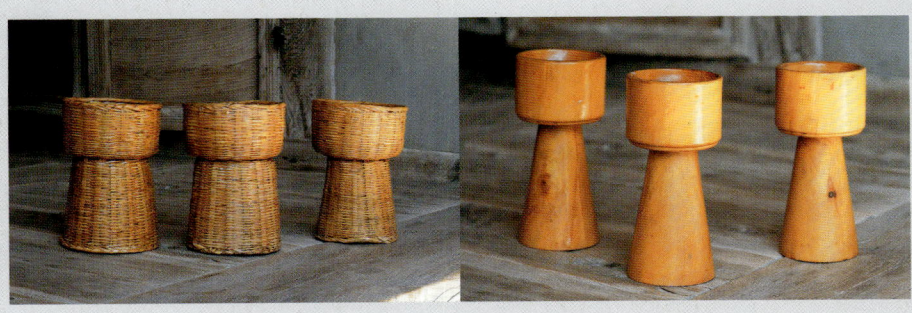

Byeon, implements made of bamboo for serving dry offerings such as fruits and dried foods

Du, wooden implements for serving moist or liquid offerings such as meat and broth

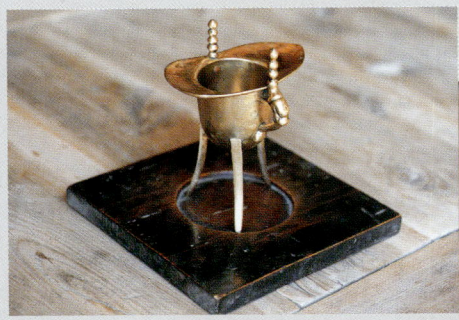

Jak, a brass goblet

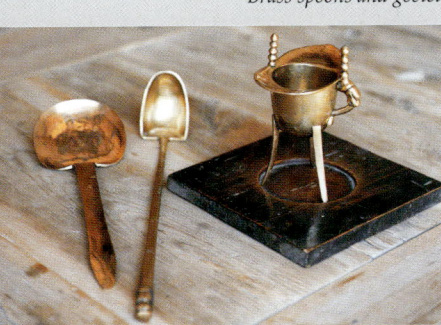

Brass spoons and goblet

Architecture of private academies 83

(4) Additional buildings

Stewards' house

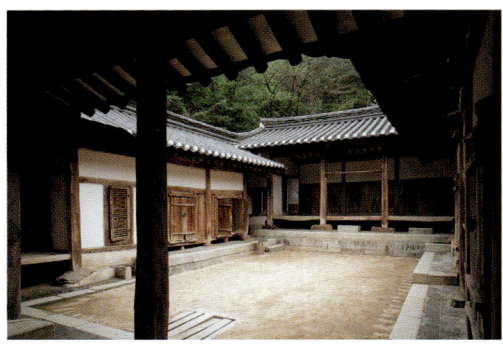

The stewards' house in Dosan seowon, which is arranged around a yard

The stewards' house (*gojiksa*) is the place where those who look after and maintain the academy live and work. Generally it is located next to the study compound and is encircled by its own wall. Normally the stewards prepare the meals of the scholars and students as well as the offerings for the memorial rites. For this reason this building also has a storage area where food and utensils are kept.

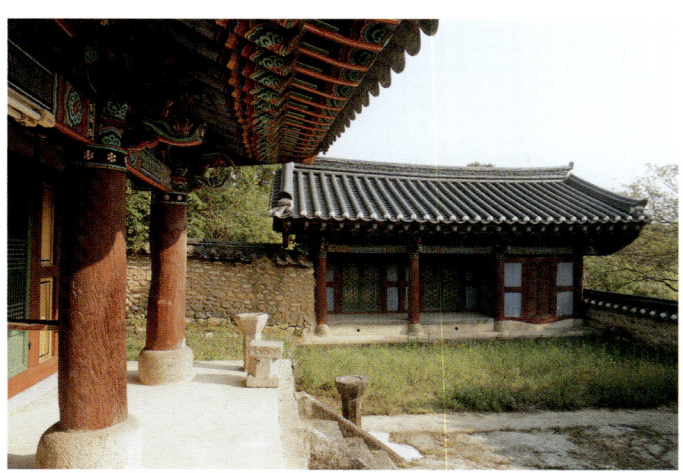

Jeonsacheong (building where sacrifices are prepared) in Namgye seowon, situated to the left in front of the shrine

The stewards' house is similar to an ordinary house in that it consists of a room, a main wood-floored room and a kitchen which are all on the ground level, but differs insofar as the inner courtyard functions as an extension of the kitchen and is used for working, and that there are no men's quarters (*sarangchae*). Generally the building is arranged in the shape of a square or an open square, although in the Jeolla-do provinces it is generally in a single line, and in the Chungcheong-do provinces in an L shape; in the Gyeongsang-do provinces either the square or open square layout is used. Food prepared in the stewards' house is transported to the study quarters through the side gate (*hyeommun*), which separates the two areas, and while the president and other prominent scholars are served individually in their rooms, the students eat together in the dormitories.

Jeonsacheong, jegigo

These two buildings belong to the shrine compound; the former (*jeonsacheong*) is used to prepare the sacrificial offerings during the memorial rites, while the storage area (*jegigo*) is used to store the ritual vessels and other ritual implements needed for the rites. Some academies do not have separate buildings, but store the ritual vessels and implements in the *jeonsacheong*.

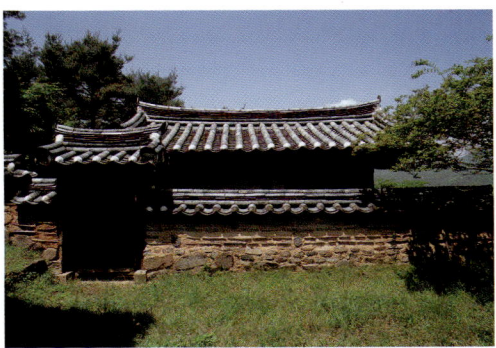

Because of their function, these buildings are located close to the shrine compound. In some academies, including Namgye seowon, Seoak seowon and Jagye seowon, these auxiliary buildings are actually located within the shrine compound, but in other academies, including Dodong seowon, Dosan seowon and Byeongsan seowon, they are located in a separate compound encircled by a wall.

Jeonsacheong, Dodong seowon

(5) Additional facilities

Saengdan

The *saengdan* is a small stone dais on which the sacrificial animal to be used in the memorial rites is inspected. The ceremony of inspecting and assessing the sacrificial animal, referred to as *saengganpum*, begins with the ritual officiants and related officers taking their places around the altar. It ends with the eulogist, standing to the west of the altar, asking whether the animal is "fat" (*dol*), and the officiant affirming by saying "adequate" (*chung*). After this everything is ready to be offered. This altar is usually placed in the shrine compound, but Namgye seowon, where it stands to the right (north) of the lecture hall, is an ex-

Stele to which the sacrificial animal is tied, Piram seowon

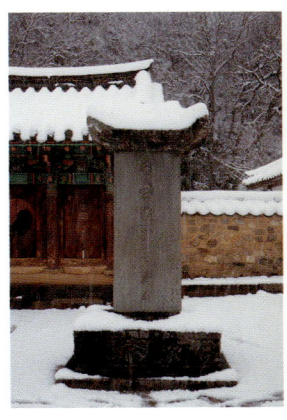

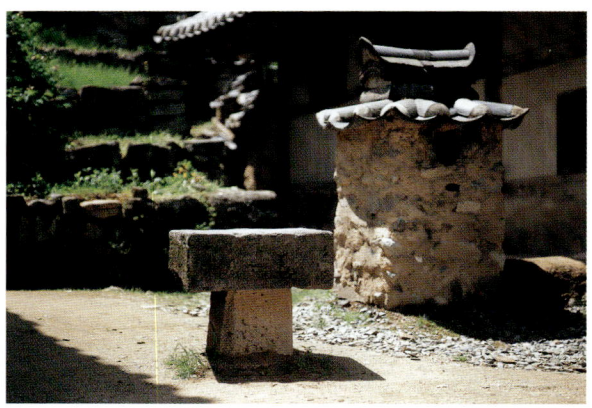

Saengdan (sacrificial altar) at Dodong seowon, situated to the left of the lecture hall

ception to this general rule. Other exceptions are Yerim seowon, where it can be found in front of the lecture hall, and Piram seowon, where instead of an altar, a stele to tie the sacrificial animal to (*gyesaengbi*) is placed in front of the main gate.

Gwansewi

The *gwansewi*, consisting of a stone prop on which a basin (called *gwanbun*) can be placed, is a place where the officiants can wash their hands before a ritual. If the shrine faces south, it is located east of the eastern stairs leading up to the shrine. Generally, the officiants stand facing the shrine from the yard in front of the shrine before moving slowly sideways, and wash their hands before climbing the eastern stairs to the shrine for the ceremony.

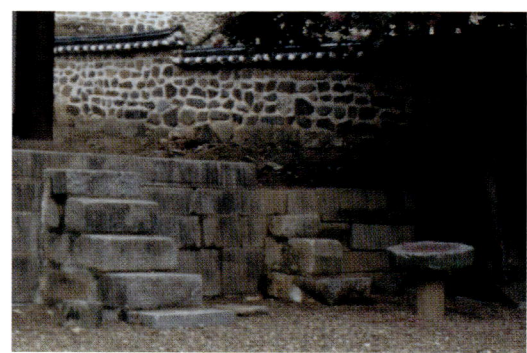

Gwansewi (basin prop), situated in front of the shrine, below its foundation platform

Mangnyewi

The *mangnyewi* is a facility pertaining to the ritual compound: It is a place for the burning and burial of the eulogy after the sacrifice is over. When the sacrificial rite is over, the eulogist climbs down the western stairs of the shrine, holding the eulogy. Going to the *mangnyewi* to

86 THE ARCHITECTURE OF KOREA'S PRIVATE ACADEMIES

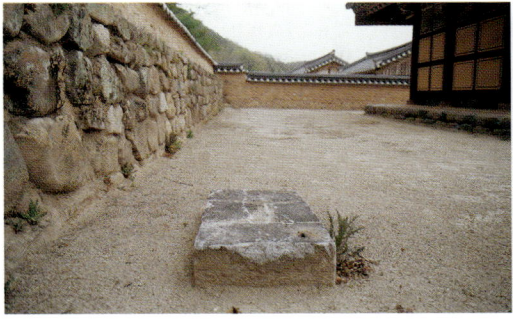

Mangnyewi, Piram seowon

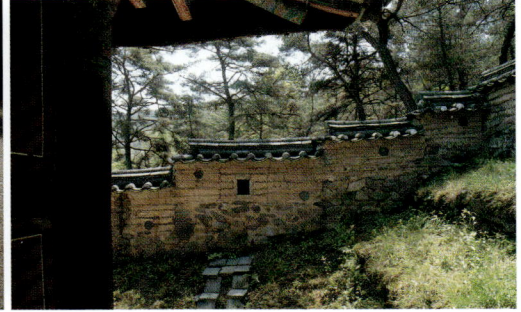

Niche in the wall for burying the remains of the eulogy, Dodong seowon.

the west of the shrine, he burns the eulogy and buries it there. Sometimes this facility is also called *mangnyowi*: "ye" means to bury, and "yo" means to burn. In Dodong seowon there is a niche in the wall where the eulogy is buried after being burnt.

Stone lanterns, *jeongnyodae*

Stone lanterns (*seokdeung*) are stone constructions on which a fire made of resinous knots of pine trees can be lit. They are usually placed in the yards in front of the lecture hall and the shrine. They are also known as *jeongnyodae* or *yogeoseok*, which is more like a lantern stand.

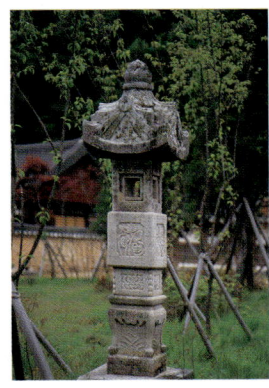

Stone lantern in front of the shrine Udongsa, Piram seowon

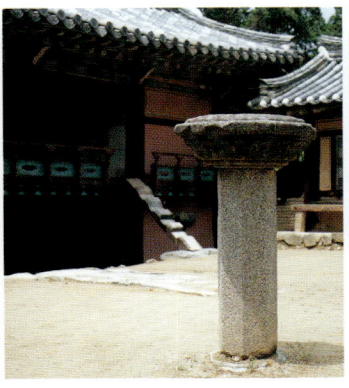

Stone lantern (jeongnyodae) in front of the lecture hall of Oksan seowon

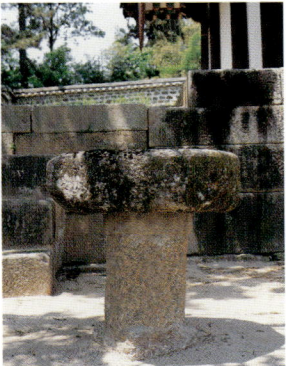

Stone lantern (jeongnyodae) in front of the shrine of Donam seowon

3) Names of private academies and buildings: a reflection of Neo-Confucian ideas

At the foundation of a new private academy, a suitable name has to be chosen. In many cases, this name is derived from the name of a local mountain, river or locality, or from a topographical feature. The same goes for the names conferred on chartered academies.

Private academies such as Dosan seowon, Oksan seowon, Byeongsan seowon, and Geumo seowon have borrowed the names of nearby mountains, i.e. Dosan, Jaoksan, Byeongsan and Geumosan. Namgye seowon was named after the Namgye stream near which Jeong Yeo-chang used to live and Deokcheon seowon after the Deok-

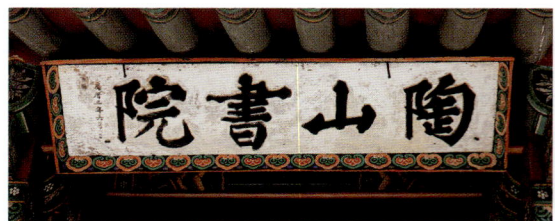

Name plaque inscribed with the name of Dosan seowon

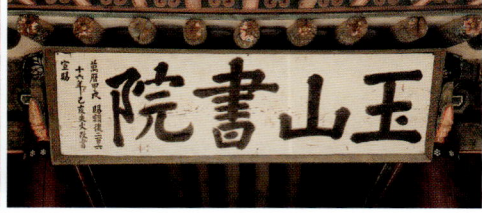

Name plaque inscribed with the name of Oksan seowon

cheon stream flowing in front of it. The name of Imgo seowon was inspired by the place-name Imgo, an epithet for Yeongcheon county where the academy is situated. Okdong seowon, dedicated to Hwang Hui (1363-1452) was named after Baegokdong, a place name in Sangju. Piram seowon and Donam seowon derive their names from nearby rock formations called "Piram" and "Donam," respectively. "Piram" refers to a sharp rock whose pointed tip resembles the point of a writing brush, and which stands at the entrance of Gisan, the village where the academy stands. "Donam" is the name of a large boulder at the foot of the mountains near a forest in Haim-ni, Yeonsan-myeon, where Donam seowon was originally located.

There are also exceptions to the general rule. Sosu seowon, the very first private academy in Korea, literally means "continuing and mending [the teaching which has fallen into ruin]" (*sosu*). "Dodong" in Dodong seowon means "the Way (*Do*, Ch. *Dao*) of Confucius has come to the East," a compliment to the scholarship of Kim Goeng-pil, to whom the academy is dedicated. Similarly, Yeokdong seowon means "the *Book of Changes* (*Yeokgyeong*, Ch. *Yijing*) has come East," a reference to words of praise uttered by Yuan scholars when they commended U Tak (1263-1342, to whom the academy is dedicated) for his thorough mastery of this classic.

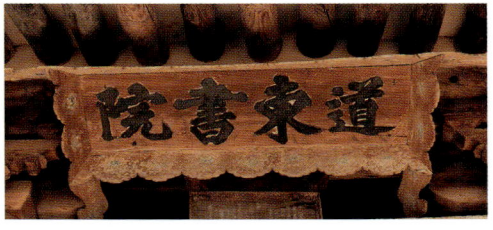

Name plaque inscribed with the name of Dodong seowon

Museong seowon, dedicated to the pioneer of Confucian studies in Korea, Choe Chi-won (857- ?), derives its name from a passage in Confucius' *Analects*. Museong is the name of a village in Lu, the country from which Confucius hailed, which appears in the *Analects*. Confucius is of course famous for his "governing through culture," based on the premise that Confucian scholars should not forget even for a single instant the correct rites (*ye*) and music (*ak*). Dongnak seowon, in which Jang Hyeon-gwang (1554-1637) is enshrined, means "A Korean place of instruction similar to that of Cheng Yi in China." "Dong", or the east, stands for Korea, while "Nak" is the first character of "Nagyang," the Korean pronunciation of Loyang, the city where the famous Neo-Confucian scholar Cheng Yi (1033-1107, pen name Icheon) and his brother Cheng Hao (1032-1085) taught.

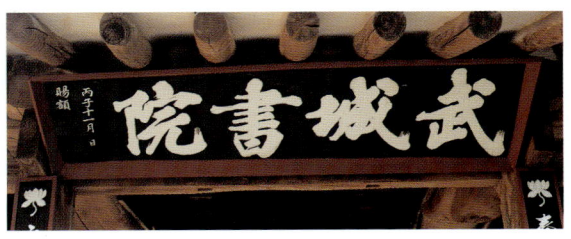

Name plaque inscribed with the name of Museong seowon

Not only the names of the academies, but also the names of all their individual buildings and rooms reflect a Neo-Confucian mindset

Architecture of private academies 89

and were chosen according to certain fundamental principles. The earlier the academy was founded, the clearer these principles are.

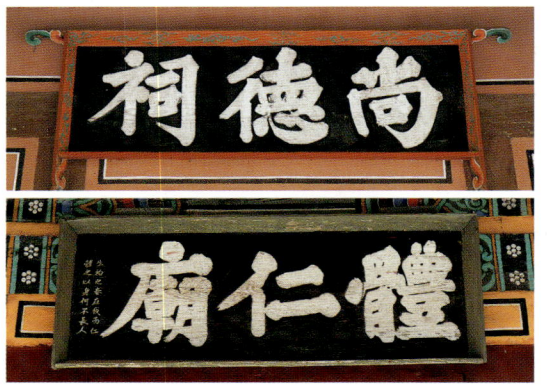

Name plaque bearing the name "Sangdeoksa," the shrine of Dosan seowon

Name plaque bearing the name "Cheinmyo," the shrine of Oksan seowon

The shrine arguably takes pride of place among *seowon* buildings, and a representative example of how its name was chosen can be seen in Dosan seowon. There the shrine is called Sangdeoksa, based on the following sentences from the "taming power of the small" (*sochuk*) hexagram in the *Book of Changes*: "the rain has fallen, and now that it has stopped virtue can be revered to the full" and "make the literary virtue beautiful." The key words in each sentence, "to revere" (*sang*) and "virtue" (*deok*) have been taken together to form the name of the shrine (Sangdeoksa, shrine of revering virtue), and thereby express the extreme virtue of the shrine's occupant, Toegye Yi Hwang. The shrine in Oksan seowon is called "Cheinmyo," which literally means "putting in practice (*che*) benevolence (*in*)," a virtue of the highest order for Neo-Confucians.

The lecture halls too were often given names drawn from the classics. The lecture hall of Namgye seowon is called Myeongseongdang, based on the phrase "in brightness (*myeong*) there is sincerity (*seong*)" from the *Doctrine of the Mean* (*Jungyong*, Ch. *Zhongyong*). The term "jungjeong" used in Dodong seowon's Jungjeongdang means "exactly right," referring to a condition in which Yin and Yang are in perfect harmony. The term also evokes the ideal mean, an uprightness that does not deviate even in the slightest way. The "Guindang" of Oksan seowon reminds us that the scholarship of ancient sages consisted simply of "pursuing (*gu*) benevolence (*in*)."

The lecture hall of Deokcheon seowon is called Gyeonguidang, a name which is also based on the *Book of Changes*, this time

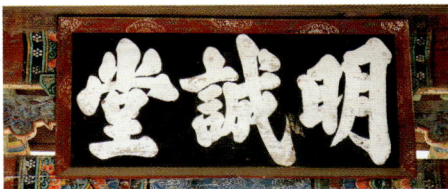

Name plaque of Namgye seowon's lecture hall, Myeongseongdang

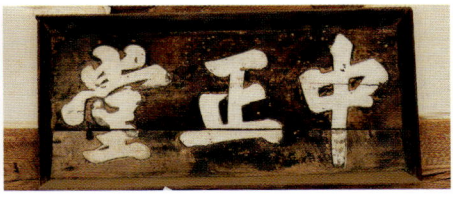

Name plaque of Dodong seowon's lecture hall, Jungjeongdang

on a line from the commentary on the hexagram "The Receptive" (*gon*): "Honesty is right, righteousness is correct; the superior man straightens himself inwardly through reverence (*gyeong*) and corrects himself outwardly through righteousness (*ui*); if reverence and righteousness are established, virtue will not be lonely." Reverence thus refers to the inner, psychological state, and righteousness to the external, formal demeanor. The lecture hall of Byeongsan seowon, then, is aptly named Ipgyodang, which means "hall where the teaching is established."

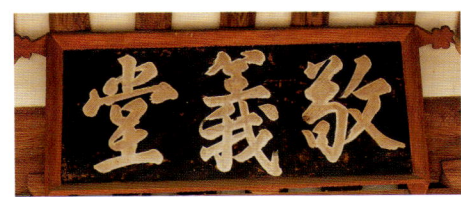

Name plaque of Deokcheon seowon's lecture hall, Gyeonguidang

Of the two side-rooms to the lecture hall in Namgye seowon, the one to the left is called Geogyeongjae and the one to the right Jibuijae. "Geogyeong" is taken from the phrase "residing in reverence to attain the utmost principle" (*geogyeong gungni*), from the "Family instructions of Master Cheng" (Ch. *Chengzi jiaxun*). "Jibui" occurs in the *Mencius*; the full saying is "gathering righteousness to live" (*jibeui isaeng*). The side-room on the left side of the Guindang lecture hall in Oksan seowon is called Yangjinjae, "yangjin" meaning to promote both simultaneously; "both" refers to "brightness" (*myeong*) and "sincerity" (*seong*), bright-

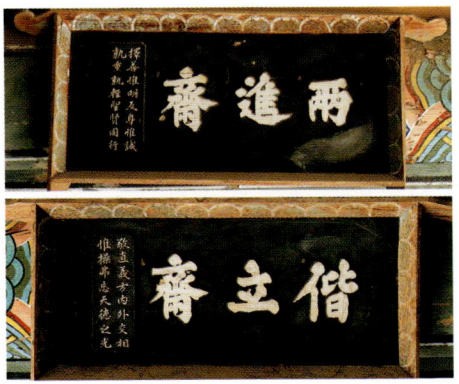

Name plaque for the left side-room of Oksan seowon's lecture hall, Yangjinjae

Name plaque for the right side-room of Oksan seowon's lecture hall, Haeripjae

Architecture of private academies

ness having the quality of revealing virtue, while every intention should be characterized by sincerity. The side room on the right bears the title Haeripjae, as in "approach everyone and everything with reverence and righteousness" (*gyeongui haerip*). "Gyeongui" (reverence and righteousness) and "myeongseong" (brightness and sincerity) are the *summum bonum* of the Neo-Confucian way of life.

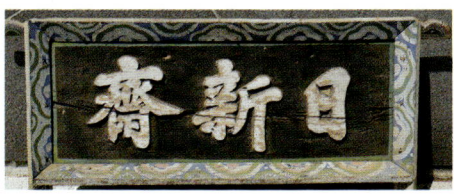

Name plaque for Sosu seowon's Ilsinjae dormitory

Name plaque for Sosu seowon's Jikbangjae dormitory

The dormitories were the places where students and scholars slept and studied. The Ilsinjae dormitory of Sosu seowon was a room used by professors and the chancellor, and its name means "renew every day" (*ilsin*), a phrase from the *Great Learning*. The Jikbangjae was used by the president; "jikbang," an expression found in the *Book of Changes*, means to "make your inner mind honest, and your outward actions straight." The names of the Hakgujae and Jirakjae dormitory buildings in Sosu seowon, both used by students, mean "to pursue scholarship" (*hakgu*) and "studying harder brings joy" (*jirak*), respectively.

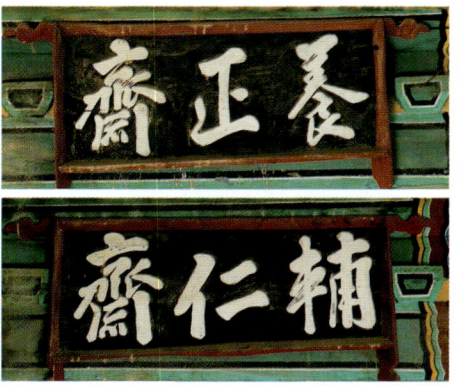

Name plaque for Namgye seowon's eastern dormitory, Yangjeongjae

Name plaque for Namgye seowon's western dormitory, Boinjae

The eastern dormitory in Namgye seowon, Yangjeongjae, is named after the phrase "to foster a work to make it straight" (*Mongi yangjeong*, from the *Book of Changes*), while the western dormitory, Boinjae, refers to the saying "achieving benevolence with friends" (*iu boin*, from the *Analects*). To the south both buildings have an upper room called Aeryeonheon and Yeongmaeheon, respectively. It is said that Jeong Yeo-chang was influenced by the poem "On Loving Lotuses" (Ch. *Ailian shuo*) of the Song scholar Zhou Dunyi (1017-1073), and had a special preference for the lotus and the plum blossom. Naming the upper floors Aeryeonheon and Yeongmaeheon thus evokes the planting of plum trees beside a pond filled with lotus flowers.

The eastern and western dormitories of Dodong seowon are called Geoinjae and Geouijae, "geoin" meaning "residing in benevolence" and "geo-ui" "residing in righteousness;" in the *Mencius* it is said, "Saying that while residing in benevolence you cannot practice righteousness is like throwing yourself away." This means that avoiding giving oneself airs, while practicing righteousness on the basis of benevolence is the most valuable way of living. The eastern dormitory of

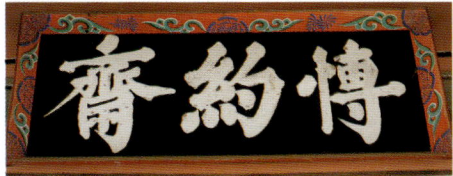

Name plaque for Dosan seowon's eastern dormitory, Bagyakjae

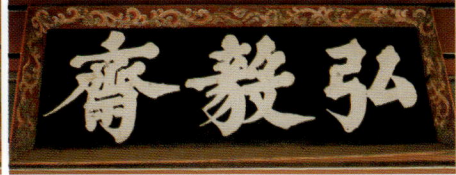

Name plaque for Dosan seowon's western dormitory, Honguijae

Oksan seowon is named Mingujae, because "in pursuing benevolence you have to be agile" (*hogo mini guji*, from the *Mencius*). The western dormitory is called Amsujae, because Zhu Xi once said that "you should cultivate yourself in tranquility" (*amyeon jasu*). Bagyakjae, the eastern dormitory in Dosan seowon, refers to the exhortation "broaden your learning, hold on to ritual" (*bangmun yangnye*), which emphasizes the importance of combining wisdom with action. The expression "hongui" in Honguijae, the western dormitory, means "broaden your mind and be resolute."

If we look at the gates or pavilion gates, the Jindomun of Dosan seowon literally means "Gate through which you go forth in the Way." The Yeongnangmun in Oksan seowon paraphrases the opening sentence of the *Analects*, "A friend coming to visit from afar, is not this a

Jindomun, the main gate to Dosan seowon

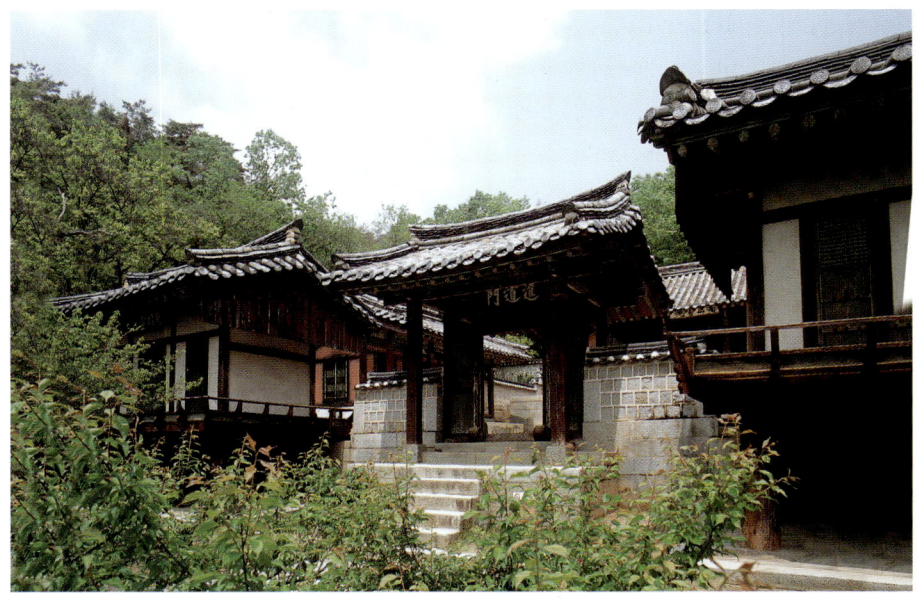

joyous occasion?" The Mubyeollu pavilion in the same academy was inspired by Zhou Dunyi's saying "nature has no borders" (*pungwol mubyeon*).

The name Suwollu of Dodong seowon evokes "reading books by the light of the moon reflected in the water," and the "hwanju" in Hwanjumun means "calling forth the root that can be the master of my mind." The following story is behind the Hwagyeollu gate-pavilion in Piram seowon: Because Kim In-hu had a bright personality and was very impartial, Song Si-yeol styled him "Hwagyeon" after an expression coined by Cheng Yi, which describes the gentleman's learning as "vast and just."

Suwollu, the gate-pavilion of Dodong seowon

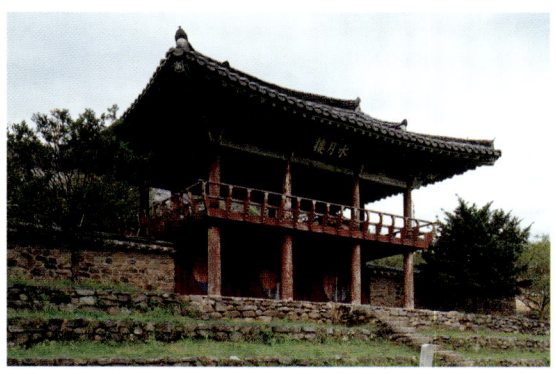

The gate pavilion of Museong seowon is called Hyeongaru, because of the first two characters in the saying "performing the music of rites is educating the masses" from the *Analects*. The Bongnyemun is the main gate of the Byeongsan academy, and

94   THE ARCHITECTURE OF KOREA'S PRIVATE ACADEMIES

"bongnye" (restoring rituals) is based on the *Analects* again: "Overcome yourself, restore rituals, and establish benevolence." In other words, it instructs people to overcome their worldly self and restrain themselves with ritual.

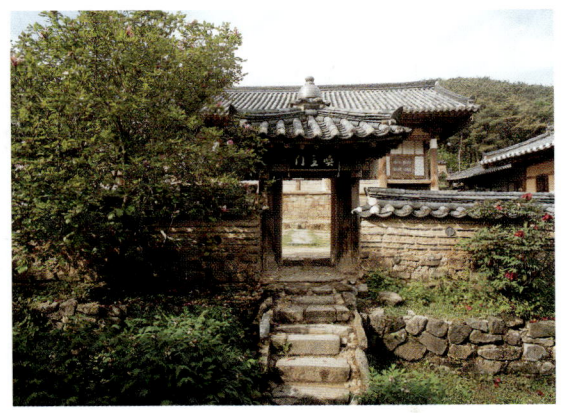

Hwanjumun, the gate to Dodong seowon's study compound

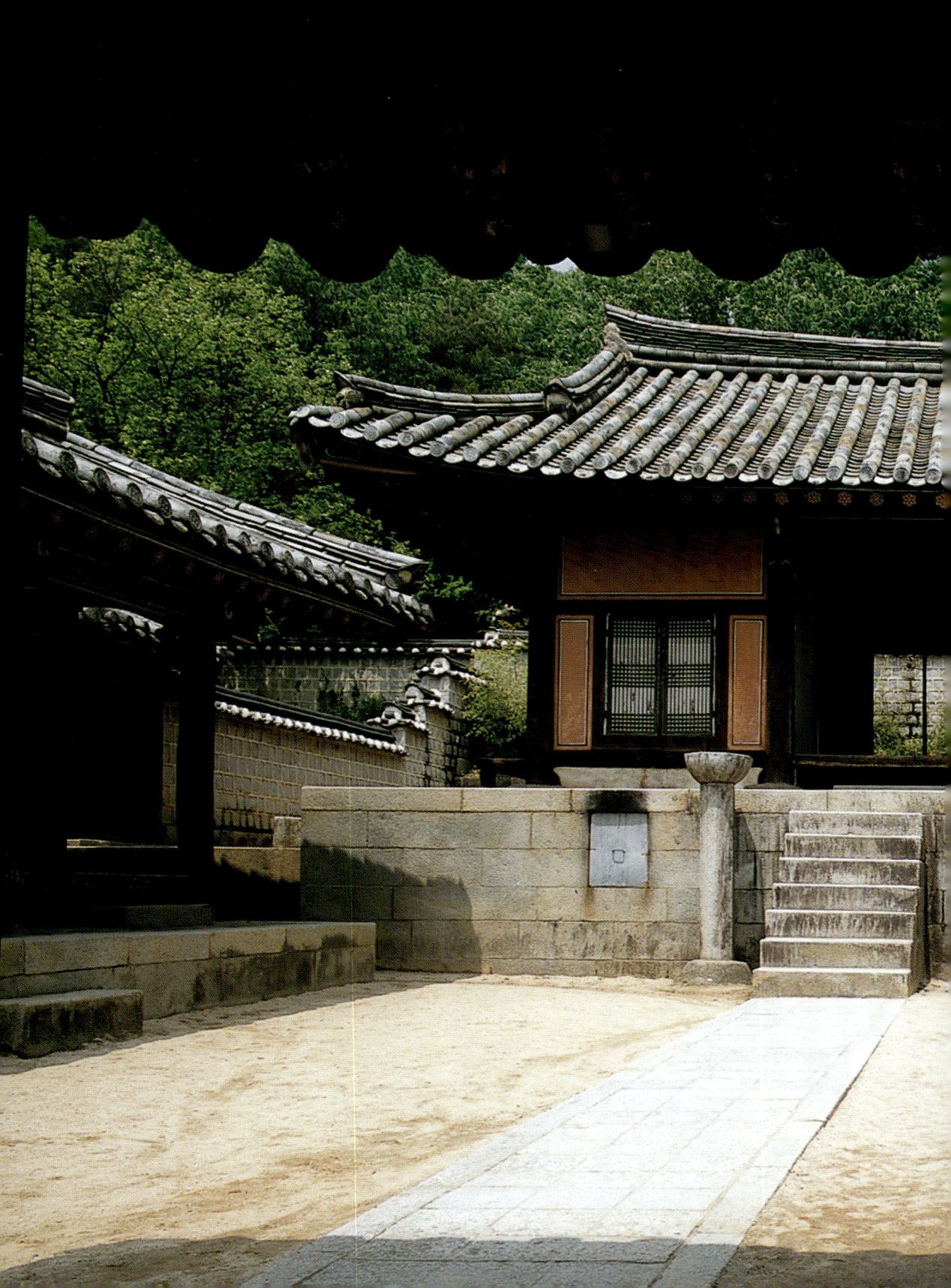

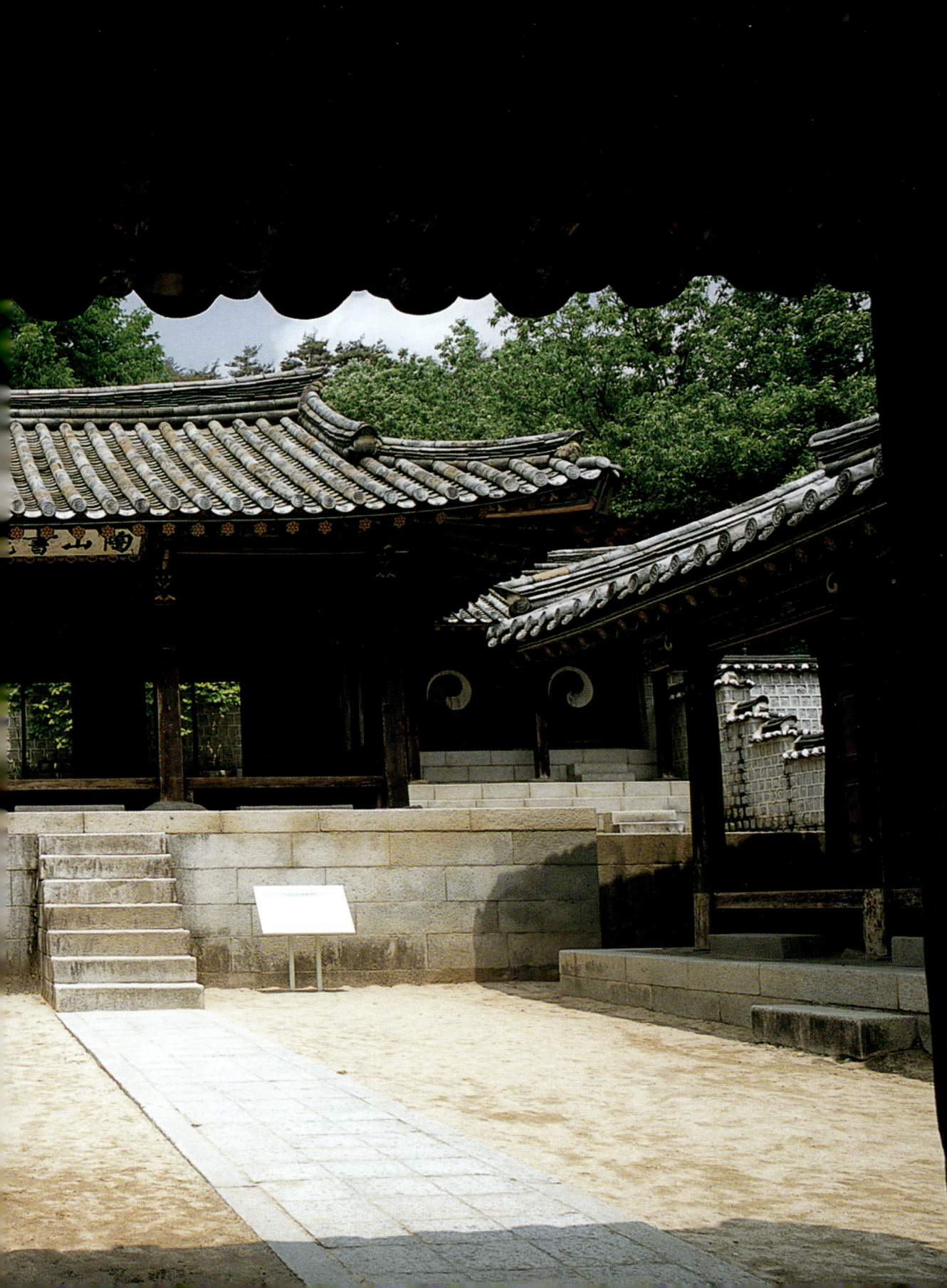

4. Examples of *seowon* architecture

1) Sosu seowon

Sosu seowon is located in 158 Naejuk-ri, Sunheung-myeon of Yeongju city in Gyeongsangbuk-do province. Celebrated as Korea's oldest private academy, it traces its origins to the eighth month of 1542, when Ju Se-bung, who had been appointed magistrate of Punggi county in the seventh month of the previous year, started construction on a shrine dedicated to An Hyang (1243–1306). It was completed on the 11th day of the eighth month of 1543, when a portrait of An Hyang was enshrined there. The same year a lecture hall was constructed east of the shrine, thus giving rise to Baegundong seowon.

An Hyang traveled together with the Goryeo king and princes on their compulsory journey to the Yuan court in the 11th month of 1289. He took this opportunity to procure the collected works of Zhu Xi as well as portraits of Confucius and his disciples, which he took back to Korea in the third month of the following year, after which he devoted himself to the study of Zhu Xi's thought. In the 12th month of 1297 he built a cloister in his backyard, where he enshrined portraits of Zhu Xi and Confucius. In 1303 he entrusted Kim Mun-jeong with the mission of obtaining more works and implements from southern China: He brought back portraits of Confucius and his 72 disciples, as well as implements to be used in the shrine for Confucius, the Six Classics and Four Books, and other philosophical works and books by Zhu Xi. In 1304 he founded the Seomhakjeon, an organization akin to modern educational foundations. With these efforts at implementing and spreading Zhu Xi studies, An Hyang can be regarded as the founding father of Korean Neo-Confucianism.

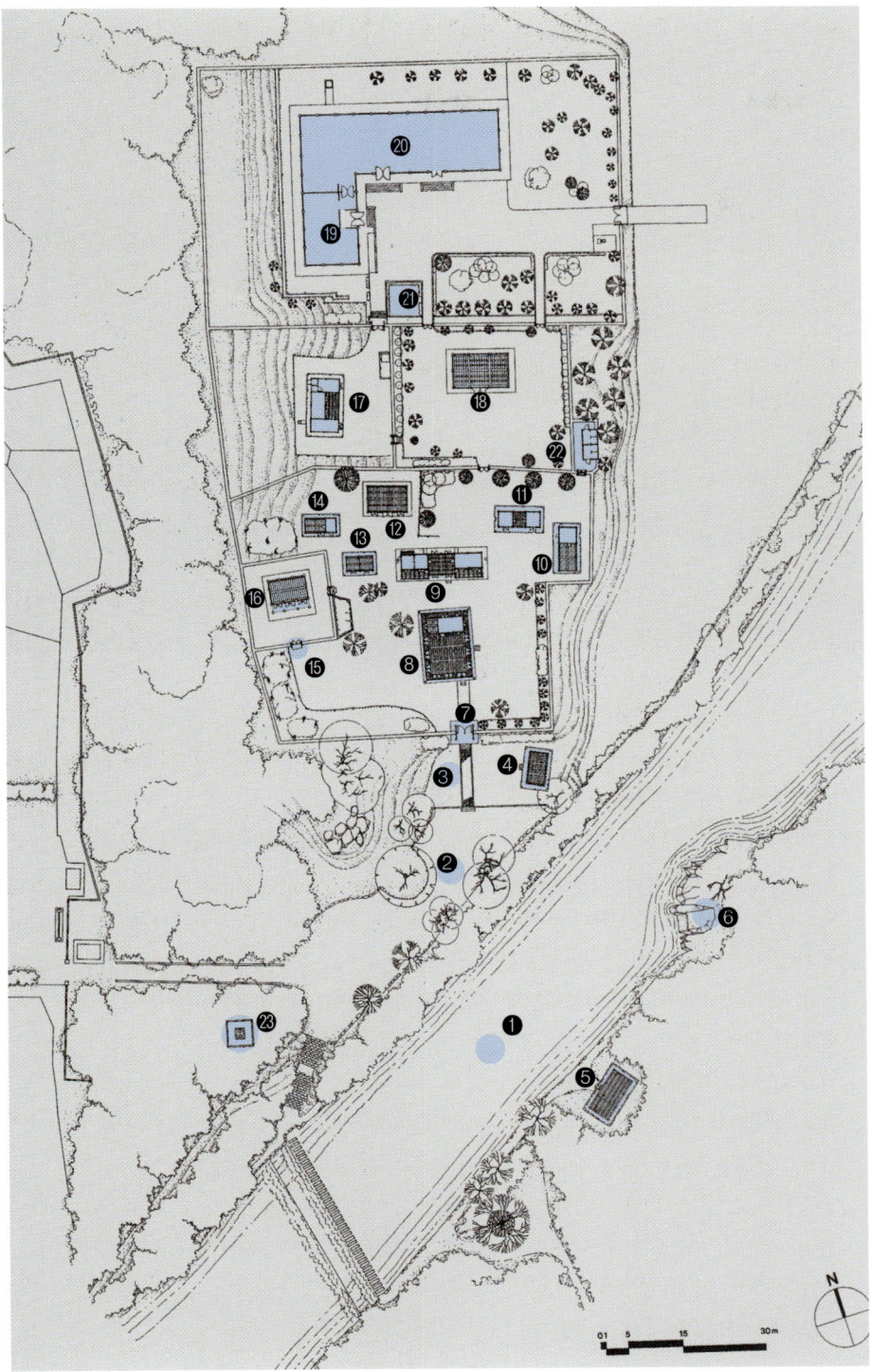

Building arrangement, Sosu seowon

1. Jukgyesu stream
2. gingko trees
3. altar for inspecting the sacrificial animal (saengdan)
4. pavilion (Gyeongnyeomjeong)
5. pavilion (Chwihandae)
6. cliff (gyeongja rock)
7. main gate
8. lecture hall (Myeongnyundang)
9. dormitories for professors and administrators (Ilsinjae, Jikbangjae)
10. dormitory for students (Jirakjae)
11. dormitory for students (Hakgujae)
12. portrait hall (Yeongjeonggak)
13. library (jangseogak)
14. building for preparing offerings (jeonsacheong)
15. spirit gate (sinmun)
16. shrine (Munseonggongmyo)
17. stewards' house (gojiksa)
18. repository of artefacts
19. exhibition hall of academy's documents
20. office
21. memorial stele (gijeokbi)
22. toilet
23. stone flagpole props (danggan jiju)

Examples of *seowon* architecture

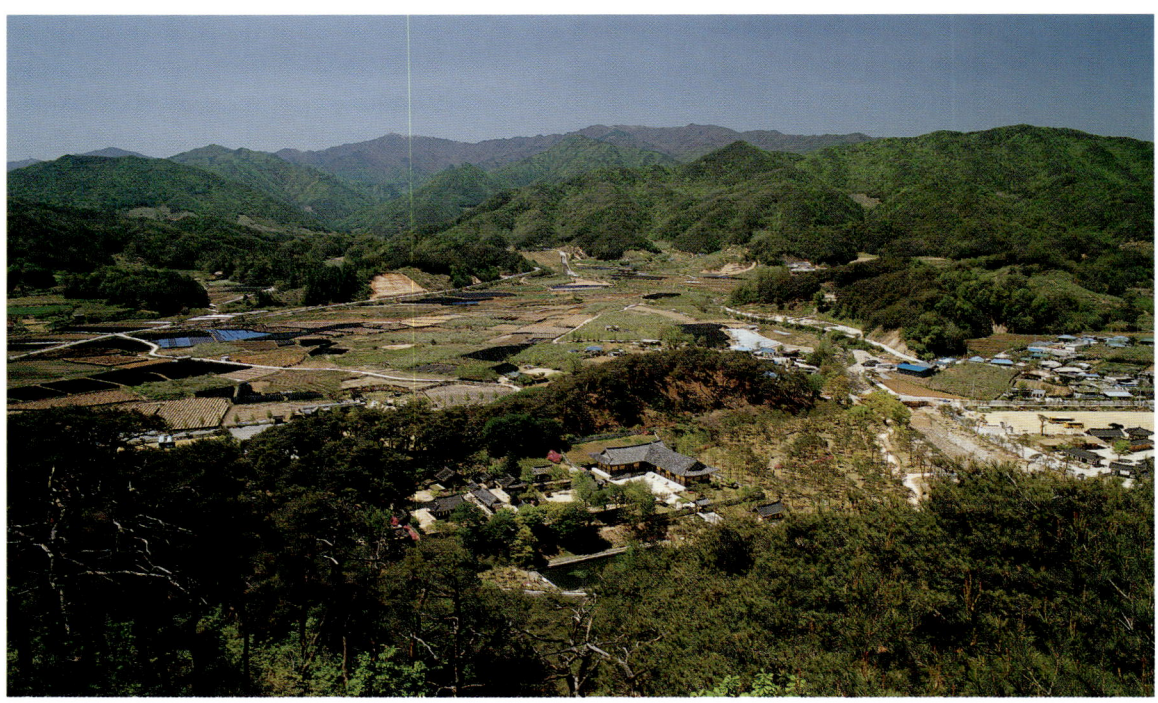

View of Sosu seowon

When he enshrined An Hyang's portrait in the newly completed shrine on the 11th day of the eighth month of 1543, Ju Se-bung also had a poem in three stanzas, titled *Jukgyesa,* read and an ode called *Dodong gok* sung in three parts of three stanzas. The *Jukgyesa* goes as follows:

> To the east the Jukgyesu stream, to the west the Sobaek range, and my lord's shrine in between.
> In the valley shrouded by one hundred clouds (Baegun) the road ahead is faint indeed.
> Fish dart in the stream, and pine trees dot the mountain slopes.
> This is where my lord used to roam, but alas he will not return.
> Come back, please come back and relieve my sadness!
>
> To the east the Jukgyesu stream, to the west the Sobaek range, and above the mountain clouds.
> In the river the moonlight is the same as of old.
> When you come riding on the jade mace (*okgyu*),

Or sometimes on the phoenix,
Please drink from my winecup to lift my feelings
And enjoy yourself to the utmost.

Before you were born, virtue was shrouded in darkness,
Morality fallen from this earth, covered in a twilight of clouds
and smoke.
But after your glorious birth the country of the Three Han
(Korea) was born anew.
You elevated righteousness as the sun in the blue sky,
And as your portrait is now enshrined in a respectful shrine,
The water of the Jukgyesu stream is clearer, the mountains in the
Taebaek range higher.

According to Ju Se-bung, when he founded the Baegundong academy, he had to overcome opposition put up by some local Confucian scholars. In the preface to his *Jukgyeji* (The Records of Jukgyesu Stream), he writes that these scholars objected as follows: "Sir Munseong (An Hyang) is already inducted in the Confucian shrine (Munmyo), and shrines are established in every locality, so what need is there for another shrine? Also, here in Sunheung there is already a county school fostering Confucian scholars, so why do we have to found a private academy?" Furthermore, "not only are we suffering from a year of bad harvests, but even if it were not for this, with your humble stature inspiring little confidence, isn't it simply too much for you to found a shrine and academy by yourself?" To this Ju Se-bung replied by clarifying his motivation for founding an academy: "To provide education and transform the people, we should start by showing respect to a wise person, so in order to uphold the tradition of An Hyang's insight into human nature and reverence, I built this shrine in his honor, and to allow Confucian scholars to cultivate themselves and study, I built his academy." For Ju

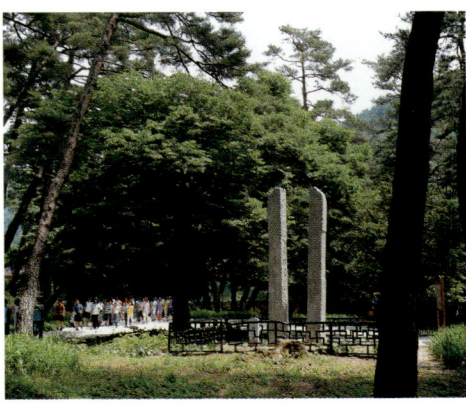

Stone flagpole props, usually found at the entrance of Buddhist temples, showing that Baegundong seowon stands on the site of the ancient temple Suksusa

Se-bung, An Hyang was the patriarch of Korean Neo-Confucianism, and to revive his teaching, he established an academy in Jukgye, where An Hyang used to live. Baegundong seowon is located at the place where the Buddhist temple Suksusa used to stand, a place where An Hyang used to reside and study.

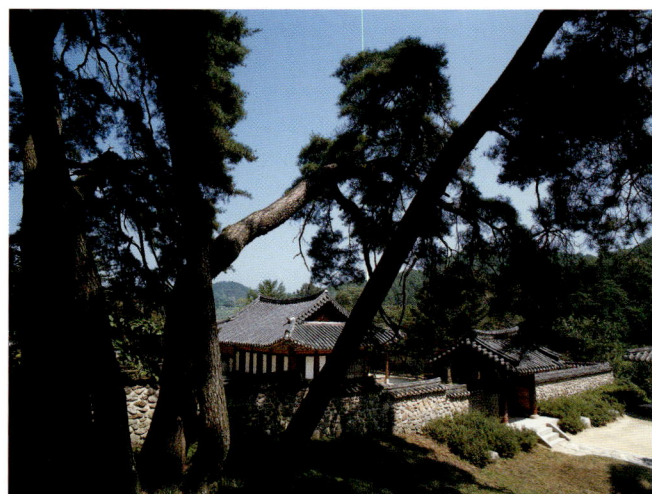

View of the entrance to Sosu seowon

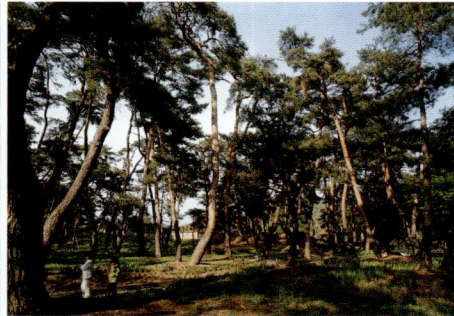

Pinetree grove at the entrance of Sosu seowon

The fact that Baegundong seowon eventually received official recognition from the state and gained fame across the country was due to the efforts of Toegye Yi Hwang, who became magistrate of Punggi in the tenth lunar month of 1548. Through the governor for Gyeongsang-do province, Sim Tong-won (1499-?), Toegye sent a petition to the court requesting a charter and state support. In response, King Myeongjong ordered Sin Gwang-han (1484-1555) to come up with a suitable name, and he decided on Sosu seowon, which means "continuing and mending [the teaching which has fallen into ruin]." In the second month of 1550 the king granted a name plaque bearing the title "Sosu seo-

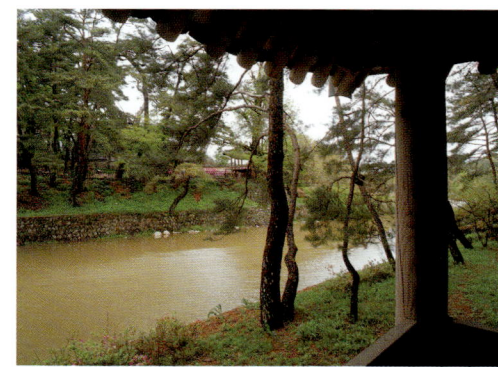

The Jukgyesu stream seen from Gyeongnyeomjeong

102 THE ARCHITECTURE OF KOREA'S PRIVATE ACADEMIES

won." This name reveals that the academy intended to restore the long-neglected intellectual heritage of An Hyang and continue his spiritual lineage. In this sense Sosu seowon is similar to the Bailudong academy, which was resurrected by Zhu Xi. Bailudong shuyuan was originally founded in the late Tang dynasty (616-907) by Li Bo as a hermitage and study. Because Li Bo always took a white deer along, he was known as the White Deer Master. After the fall of the Tang dynasty, during the Five Dynasties period (907-960), this place became known as the Lushan Guozijian (National Academy on Mt. Lushan) or the Lushan Guoxue (National School on Mt. Lushan), and in the early Song period it finally acquired its present name. After it had fallen into disrepair, Zhu Xi resurrected it as a private academy.

Two gingko trees stand near the entrance to the Sosu academy. They stand on a slightly elevated surface, thus marking the entrance to the academy's domain. On the left side of the road leading to the main gate stands the *seongsaengdan* altar, while the Gyeongnyeomjeong pavilion, from where the Jukgyesu stream can be seen flowing towards the academy's east side, can be seen on the right.

The *seongsaengdan* is an altar that was used to inspect the animals to be sacrificed for the memorial rites. Such altars were usually placed near the shrine, but in the case of Sosu seowon it stands near the entrance. Gyeongnyeomjeong straddles the space between the academy and its natural environs, and hugs the Jukgyesu stream, which flows north to south from the academy's eastern side. It offers wonderful views of the surrounding landscapes and played an important role not only as a place where students and scholars could hold meetings or poetry gatherings, but also where they could enjoy the scenery and lift their spirits.

East of Gyeongnyeomjeong, on the other side of the stream, a cliff known as the Gyeongja rock rises up straight from the bank of the stream. Its name is derived from the character "gyeong" (reverence) en-

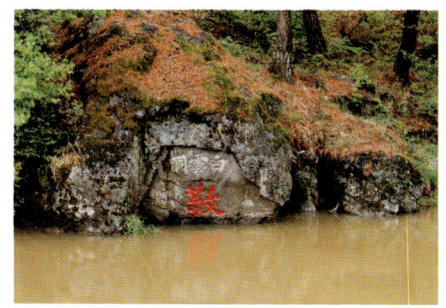

Gyeongja rock

graved on it, and is said to have been written by Ju Se-bung himself after the scholar founded the academy. "Reverence" is a key directive for the Neo-Confucian scholars, a central concept in the discourse about cultivating the mind, which actually means the straightening of one's inner self. It is therefore also translated as "reverential seriousness" or "mindfulness" to reflect its religious dimension within Neo-Confucian discourse. When Toegye was magistrate of Punggi, he planted conifers and bamboo on this spot and called it Chwihandae. Above the "gyeong" character he wrote the name "Baegundong" and had the letters carved out, and it is said that he used to enjoy the scenery here.

Interior of Myeongnyundang

Passing through the main gate, you immediately face the Myeongnyundang lecture hall. The hall is oriented north-south lengthwise, and it faces east. On the side facing the main gate hangs a board reading "Baegundong." Most lecture halls comprise five bays lengthwise, but in the case of Sosu seowon it comprises a main wood-floored

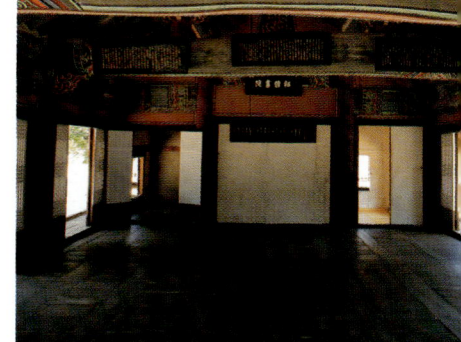

Myeongnyundang, the lecture hall of Sosu seowon

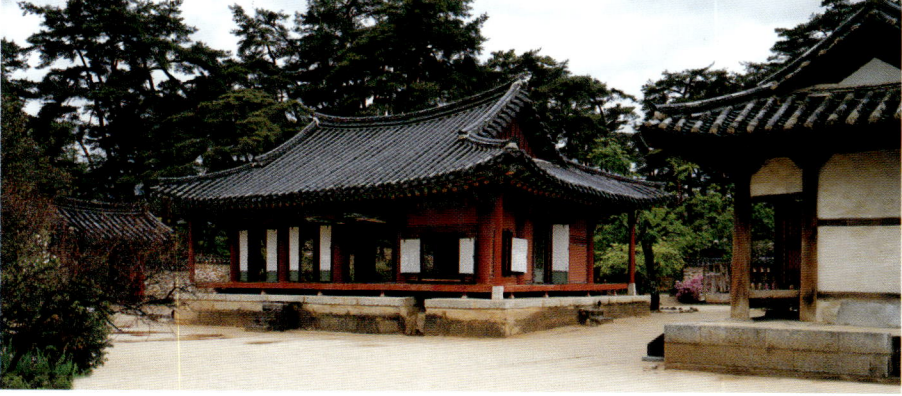

104 THE ARCHITECTURE OF KOREA'S PRIVATE ACADEMIES

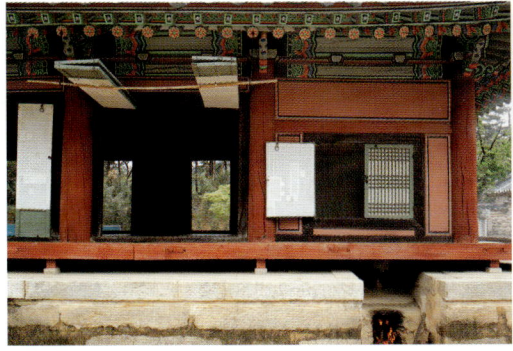

One-kan side room next to the main wood-floored hall of Myeongnyundang

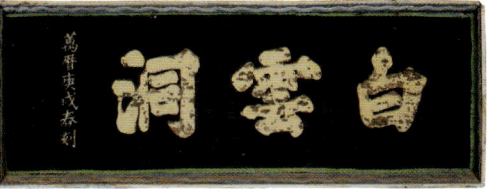

Name plaque bearing the title "Baegundong"

room of three bays with only a small *ondol*-heated room of one bay on one side of the lecture hall. On the north side of the main floored hall hangs a board reading "Sosu seowon" inscribed by King Myeongjong himself. As many as 4,000 students passed through this lecture hall, the majority belonging to Toegye's academic lineage.

The Ilsinjae and Jikbangjae buildings are located north of the lecture hall and are used both as offices and as dormitories for the president, professors and administrators. Unlike other private academies, where the dormitories are invariably divided into two different buildings, the eastern and western dormitories, here they are combined into a single building, and the two parts can only be distinguished by the name plaques. The dormitory building measures six *kan* in length and

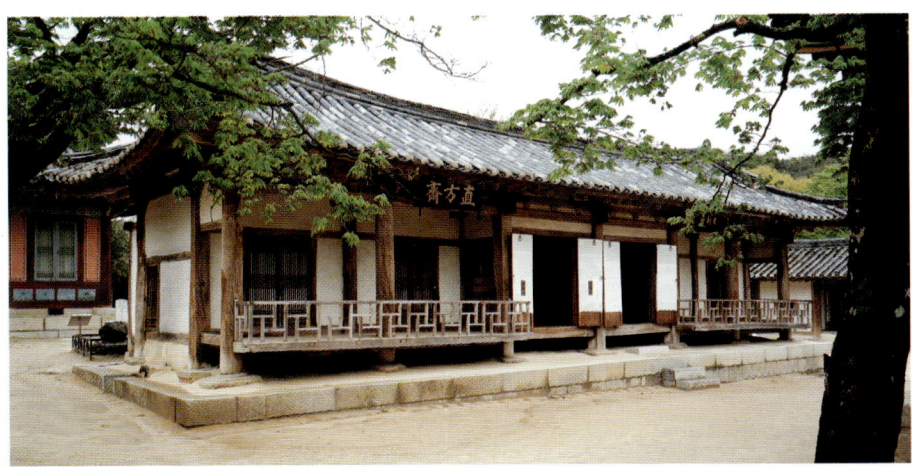

Ilsinjae and Jikbangjae, the dormitories for professors and scholars

Examples of *seowon* architecture 105

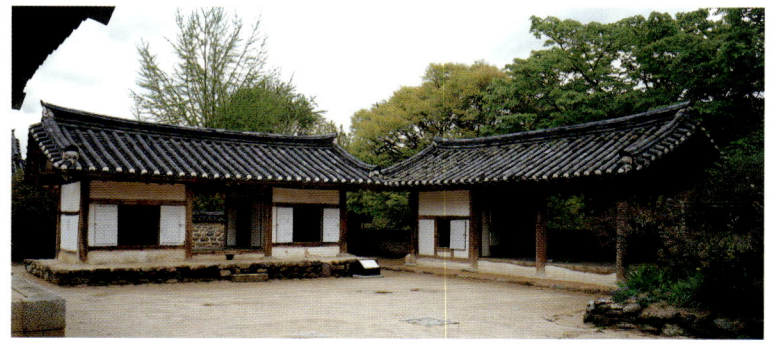

Hakgujae and Jirakjae, the dormitories for students

one and a half *kan* in width, and consists of an *umul* (well, 井) patterned wooden floor for the two *kan* in the middle, and two *kan* of side-rooms on each side, which also have an extension of the wooden floor (*toenmaru*, a kind of ledge) in front.

To the northeast of this dormitory stand the L-shaped Hakgujae and Jirakjae dormitories where students used to study and sleep. Since this building housed students rather than professors, its status is lower, and this lower status is reflected in the construction: The foundation platform is lower, and the building itself is smaller. The south-facing Hakgujae measures three *kan* lengthwise and one *kan* in width, has a pitched roof, an *umul*-shape patterned wooden floor in the middle, which is completely open at the front and back, and heated *ondol* rooms of one *kan* each on the sides. The west-facing Jirakjae has a single-*kan ondol* room to the north while the rest of the building consists of a floored room which is open on all the external sides.

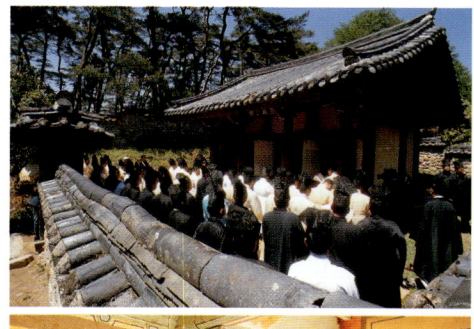

Memorial ritual at Munseonggongmyo, the shrine to An Hyang

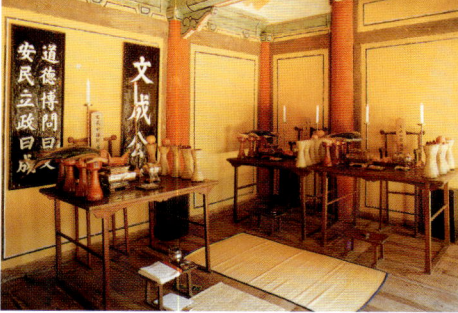

Offerings to the spirit tablet of An Hyang, posthumously styled Munseonggong

The shrine, called Munseonggongmyo, is located on the western edge of the academy compound, in the remotest and most solemn corner, and is encircled by a wall. The shrine measures three *kan* by three, and has an extension of

106 THE ARCHITECTURE OF KOREA'S PRIVATE ACADEMIES

the wooden floor (*toenmaru*) at the front. An Hyang is enshrined as the main object of veneration, while An Chuk (1287-1348) and An Bo (1302-1357) were additionally enshrined in 1544, and Ju Se-bung in 1633.

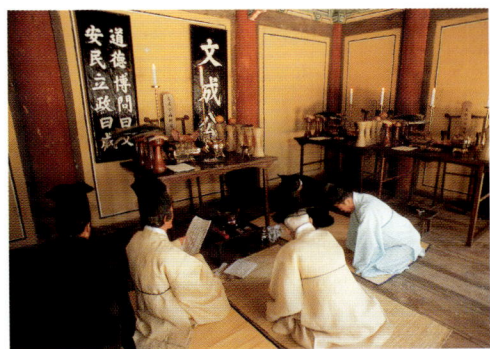

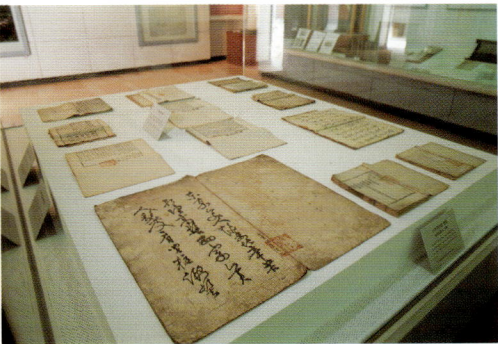

Documents relating to Sosu seowon displayed in the academy's repository

Memorial rite inside Munseonggongmyo

Sosu seowon furthermore has a library, known as Jangseogak, a building for sacrificial services called Jeonsacheong, the Yeongjeonggak portrait hall, as well as some recent buildings such as a repository for artefacts and the Chunghyo document center. As for its general layout, Sosu seowon does not yet display the typical pattern in which the lecture hall is in front of the shrine and the dormitories in front of the lecture hall.

2) Dosan seowon

Dosan seowon was founded by disciples of Toegye, one of the greatest Confucian philosophers of the Joseon period and the archetypal scholar-official, shortly after his death. The present Dosan private academy comprises the compound of the Dosan private school, used by Toegye himself for the study of Neo-Confucianism and the training of students, and Dosan seowon, established by Toegye's students to commemorate his scholarship and virtue. The buildings located at the front of the present complex belong to the private school, while those behind it belong to the academy proper.

General view of Dosan seowon. Towards the front of the complex is Dosan seodang, founded by Toegye as a place where he could instruct his students. The rest of the complex is the private academy founded after Toegye's death by his students as a token of respect for his scholarship and virtue.

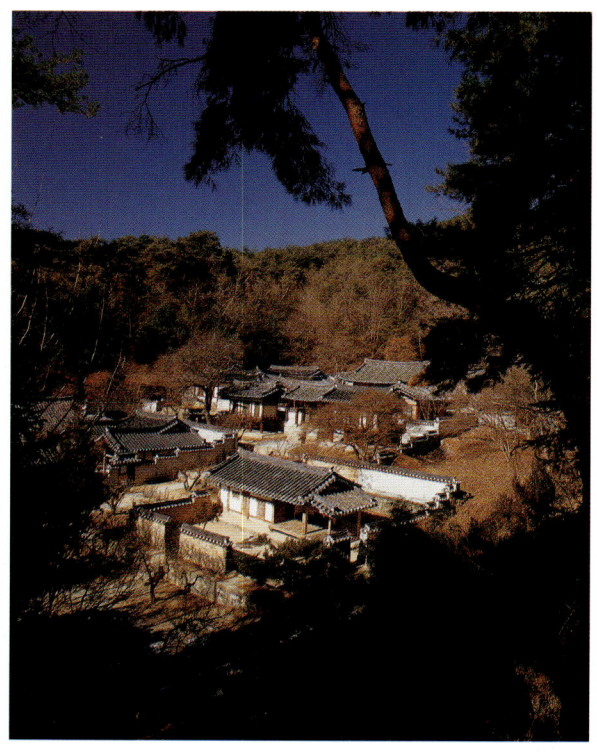

Even before Toegye built the Dosan private school, he had established buildings for study and the training of students. In his later years he mustered the courage to quit his official career and retreat to the countryside to cultivate his mind and find a new way to organize Neo-Confucianism as a system; thus he became the outstanding example of the Joseon Neo-Confucian scholar, as well as an educator who nurtured many students. Both in terms of his scholarship and in terms of his reputation he is simply unrivaled among Joseon-era scholars. Even now, more than four centuries after his death, his work is appearing ever more impressive in the light of new studies.

Toegye retired from office in 1546 at the age of 46, and built the Yangjinam hermitage on the southern foot of Mt. Geonjisan in Yean, where he started his search for the true Way in earnest. At this time he changed the local place name from Togye (rabbit stream) to Toegye (retreating stream) and adopted this as his pen name.

Gyesang seodang, reconstructed in 2000

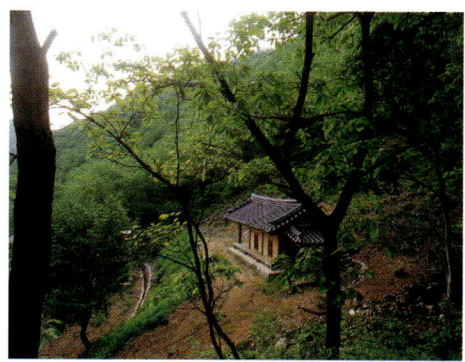

Then in 1548 he received a local appointment as magistrate of Danyang, and in the 10th month of the same

108 THE ARCHITECTURE OF KOREA'S PRIVATE ACADEMIES

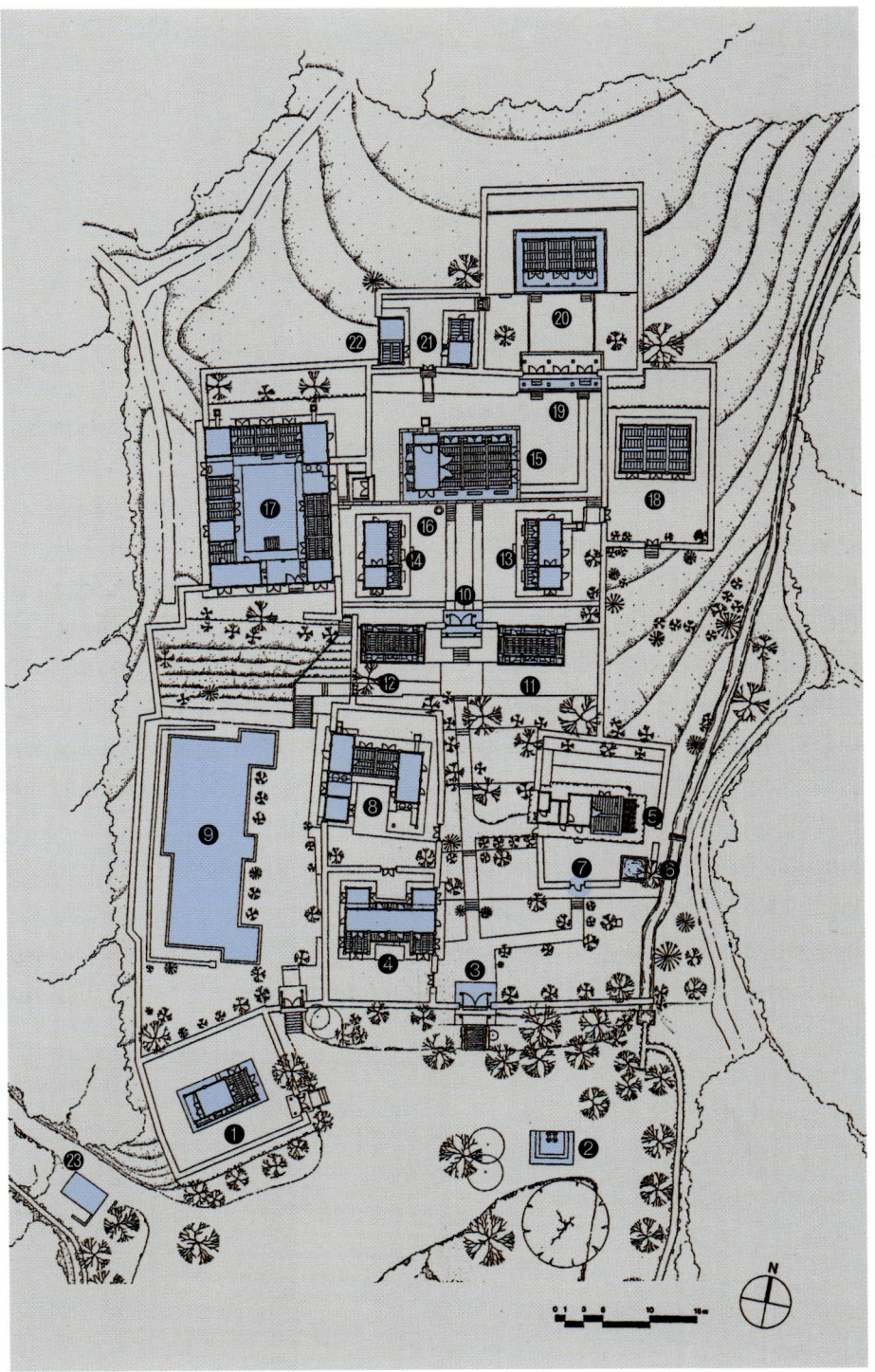

Building arrangement, Dosan seowon

1. student dormitory (Yeongnak seojae)
2. well (Yeoljeong)
3. main gate
4. student dormitory (Nongun jeongsa)
5. Dosan private school (Dosan seodang)
6. pond (Jeongudang)
7. entrance to Dosan seodang (Yujeongmun)
8. lower stewards' house (ha gojiksa)
9. exhibition hall of academy's documents (Okjingak)
10. main gate to the academy (Jindomun)
11. east library (Dong Gwangmyeongsil)
12. west library (Seo Gwangmyeongsil)
13. eastern dormitory (Bagyakjae)
14. western dormitory (Honguijae)
15. lecture hall (Jeongyodang)
16. stone lantern (jeongnyodae)
17. upper stewards' house (sang gojiksa)
18. storehouse for printing blocks (jangpangak)
19. spirit gate (naesammun)
20. shrine (Sangdeoksa)
21. ritual implements store (jegigo)
22. libations hall (jucheong)
23. toilet

Examples of *seowon* architecture

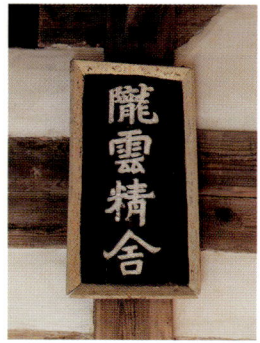

Name plaque of Nongun jeongsa

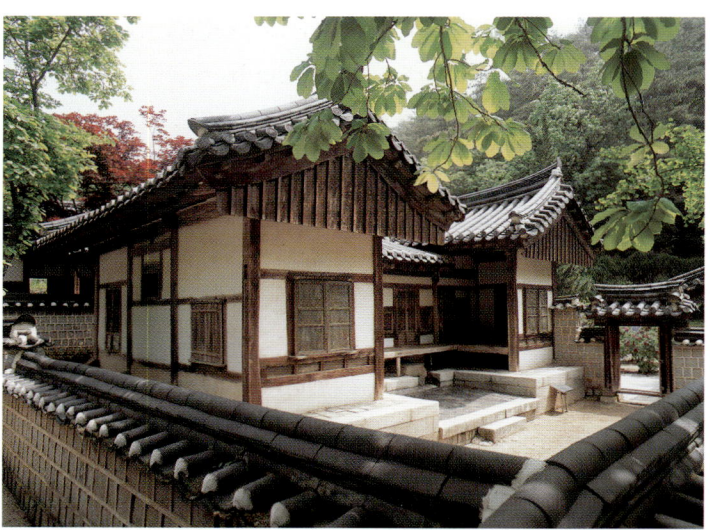

Nongun jeongsa, the student dormitory of Dosan seodang

year he was transferred to Punggi. After applying for a royal warrant for Baegundong seowon in the first month of 1549, he retired again at the beginning of the 12th month of that year. In the second month of 1550 he erected a small building west of Toegye in Sanggye, which he called Hanseoam hermitage. It was a simple three-*kan* building consisting of an inner room, an open wood-floored room and a kitchen. On the philosophy of his retirement and the life ahead of him, Toegye had the following to say in his poems: "If they mention wealth, I reply with benevolence, if they mention an official career, I reply with righteousness" and "Now the thing I have to do... having retreated quietly in my hometown... is to foster many good people and straighten the essential order of Heaven and Earth..." These fragments of poems reveal his firm resolve to retreat to his home village and devote himself to studying, training students and generally finding a way of making society more orderly.

Later it became necessary to build a larger space to

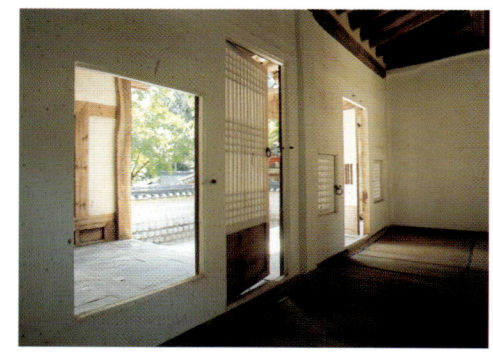

Interior of Nongun jeongsa (cloister)

110 THE ARCHITECTURE OF KOREA'S PRIVATE ACADEMIES

receive the students who flocked to him from all over the country, so in 1551 the Gyesang seodang private academy was built in a valley northeast of Hanseoam, marking the beginning of his systematic education of students. When Gyesang seodang was first built, it was a spartan house without *ondol* heating.

Since Gyesang seodang was small and many students wanted to study with Toegye, soon he had to build a new school. Dosan seodang was built on the other side of the mountain, on the edge of Mt. Dosan, but even after it was finished Toegye traveled to and fro from Gyesang seodang, which was also the place where he died. In 1557, when Toegye was 57, land was procured south of Mt. Dosan, and in 1558 the ground was prepared and building started. In 1560 work was completed, although the student dormitory, Nongun jeongsa, was finished only the year after. Toegye expressed his feelings of joy on finding the place for Dosan seodang in several poems, as in the following two:

> In the driving wind and rain, not one desk in Gyesang is safe.
> Having looked everywhere in the forest for a place to move to,
> How could I know that the place for everlasting practice
> Was next to the place where plants are dug and fish caught?
> Flowers meet me and smile as if they hold deep feelings.
> The sound of birds seeking a mate extends this meaning.
> Moving across numerous small trails, I pledge to settle down
> And share the joy of this beauty with the world.

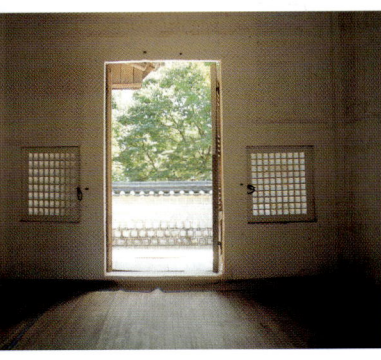

Windows and doors seen from the inside of Nongun jeongsa

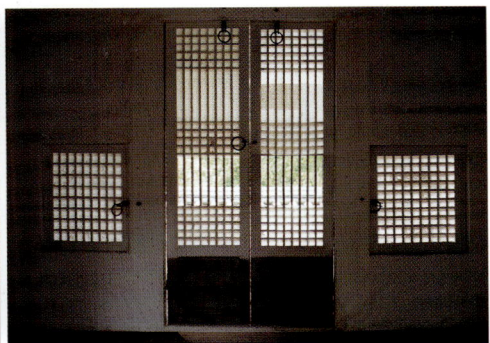

Windows and doors in Nongun jeongsa

On the southern foot of Mt. Dosan the clouds are thick,
And a small string-like spring trickles from the northeast.
The brilliant birds of dusk dally at the water's edge,
And the exquisite flowers of spring add splendor to rocks and forest.
Settling down in quietude, the feelings naturally come forth.
Returning late to this place is truly a joy.
After groping about for harmony, is it really found?
Now all I wish is to learn the words from ancient scriptures by heart.

As mentioned before, Toegye thought that the location of a private academy had to meet two criteria: It should be connected to a former sage worthy of respect, and the environment should be conducive to cultivating the mind and study. Dosan seowon met both these criteria of location, the human one and the geographic one. Dosan seowon is thus not just the place where Toegye used to lecture and study, it is also an area of outstanding natural beauty. The natural conditions of the academy are of course the same as those of the private school.

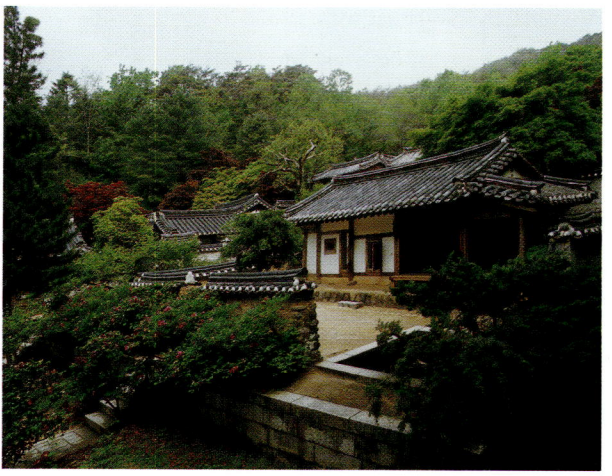

General view of Dosan seodang

In the 11th month of 1561, the year after he finished Dosan seodang, Toegye wrote his "Various Hymns of Dosan" (*Dosan jabyeong*). In the accompanying explanation to this collection, he wrote about the landscape surrounding the school and other factors that led him to compose these poems. "Originally I found a place higher up the Toegye stream," he writes, "and built a simple single-*kan* house beside the stream and decided to make it a place to store books and broaden my mind. But even after moving three times, the wind and rain kept destroying it. Also, upstream it was very desolate and not suitable for broadening the mind, so I decided to move once more and obtained some land south of the mountain."

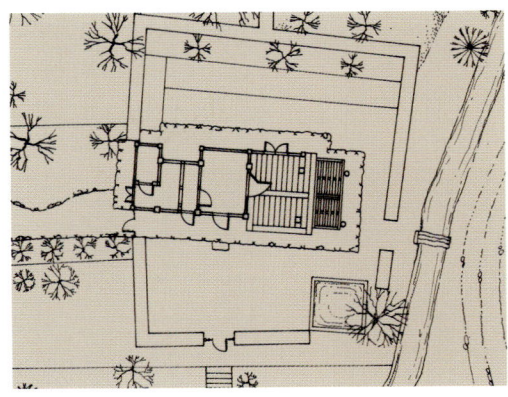

Ground plan, Dosan seodang

Dosan seodang was a small, south-facing building measuring three *kan*. The westernmost of these three bays was occupied by a small kitchen shed, the *ondol*-heated middle room was the Wallakjae, Toegye's living quarters, and the easternmost room was a wooden-floored veranda called Amseoheon. The reason the building faced south was to facilitate the performance of rites. The location of the studio (Wallakjae) to the west and the veranda to the east meant that they faced the plants and flowers in the garden, so that their life-force could be admired. In Toegye's studio there were bookshelves holding more than a thousand volumes, while a flower pot, a desk, an ink-grinding slab, a stick, bedding, a rush-mat, an incense burner, and an armillary sphere were arranged along the southern wall. In a small storage space carved out in the back wall, he kept a clothing chest and a letterbox, and apart from these things he had no other belongings.

East of the private school, on an uneven surface, Toegye dug a pond in which he planted lotus flowers, calling it Jeongudang pond. East of this lotus pond he dug a spring called Mongcheon, and above it, at the foot of the mountain, constructed a level terrace facing Amseoheon, on which he planted the so-called four friends – plum tree, bamboo, orchid and chrysanthemum – and which he called Jeorusa. The fact that the Jeongudang, Jeorusa, and further the Nakdonggang river can all be seen from the Amseoheon well expresses Toegye's Neo-Confucian pursuit of unity with nature.

Jeongudang, the pond in front of Dosan seodang

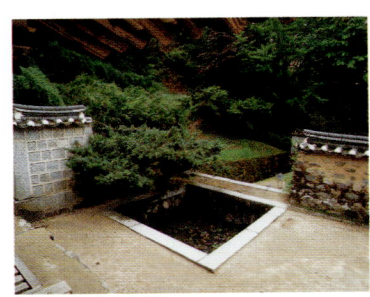

Among the "four friends," Toegye showed a special attachment to the plum tree. When all things are still frozen

Examples of *seowon* architecture

in winter, the plum blossoms are the first flowers to open. Scholar-officials of the Joseon period made this a symbol of the spirit of the ideal scholar-official, who would not succumb to immorality but would display a spirit of integrity and aloofness. Among the poems he wrote, more than 100 deal with the plum blossom. He compared the plum blossom to jade and hail, and was said to be deeply interested in its fragile appearance. He summed up its characteristics as true, chaste, tough and bitter. When he lay on his deathbed, he did not leave behind any last words, but just reminded his followers "to water the plum trees." This can be called the final simple expression of his love for the plum blossom.

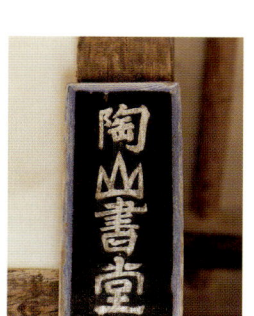

Name plaque of Dosan seodang, inscribed by Toegye himself

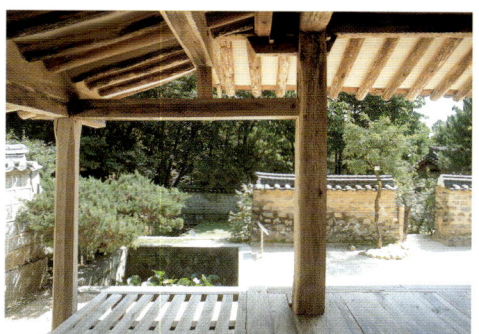

View from the veranda of Dosan seodang

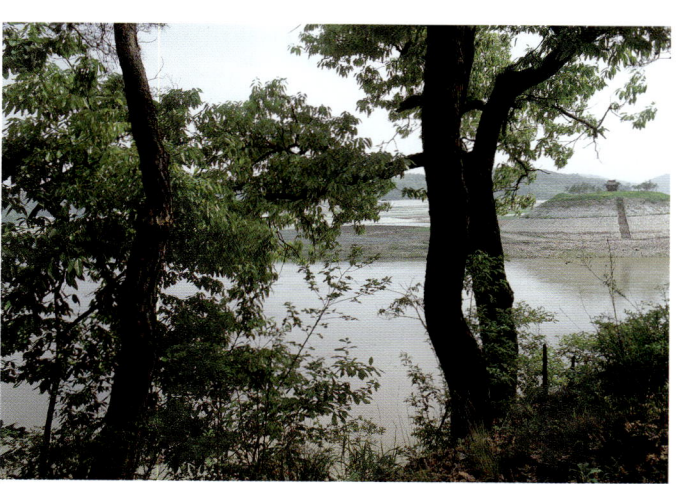

View of the Nakdonggang river from Cheonyeondae, a terrace in front of Dosan seowon

At the entrance to his private school, Toegye erected a gate made of wicker, which he named Yujeongmun. If you open the south-facing door of the Wallakjae, this gate can be seen straight in front. Its name is derived from the description of the "treading, conduct" (*i*) hexagram in

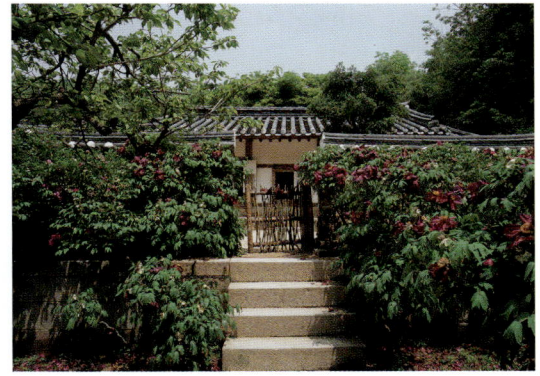

Yujeongmun, the entrance to Dosan seodang

the *Book of Changes*: "treading the Way is a matter of broad and even effort, the hidden scholar with a straight mind will obtain good fortune."

South of the wide yard in front of the present-day entrance to Dosan seowon there used to be a road leading to Gokguam hermitage, the entrance to Dosan seodang. Before the Andong dam was constructed, to get to Dosan seowon from the city of Andong, you had to pass through Yean and Buncheon villages, then follow the western bank of the Nakdonggang river upstream, then go around a small hill and take a small path up towards Gokguam. Going up to Gokguam and then towards the academy's entrance, the landscape unfolding around you was dramatic. But after the Andong dam was completed in 1976 this road became submerged, and the new access road no longer offers this dramatic scenery. The wide road that now leads to Dosan seowon, together with the parking lot and the surrounding terraces were all constructed in 1970.

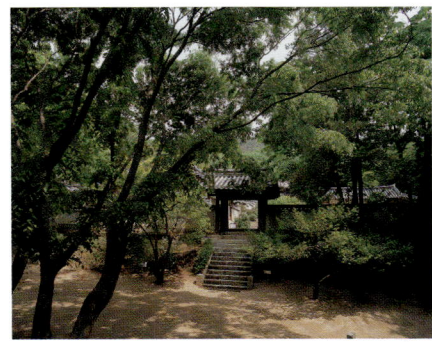

Entrance to Dosan seowon

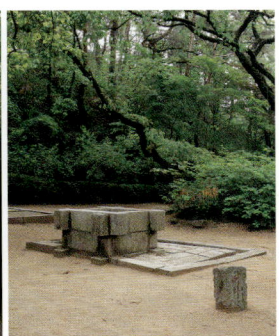

The Yeoljeong well, located east of the entrance to Dosan seowon

In Dosan seodang, the space created by Amseoheon, Jeorusa, Yujeongmun, and Cheonyeondae functions as an extension of nature. When construction was finished, Toegye said about this place that "(in spring) the mountain birds sing happily, (in summer) the plants and trees grow dense and tall, (in autumn) wind and frost make it cold, and (in winter) the moon-

Examples of *seowon* architecture 115

light shines on a frozen snowscape; different in every season the landscape does not cease to excite me." In this place he could rid himself of worldly afflictions, enjoy everything between the universe and nature, and thus endeavor to find the origin of all things and investigate their raison d'être.

Private academies were established in or near beautiful landscapes in view of the "Unity of Heaven and Man" theory, which regards man and nature as one. In the architecture of the private academies, this principle was realized by managing the way buildings related to nature. Through the design of the academies' buildings and the careful adaptation of surrounding natural features, Toegye attempted to integrate nature and architecture, and this idea also underlay the construction of Dosan seowon after his death.

After the three-year mourning period for Toegye was over, in the spring of 1574 his students and local scholars agreed that "since Dosan is the place where our master discoursed on the Way, it is impossible not to have a private academy here." So they prepared the ground right behind Dosan seodang and started building Dosan seowon. Construction was finished in the eighth month of 1575, and at the same time King Seonjo conferred a warrant naming the academy "Dosan seowon." In the second month of 1576 the shrine was finished, and Toegye's spirit tablet was enshrined there.

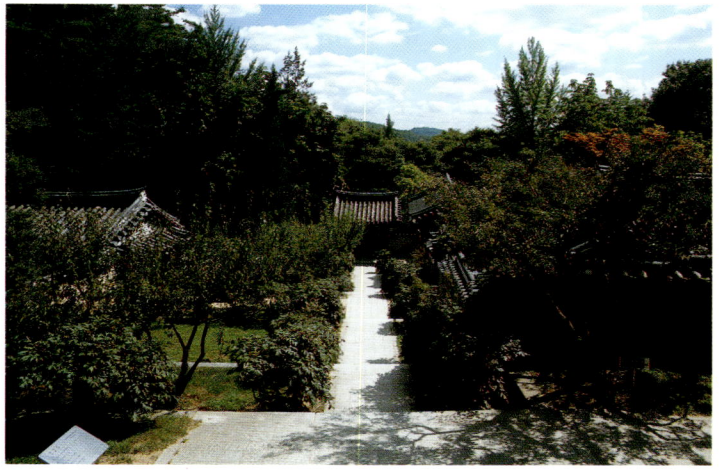

View from Jindomun (the main gate of Dosan seowon) towards the outside

The main gate to the academy is called Jindomun. Looking out from this gate towards the landscape in front of the academy, the Andong lake, gathering the water from the Nakdonggang, unfolds far and wide towards the south.

116 THE ARCHITECTURE OF KOREA'S PRIVATE ACADEMIES

At the center of the study area, the Jeongyodang lecture hall is constructed on top of a high platform, with the two dormitory wings laid out in stern symmetry on either side of its front yard, a layout designed to reflect the high standards of this center of learning. The Jeongyodang, where scholars cultivated their minds and educated stu-

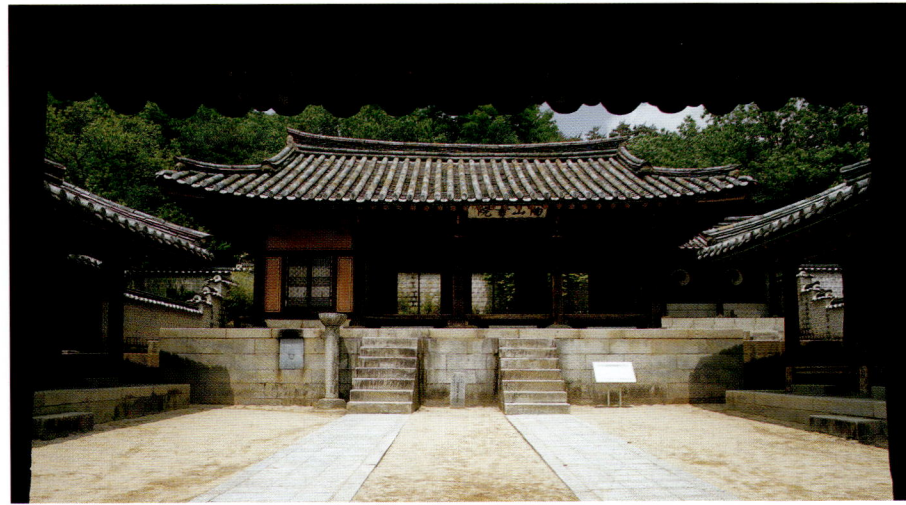

Jeongyodang, the lecture hall of Dosan seowon

dents, measures four *kan* by two, and consists of a three-*kan* wood-floored main hall and a one-*kan ondol*-room called Hanjonjae. The calligraphy on the board inscribed with the letters "Dosan seowon" that hangs outside the Jeongyodang is said to have been executed by the eminent calligrapher Han Seok-bong (1543-1605) in the presence of the king.

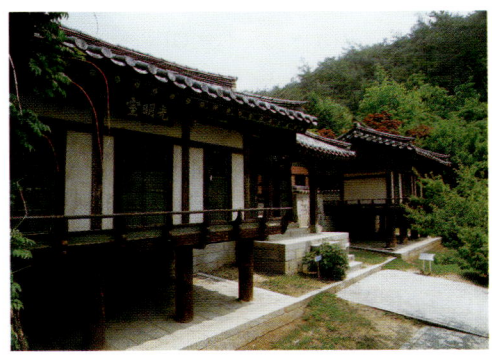

The eastern dormitory, called Bagyakjae, and the western dormitory, called Honguijae, are buildings of the same size, which stand face to face on either side of the yard in front of the lecture hall. They measure three

The Dong (east) Gwangmyeongsil and Seo (west) Gwangmyeongsil, located on either side of the main gate, Jindomun.

Examples of *seowon* architecture 117

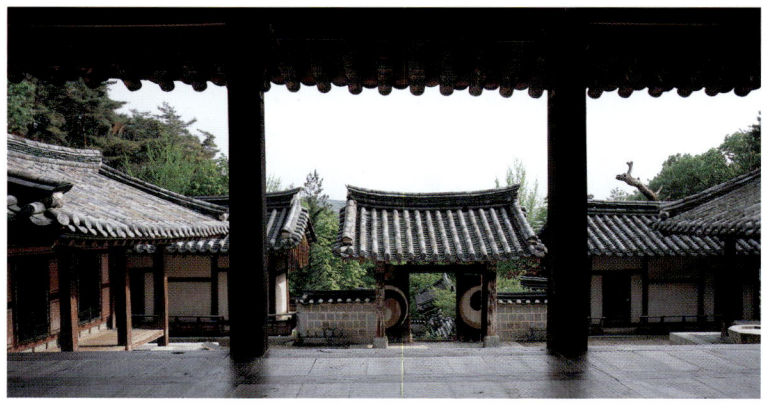
View from the main wood-floored room of Jeongyodang

kan by one. At the front they have an open porch that protrudes half a bay outside the building proper, while the three *kan* of the building all have *ondol*. Each building is divided into two rooms, one measuring two *kan* and the other one *kan*, connected by a door that cannot be shut.

On either side of Jindomun there are structures called *Dong* (east) *Gwangmyeongsil* and *Seo* (west) *Gwangmyeongsil*, which are joined to the wall. These buildings are used to store the books bestowed by the king, the books used by Toegye, books transferred from the abolished Yeokdong seowon, and the literary collections (*munjip*) of students of Toegye and other scholars. They are built in the style of pavilions, with the floor elevated above the ground to prevent moisture from seeping up. Seen from outside Jindomun they are two-storied buildings, but seen from the inside they have only a single story, and it is also from this side that the buildings can be accessed. The Jangpangak, used to store woodblocks for printing, is a separate building located east of the lecture hall, which is precisely one level higher than the eastern dormitory and one level lower than the lecture hall.

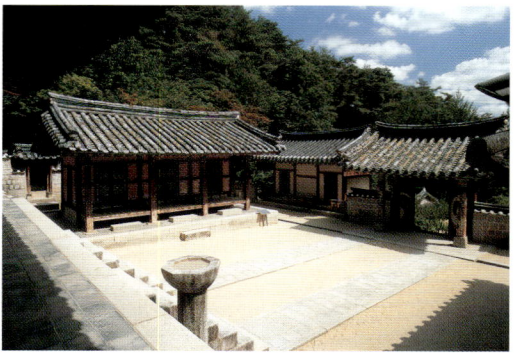
The study compound of Dosan seowon

West of the Jeongyodang lecture hall is the Sang (Upper) Gojiksa, the residence of the stewards (*gojik*), who manage the academy's af-

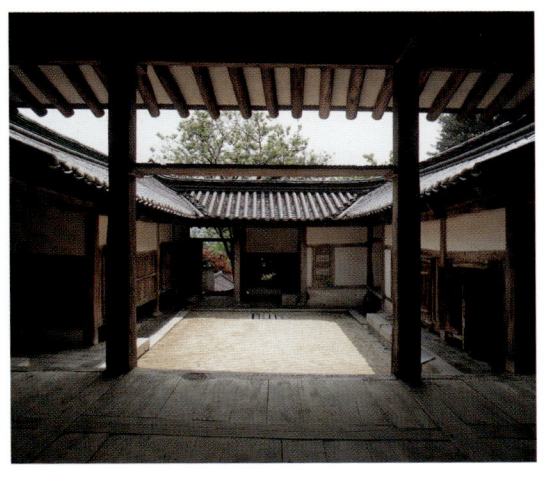

The Upper Gojiksa, the house of the stewards, the private academy's caretakers

fairs. Its ground plan resembles that of ordinary residences in the Andong area, with buildings arranged in the shape of a square. With this ground plan, the buildings are cool in summer and protected against the cold wind on all sides in winter.

The ritual compound is situated behind the lecture area. The shrine, called Sangdeoksa, measures three *kan* by two. At the front, there is a covered porch that extends half a *kan* outside the building proper, with the one and a half *kan* behind it occupied by an *umul*-patterned main wood-floored hall, which makes up the inner space. Inside the shrine, facing south in the middle of the northern wall, is the spirit tablet for Toegye as the main ritual occupant, while on the east wall, facing west, the subordinate ritual occupant Jo Mok (pen name Wolcheon, 1524-1606) is enshrined. The memorial rites in this shrine are held twice a year, on the *jungjeong* day of the second and eighth months.

Unlike other academies, in Dosan seowon the functions of the Jeonsacheong (house for preparing offerings) have been divided between two buildings, namely, the ritual implements store (*jegigo*) and the libations hall (*jucheong*), located southwest of the ritual hall on lower ground; interestingly, the buildings give access to both the shrine's yard and the backyard of the lecture hall. The buildings stand face to face with the *jegi-*

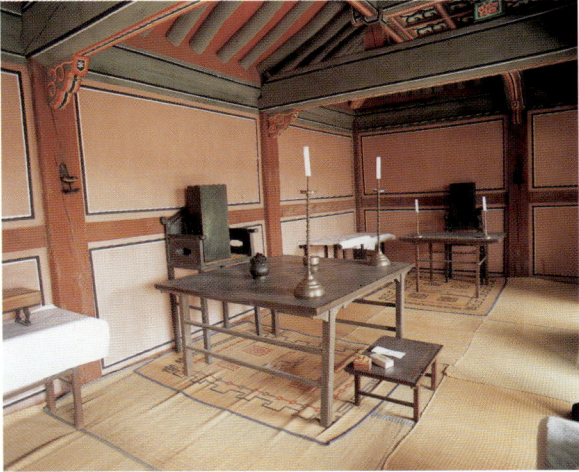

Interior of Sangdeoksa, the shrine housing Toegye and Jo Mok's spirit tablets

Examples of *seowon* architecture 119

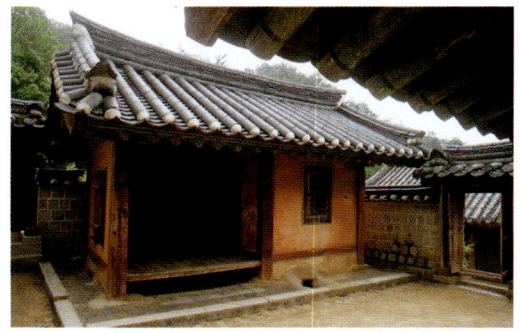

The ritual-implement store at Dosan seowon, comprising an ondol room and a wood-floored room

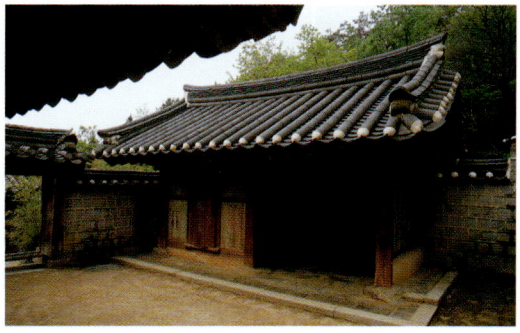

The libations hall (jucheong) at Dosan seowon, consisting of a wood-floored room and a room with a tiled floor

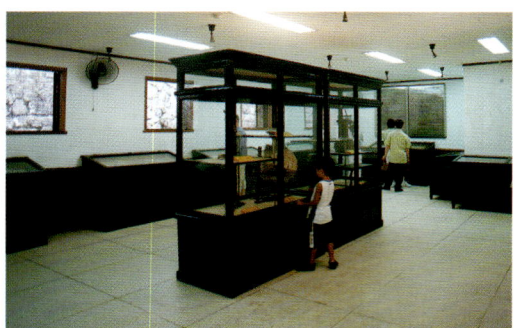

Some of Toegye's belongings displayed in Okjingak, the exhibition hall of Dosan seowon

go to the east and the *jucheong* to the west. The *jegigo* consists of two *kan*, a one-*kan ondol*-room and a one-*kan* veranda. As for the *jucheong*, one room has a wooden floor and the other room a brick-tiled floor that is open towards the outside.

3) Oksan seowon

Oksan seowon was founded in 1573 to commemorate the virtue and scholarship of Yi Eon-jeok (1491-1553), pen name Hoejae. In 1574 it received a warrant conferring the name "Oksan."

Yi Eon-jeok, active during the reign of King Jungjong, played a pioneering role in the development of Neo-Confucian philosophy: By adhering to Zhu Xi's position that principle preceded material energy, he adumbrated the Neo-Confucian orthodoxy and established its trends and nature. His pen name Hoejae bears out his admiration for Zhu Xi,

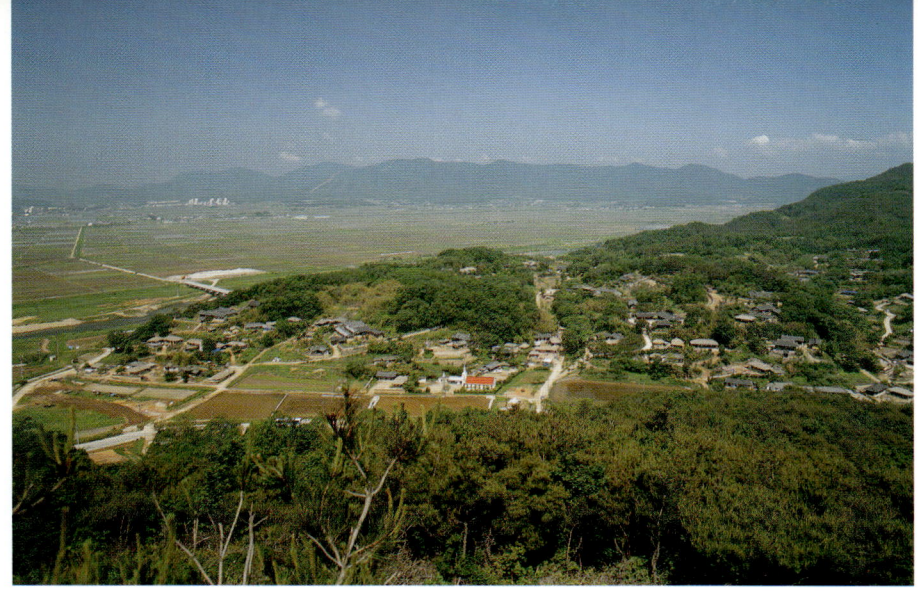

Yangdong village, the birthplace of Yi Eon-jeok

for the first character, "hoe", is taken from Zhu Xi's own pen name Hoeam (Ch. Huiyan). Toegye essentially continued Yi Eon-jeok's Neo-Confucian scholarship. In the ninth month of 1610 Yi Eon-jeok was inducted in the Confucian shrine together with Kim Goeng-pil, Jeong Yeo-chang, Jo Gwang-jo and Toegye. They were called the "Five Sages of the East" because they were deemed to represent the pinnacle of Korea's Neo-Confucian tradition.

Yi Eon-jeok hailed from the village of Yangdong near Gyeongju. Yangdong is a village that to this day has preserved the largest concentration of *yangban* houses in Korea, and thus offers a window into the past. In his later years he retired from office and retreated to a place not far from Yangdong, a riverbank in Oksan, Angang-eup, Gyeongju, where he built a residence. It consisted of the inner rooms where he lived, the men's quarters, called Dongnakdang, facing the stream, and a pavilion called Gyejeong; here he made nature his friend and devoted himself exclusively to the study of Neo-Confucianism for six years. Because of this association with Yi Eon-jeok, after his death, on a spot about 700 meters southeast of Dongnakdang, Oksan seowon was founded.

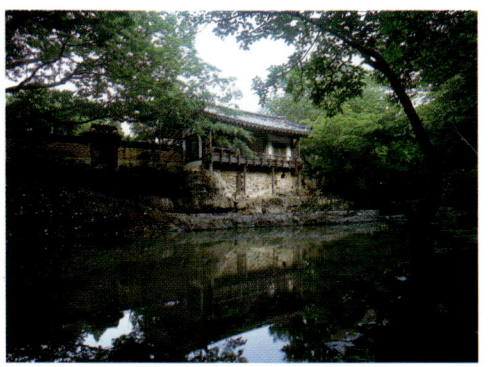

Gyejeong pavilion, which looks out over a valley

Examples of *seowon* architecture 121

Building arrangement, Oksan seowon

1. stream (Jagye)
2. rock terrace (Sesimdae)
3. main gate (Yeongnangmun)
4. Myeongdangsu stream
5. pavilion (Mubyeollu)
6. eastern dormitory (Mingujae)
7. western dormitory (Amsujae)
8. stone lantern (jeongnyodae)
9. lecture hall (Guindang)
10. spirit gate (Cheinmun)
11. shrine (Cheinmyo)
12. stele pavilion (sindobigak)
13. building for preparing offerings (jeonsacheong)
14. classics pavilion (Gyeonggak)
15. storehouse for printing blocks (pangak)
16. repository of academy's documents (Cheongbungak)
17. stewards' house (gojiksa)
18. toilet

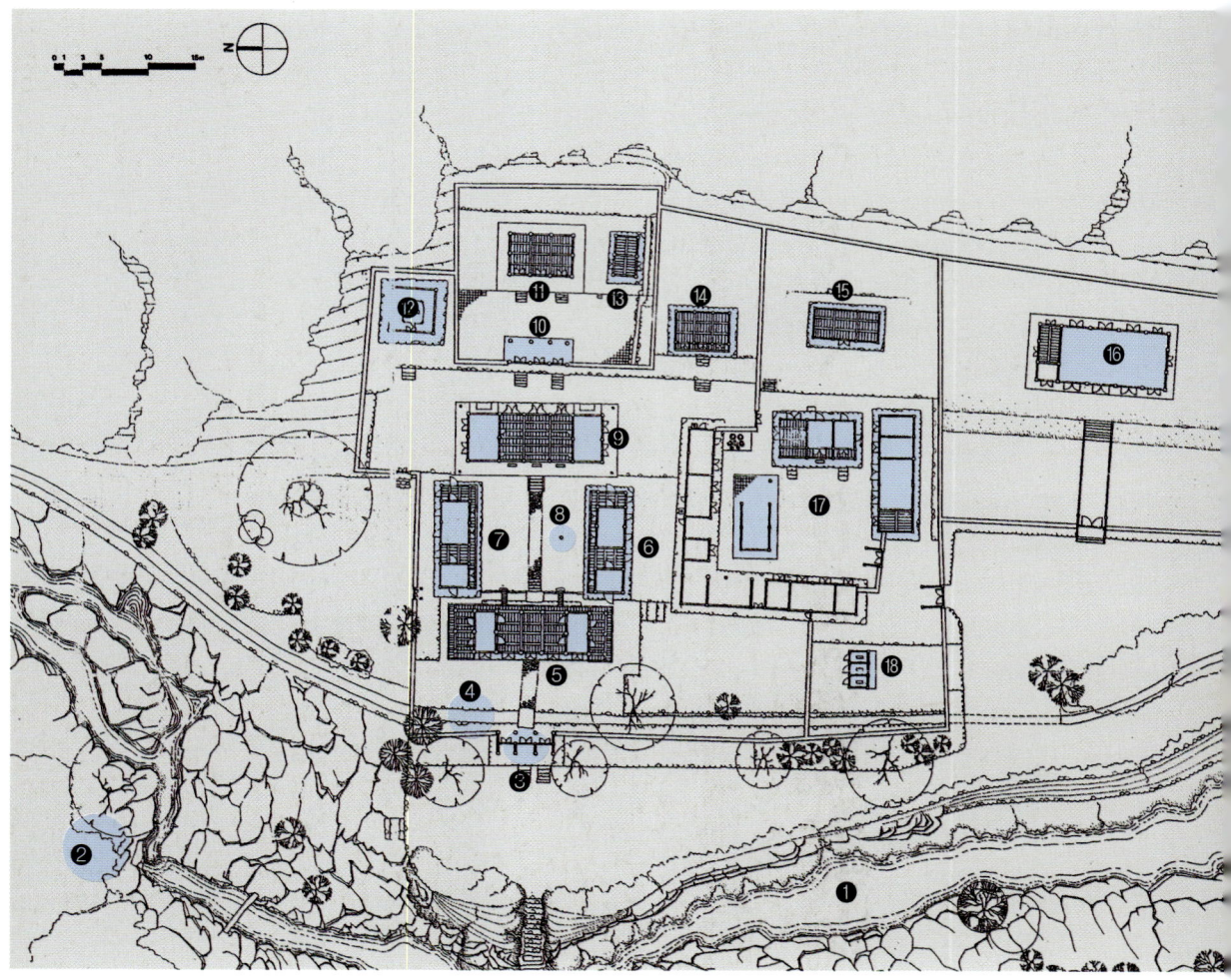

122 THE ARCHITECTURE OF KOREA'S PRIVATE ACADEMIES

Dongnakdang, while appearing very individual and hidden, seems to blend in with nature. Built close to the ground, its arrangement and spatial structure is in tune with nature and is an outstanding example of the environment where scholars secluded themselves in a valley to study and lived like hermits. The buildings form a living environment imbued with the simple and comfortable feeling of the scholar's life.

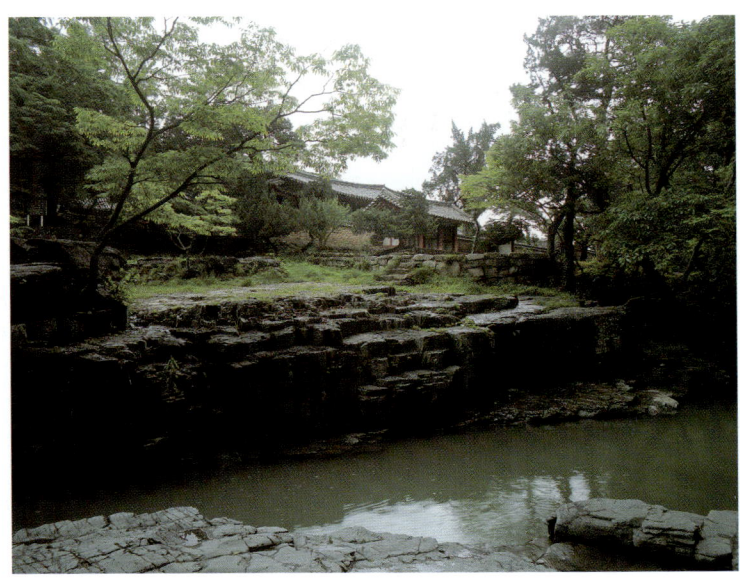

Oksan seowon seen from Sesimdae

The Gyejeong pavilion, which hugs the stream north of Dongnakdang, was built by Yi Eon-jeok's father, and its simple style is somewhat different from that of Dongnakdang. The roof, which is so low that you can hit your head when standing, and the low eaves give the building an impression of softness and meekness, but this small scale also tends to subdue the viewer. The unadorned vivacity and leisure of the building's structure tend to overwhelm the visitor, because when you sit inside, the completely unobstructed scenery of the valley in front makes you forget everything. And if you sit aimlessly watching

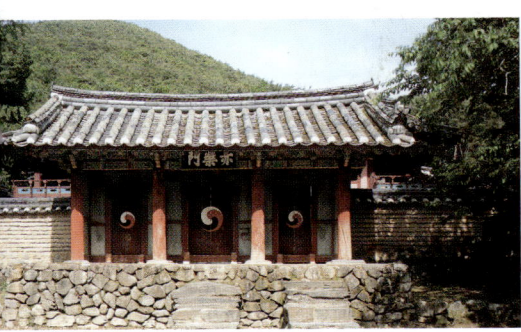

Yeongnangmun, the outer or main gate of Oksan seowon

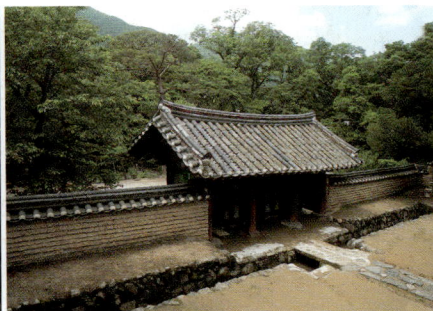

The Myeongdangsu, a geomantically auspicious stream that flows between Yeongnangmun and Mubyeollu

Examples of *seowon* architecture 123

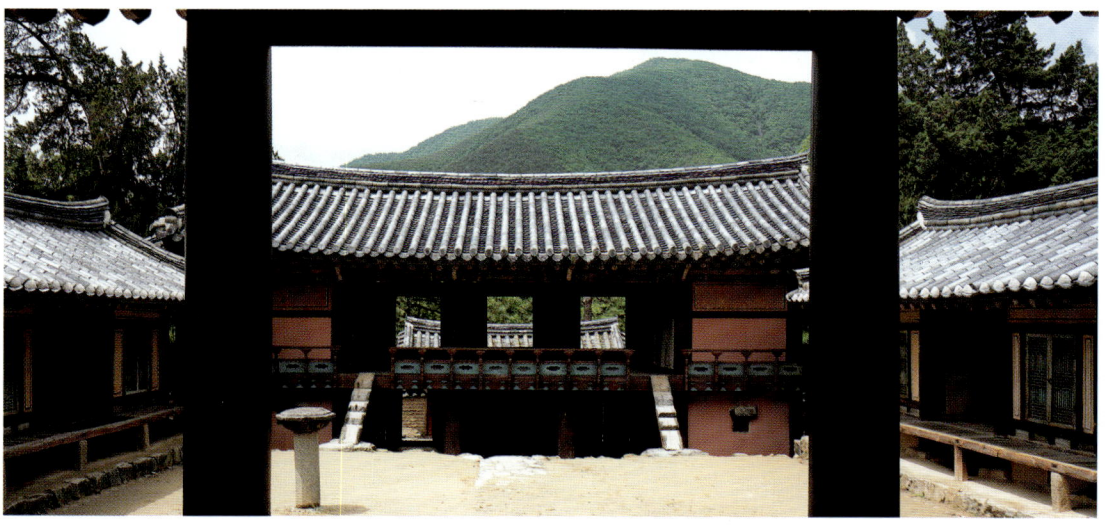

Mubyeollu and the study compound seen from Guindang, the lecture hall

the water flow down, you will start ruminating on questions such as: Why does nature always draw your eyes to it? Should you reject desire? Wherein lies the value of life?

Oksan seowon faces west, but on three sides – east, west and north – it is hemmed in by mountains. Only the southern side is open. The mountain facing the academy on its western, or frontal, side is Mt. Muhaksan, which is part of a range branching off from Mt. Jaoksan in the north. In the valley in front of the academy, the water flowing from north to south forms a series of waterfalls known as Yongchu, and the fast-flowing water hitting the rocks produces a thundering noise. The academy also faces the Sesimdae terrace in the valley area. Sesimdae is a large, flat boulder, and its meaning, "terrace to wash the mind", reveals that it was considered a place where the swift flowing water could refresh the mind and where the companionship of nature was conducive to study.

Mubyeollu

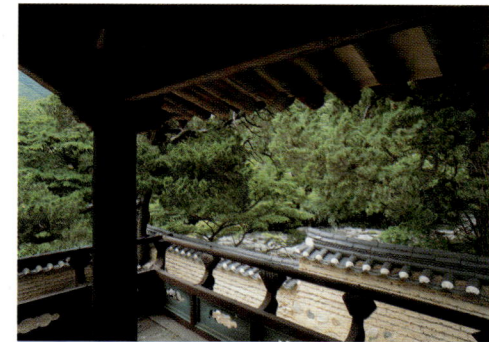

124 THE ARCHITECTURE OF KOREA'S PRIVATE ACADEMIES

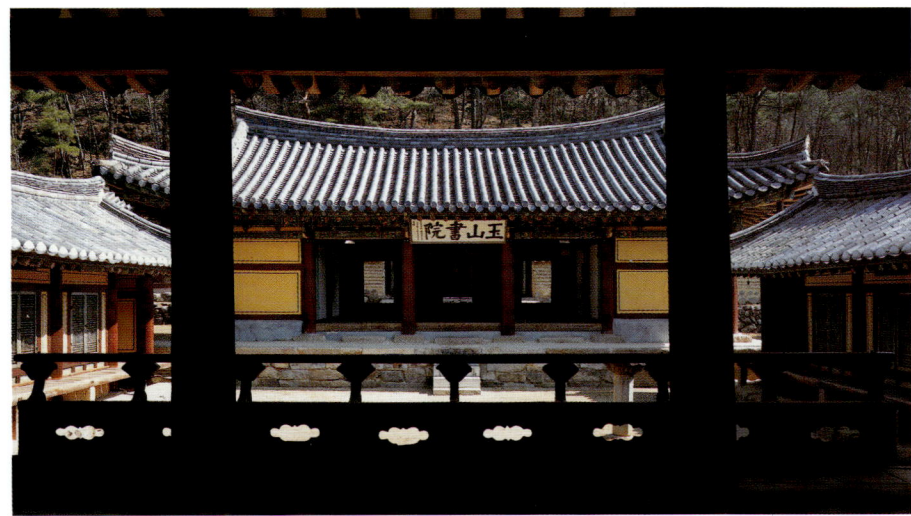

Guindang seen from Mubyeollu, together with the eastern and western dormitories

Passing through Yeongnangmun, the academy's outer gate, and over a small stream you reach the Mubyeollu pavilion, a two-story building with a loft. The small stream between the gate and the pavilion, which draws its water from the valley stream, is known in geomantic terms as the *myeongdangsu*, the watercourse flowing in front of an auspicious site, because it retains the energy for that auspicious site – the site where the academy is located. The name of the outer gate, Yeongnangmun (lit. "also-joy gate"), is inspired by a famous passage in the *Analects*: "When a friend comes to visit from afar, is not this a joy too?"

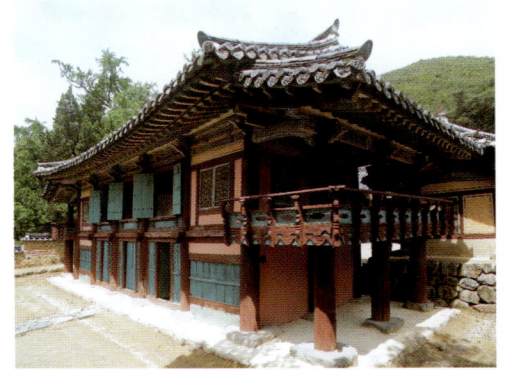

Elevated veranda (numaru) of Mubyeollu

Mubyeollu, literally "boundless pavilion," is a seven-*kan*-long building; the middle section consists of three bays with a wooden floor, flanked by a one-*kan ondol* room on each side, and with a one-*kan* extension of the wooden floor of the rooms at each end of the building. Towards the academy side, the front yard of the lecture hall can be seen through the eaves, and towards the outside the mountains and valleys unfold and seem to enter the building as if there is no separation be-

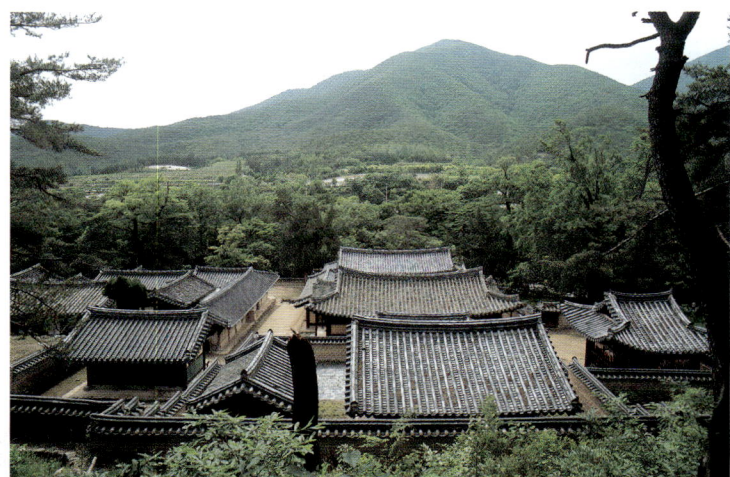

View from behind Oksan seowon towards the front

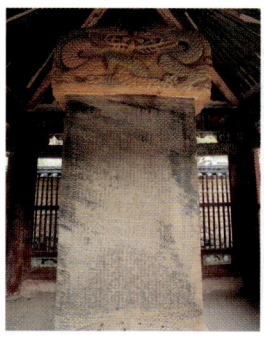

Stele in Sindobigak

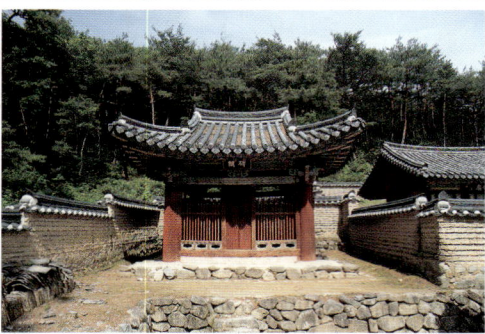

Sindobigak (funerary stele pavilion), which is located to the right of Cheinmyo, the shrine of Oksan seowon

tween nature and building. The building is designed to face inwards: Towards the outside the floored rooms in the middle of the Mubyeollu have thin wooden walls, sections of which can be opened to enlarge or contract the inner space, but towards the inside there is no wall, so that the building is always open toward the lecture hall. Seen from the outer gate Mubyeollu has two stories, but from the lecture hall only the top story is visible.

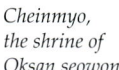

Cheinmyo, the shrine of Oksan seowon

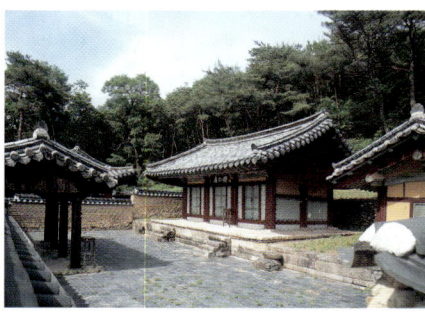

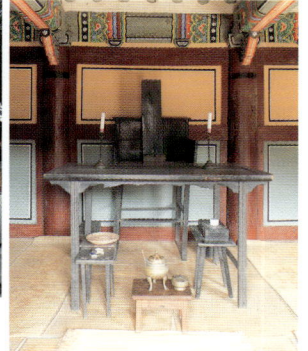

Interior of Cheinmyo

126 THE ARCHITECTURE OF KOREA'S PRIVATE ACADEMIES

The study compound consists of the Guindang lecture hall, which faces Mubyeollu, and the two dormitories in front of it. Guindang has a three-bay main floored room in the middle, flanked by two one-bay *ondol* rooms on either side. Looking out from Guindang across the front yard and beyond Mubyeollu, the landscape can be taken in at a glance. The board inscribed with the letters "Oksan seowon" hanging at the front of the building is executed in the calligraphy of Kim Jeong-hui (pen name Chusa 1786-1856), while the board with the same letters hanging at the front of the main floored room dates to the time the

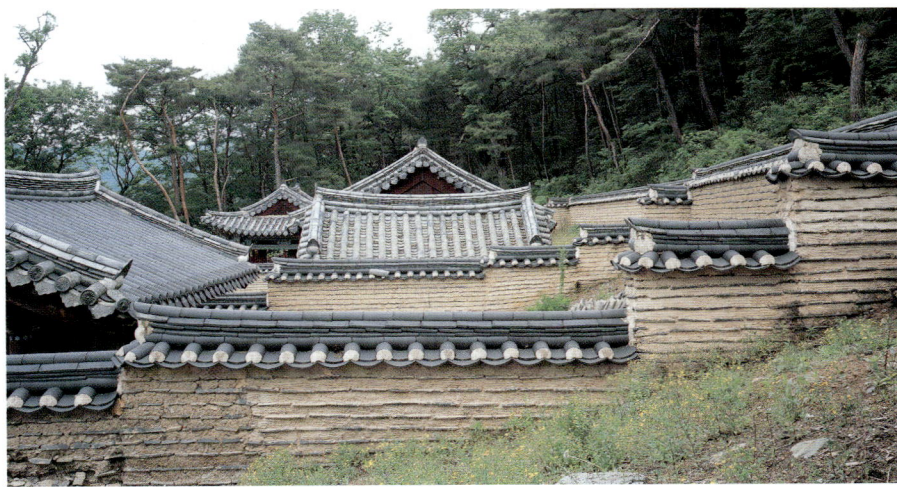

Oksan seowon's outer perimeter and wall seen from behind

academy was chartered, and carries the calligraphy of Yi San-hae (pen name Agye, 1538-1609). The boards carrying the names of Mubyeollu and Guindang were executed by Han Seok-bong.

Behind Guindang is Cheinmun, the inner gate, which leads to the walled compound where the shrine, called Cheinmyo, and the room for preparing the offerings can be found. Outside the wall of this compound, you will find the Gyeonggak (classics pavilion) to the left, and the Sindobigak, the pavilion for housing stele, to the right. Outside the academy compound, on the northern side, are the stewards' quarters and a pavilion for storing the printing blocks of scholars' collected works (*munjip*).

Examples of *seowon* architecture 127

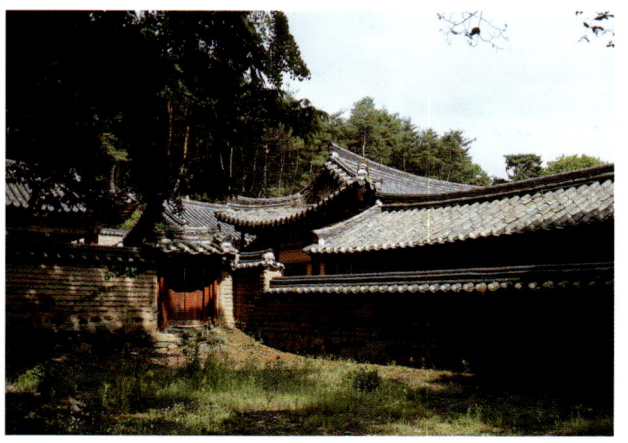

Oksan seowon's outer perimeter and wall seen from the valley

The building layout of Oksan seowon consists of a succession of buildings starting with the main gate, a pavilion, lecture halls and so on, forming several layers of spaces, compounds that are centered around a yard and laid out in a straight line along a central axis. Although following a geometric pattern, the layout plan is in harmony with the surrounding natural landscape. The spaces around Mubyeollu, Guindang, and Cheinmyo form centers around which distinct compounds are built. The large spaces sunk between compounds, through which a path runs, the heaping up of roof ridges, and the continuation of spatial construction in the encircling walls are all elements that help define the characteristic vernacular of Oksan seowon's architectural space.

4) Namgye seowon

Namgye seowon, located at 586-1 Wonpyeong-ni, Sudong-myeon, Hamyang-gun, was founded in 1552 in honor of Jeong Yeo-chang (pen name Ildu, 1450-1504), and received its name and charter in 1566. The name "Namgye" is borrowed from the stream that flows beside the academy. After Sosu seowon in Punggi and Munheon seowon in Haeju this is one of the oldest private academies in Korea.

Traditionally, Hamyang, where the academy is situated, is paired with Andong, as in the expression "Andong to the left and Hamyang to the right." Viewed from the center, Hanyang (present-day Seoul), Andong was situated to the left of the Nakdonggang river and Hamyang to the right of it, and both were famous for producing many talented people and grand lineages and as seats of learning. If Andong

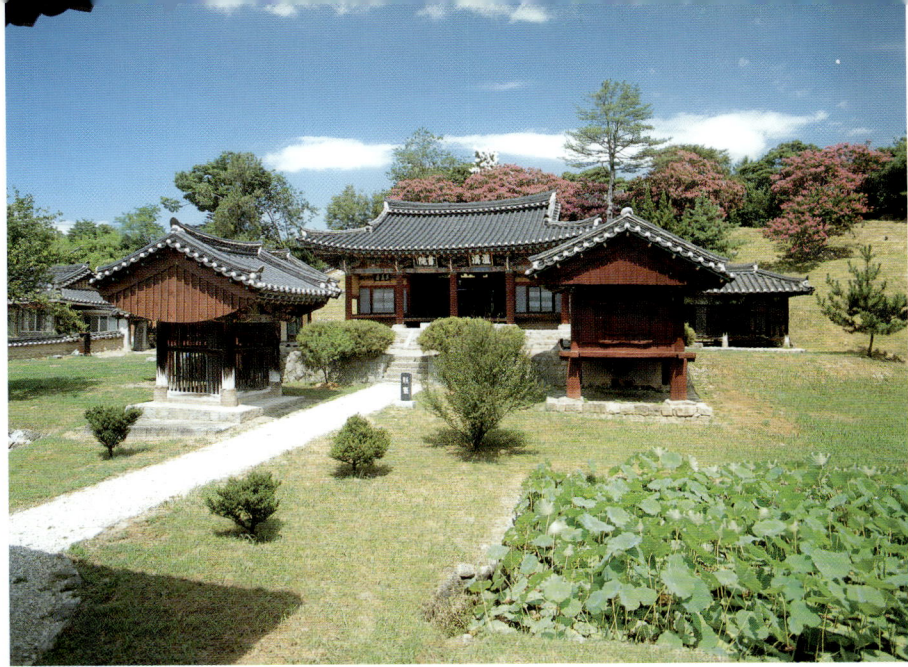

General view of Namgye seowon

is famous for Toegye Yi Hwang, then Hamyang's answer to Toegye is Jeong Yeo-chang, worshiped in Namgye seowon.

Jeong Yeo-chang was born in Gaepyeong-ni, Jigok-myeon in Hamyang, situated to the northwest of the academy. The so-called "residence of Jeong Yeo-chang," built on the place where he was born, reflects the typical features of a *yangban* dwelling of the Joseon period in the arrangement of its buildings, the arrangement of external space, and the construction of the Seokgasan artificial mountain garden in front of the men's quarters (*sarangchae*). He studied Neo-Confucianism under the tutelage of Kim Jong-jik, during which time he also sealed a firm bond of friendship with Kim Goeng-pil. At the outbreak of the 1498 literati purge he was branded as a member of the *sarim* because of his link to Kim Jong-jik and exiled to Jongseong in Ham-

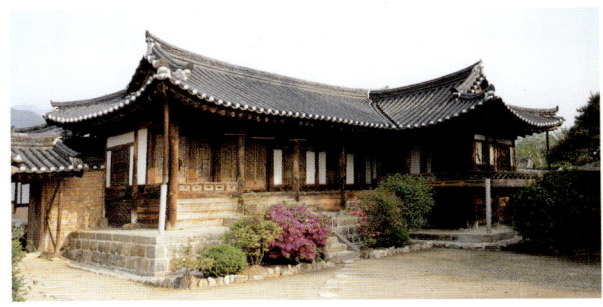

Jeong Yeo-chang's former residence

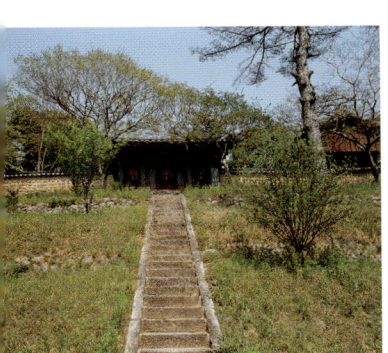

Steps leading up to the sinmun (spirit gate) of Namgye seowon

Examples of *seowon* architecture 129

Building arrangement, Namgye seowon

1. red arrow gate (hongsalmun)
2. dismounting stone (hamaseok)
3. gate pavilion (Pungyeongnu)
4. pond
5. memorial stele pavilion
6. eastern dormitory (Yangjeongjae)
7. western dormitory (Boinjae)
8. lecture hall (Myeongseongdang)
9. storehouse for printing blocks (jangpangak)
10. altar for inspecting the sacrificial animal (saengdan)
11. spirit gate (Jundomun)
12. shrine (sadang)
13. washbasin (gwansewi)
14. building for preparing offerings (jeonsacheong)
15. stewards' house (gojiksa)
16. toilet

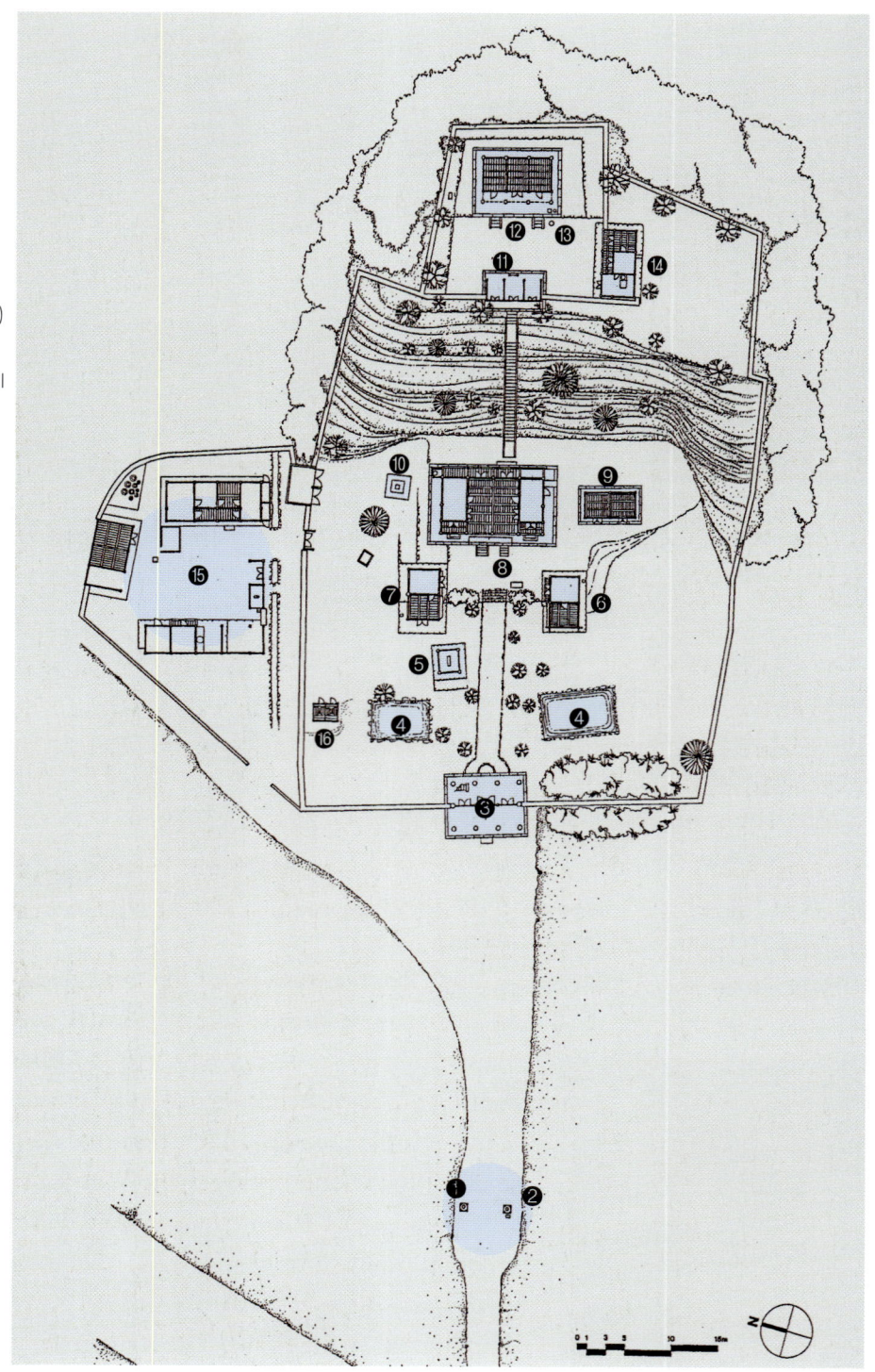

130 THE ARCHITECTURE OF KOREA'S PRIVATE ACADEMIES

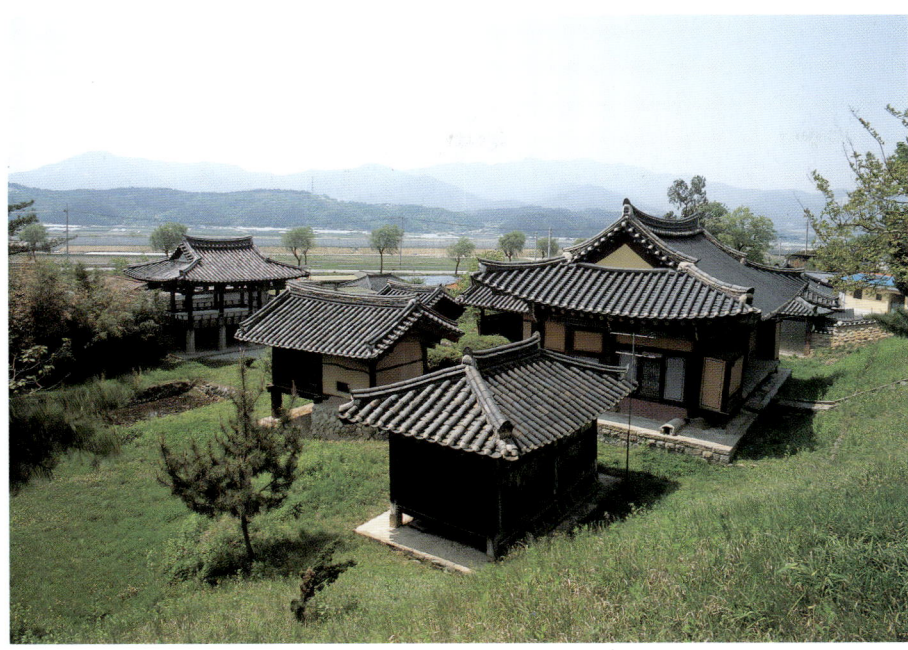

View of Namgye seowon from the shrine

gyeong-do province, where he later died. His pen name, Ildu, was made in self-deprecation, as it likens him to a moth. It was inspired by the phrase "Just a single moth between Heaven and earth," coined by the Chinese Neo-Confucian scholar Cheng Yi.

Unlike Sosu seowon, the first private academy of the Joseon period, in Namgye seowon the buildings were arranged according to a specific pattern: Buildings belonging to the ritual compound were located at the back, while those pertaining to the study compound were located at the front of the academy. This makes Namgye seowon a representative example of the typical layout of early private academies.

The shrine, completed in 1561, is built high on a climbing slope, and can be reached via a steep stairway behind the lecture hall. It exudes a

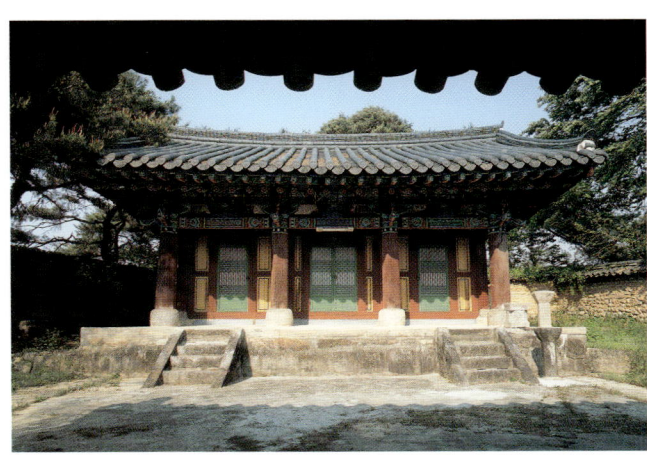

Namgye seowon's shrine

Examples of *seowon* architecture 131

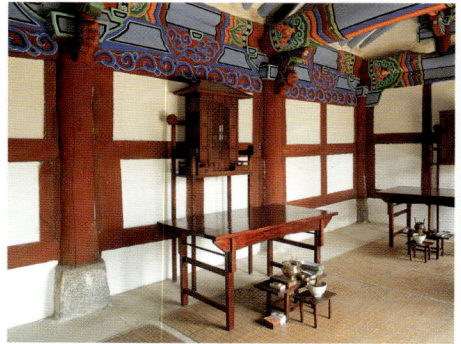
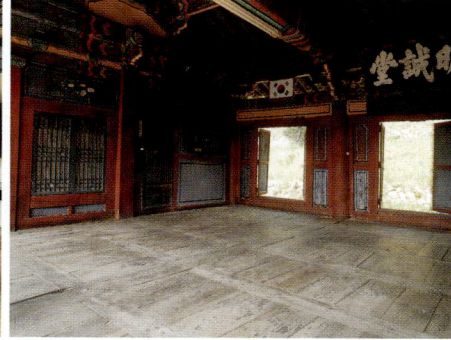

Interior of the shrine at Namgye seowon

Main wood-floored room of the lecture hall at Namgye seowon

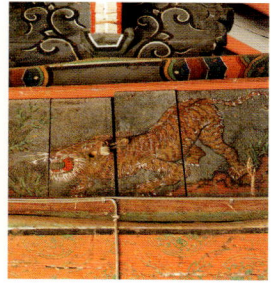

Dancheong decoration in the main wood-floored room of the lecture hall at Namgye seowon

stern image, and contrasts sharply but positively with the lecture hall. In front of the shrine and to its southwest stands Jeonsacheong, a north-facing building where ritual utensils are stored and sacrificial meals prepared. Within the shrine, Jeong Yeo-chang's tablet occupies the main place in the center, flanked by those of Jeong On (1569-1641) and Gang Ik (1523-1567). Looking down from the shrine on the academy and its surrounds, one can see how the academy is surrounded by the mountain ranges stretching out from Mt. Yeonhwasan, how the Namgye stream, originating from Mt. Deogyusan, forms the Hwarim *gugok* (nine bends), and how the academy's "front mountain," Mt. Baegamsan rises up on the other side of a broad plane.

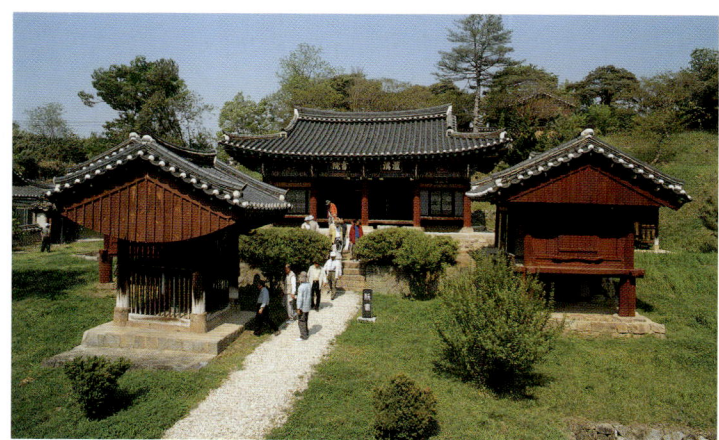

Study compound, Namgye seowon

Lecture hall, Namgye seowon

The lecture hall at the heart of the study compound, Myeongseongdang, was finished in 1559 and is four *kan* long. The central two bays are the main floored hall, which is flanked by one *ondol* room on each side. The name of the lecture hall, "myeongseong" (bright sincerity), is taken from the *Doctrine of the Mean*: "If there is brightness there is sincerity." Not only is the name an attempt to reflect in architecture the importance of self-cultivation for Neo-Confucianism, it is also a place which prompts people to look up to the scholarship and spiritual tradition of Jeong Yeo-chang.

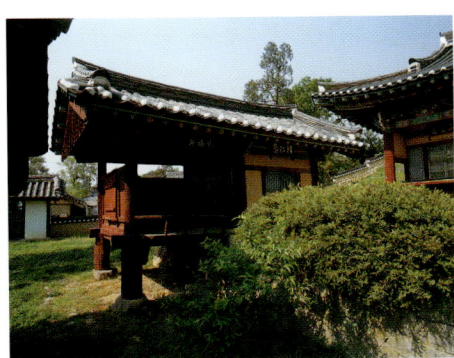

Boinjae, the western dormitory of Namgye seowon

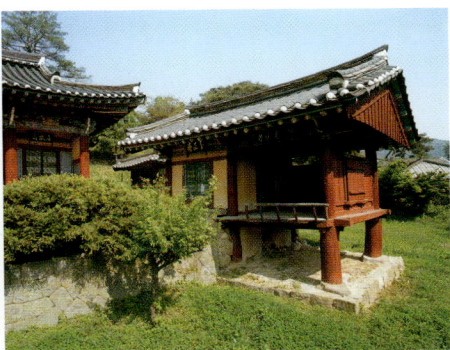

Yangjeongjae, the eastern dormitory of Namgye seowon

Examples of *seowon* architecture

Pungyeongnu

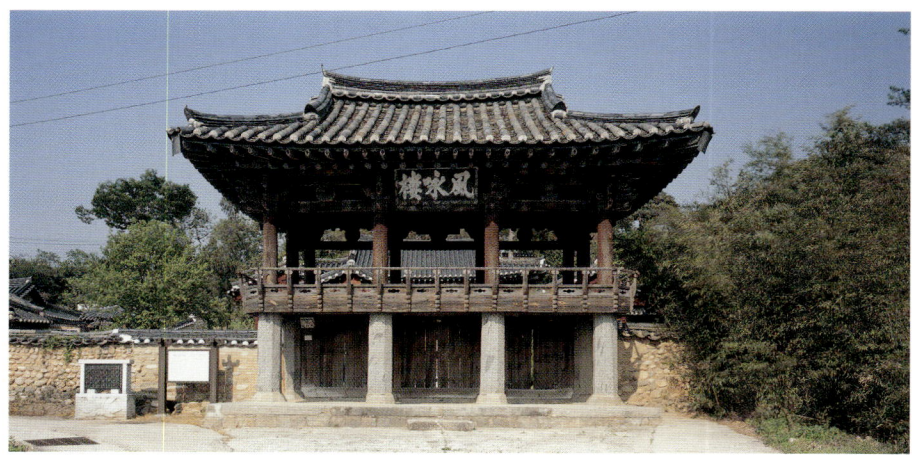

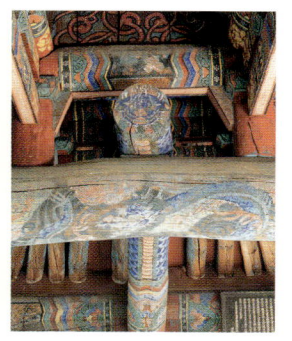

Dancheong decoration covering the beams inside Pungyeongnu

On the yard in front of the lecture hall, the eastern dormitory Yangjeongjae and the western dormitory Boinjae stand face to face with each other. Both buildings measure two *kan* in surface area. The one-*kan* rooms closest to the lecture hall have *ondol* heating, while the remaining rooms comprise open verandas called Aeryeonheon and Yeongmaeheon, respectively. Adapting to the sloping terrain on which the academy is built, the buildings are one level higher than the pavilion gate. To improve the view from the verandas, built on the lower side, their space is extended to the natural landscape outside. A peculiar feature of this *seowon* is that it has two lotus ponds: Beneath each of the verandas of the dormitories, at the side of the pavilion gate a pair of lotus ponds was created in 1564. It is said that Zhou Dunyi's "On loving lotuses" inspired Jeong Yeo-chang's love of plum blossoms and lotuses. This love is reflected in the name of the dormitories (Aeryeon means "to love lotuses," Yeongmae "chanting about the plums"), the plum trees planted around the ponds, and the lotuses planted in the ponds.

Looking at the academy from the second-story loft of the Pungyeongnu gate-pavilion, one can see that the buildings have been arranged naturally on the slope, but that they also regulated freedom. Generally, the layout can be characterized by its large and open spirit and dignified pose.

5) Dodong seowon

Dodong seowon is dedicated to Kim Goeng-pil (pen name Hanhwondang, 1454-1504) and is currently located in Dodong-ni 35, Guji-myeon, Dalseong-gun, Daegu. From Hyeonpung, the academy can be reached by following the right bank of the Nakdonggang river from the Guji-myeon district office for about four kilometers.

This private academy was founded in 1568 and was originally located in Ssangye-dong, at the foot of Mt. Biseulsan in Hyeonpung. However, these buildings were destroyed in 1597 during the second phase of the Hideyoshi invasions, and in 1605 it was rebuilt in its present location under the name Borodong seowon. In 1607 a royal warrant

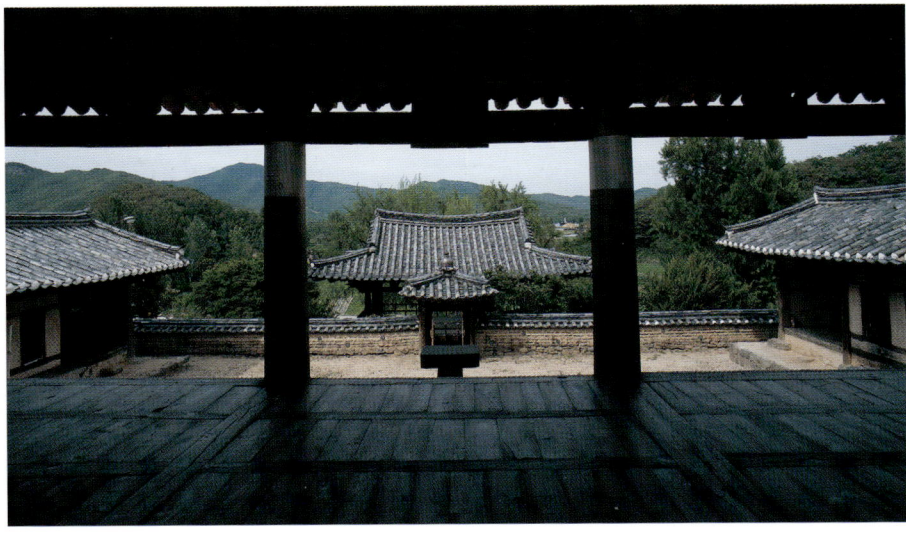

View from Jungjeongdang towards the front

gave the academy its present name, Dodong seowon. This new title reprises Toegye's praise of Kim Goeng-pil as the "patriarch of the Learning of the Way in the Country to the East," "Dodong" literally meaning "the Way (*Do*) has come to the East (*Dong*);" in other words, the academy's name evokes the fact that Kim Goeng-pil brought Confucius' true teachings to Korea.

Building Arrangement, Dodong seowon

1. gingko tree
2. memorial stele (sindobi)
3. gate pavilion (Suwollu)
4. main gate (Hwanjumun)
5. eastern dormitory (Geoinjae)
6. western dormitory (Geogyeongjae)
7. lecture hall (Jungjeongdang)
8. storehouse for printing blocks (jangpangak)
9. altar for inspecting the sacrificial animal (saengdan)
10. spirit gate (naesammun)
11. stone lantern (seokdeung)
12. shrine (sadang)
13. place to burn the eulogy after a sacrifice (gam)
14. storage for ritual vessels (jeungbanso)
15. building for preparing offerings (jeonsacheong)
16. storage
17. toilet

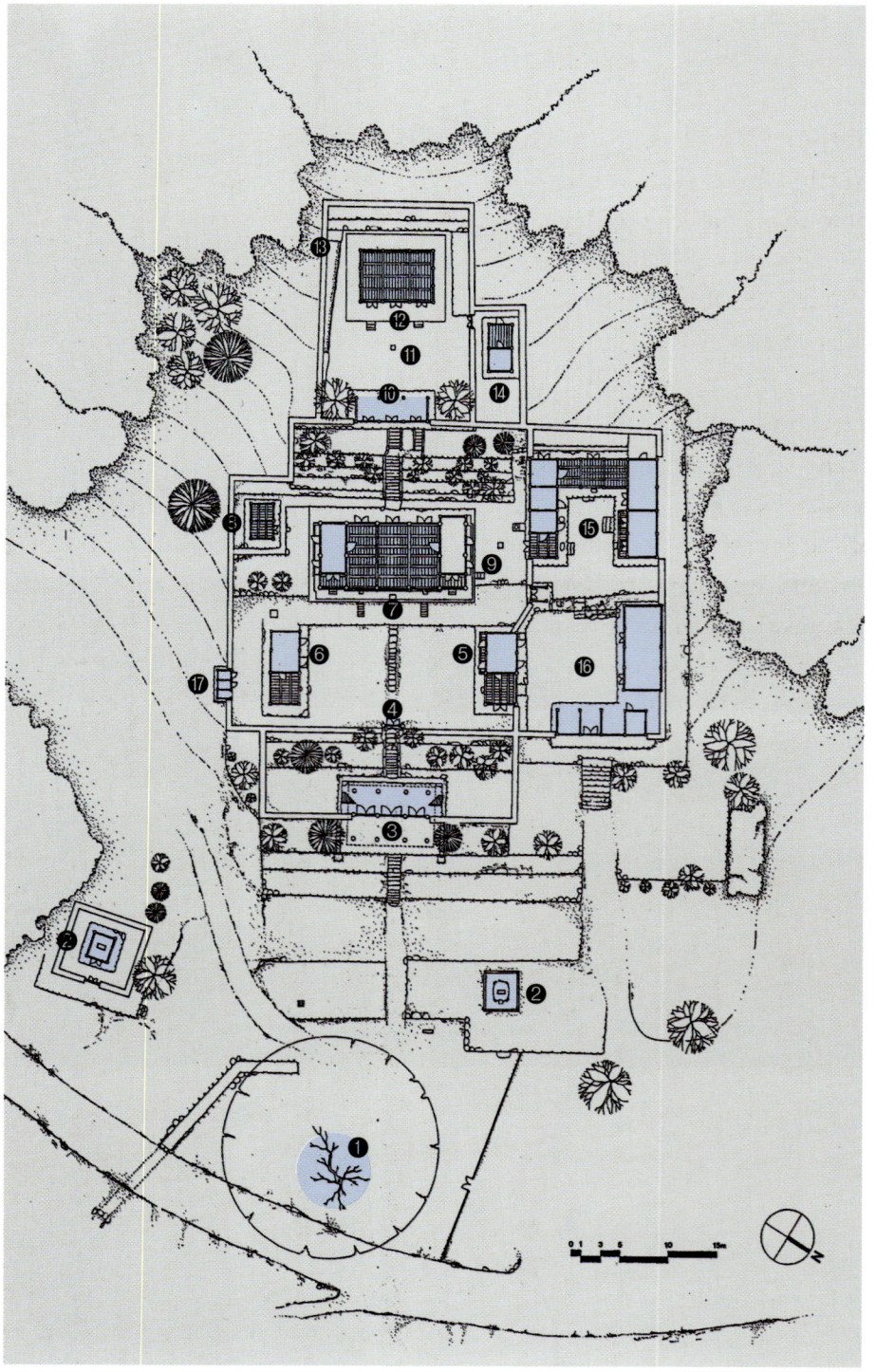

136 THE ARCHITECTURE OF KOREA'S PRIVATE ACADEMIES

Kim Goeng-pil's connection with Hyeonpung started with his great-grandfather Kim Jung-gon, who settled here after marrying into the Gwak clan of Hyeonpung. He spent a carefree and unrestrained youth in Sollye village, south of Mt. Daenisan in Hyeonpung, and at the age of 18 married into a family of Yaro, in Hapcheon-gun. In a

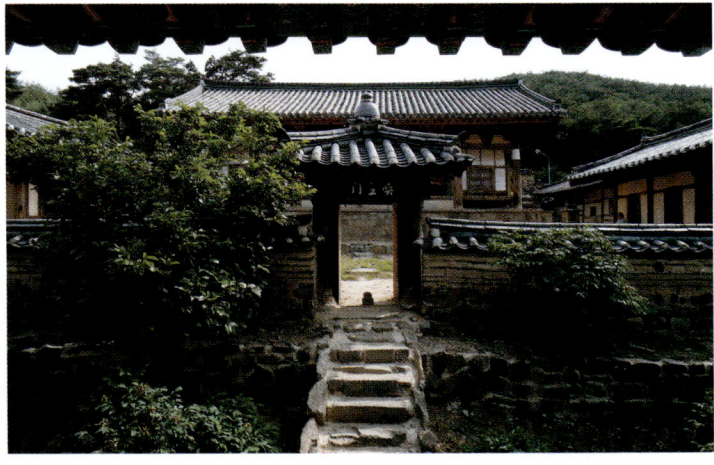

The study compound of Dodong seowon seen from Suwollu

valley near his in-laws' home he built a small study called Hanhwondang, where he devoted himself to studying. Around the same time he became a disciple of Kim Jong-jik (1431-1492), who was magistrate of the nearby Hamyang county, and studied the *Elementary Learning* with him. Thus he continued the lineage of Neo-Confucian study that started with Jeong Mong-ju and was passed on to his teacher Kim Jong-jik. He

Bracketing and rafters of Jungjeongdang

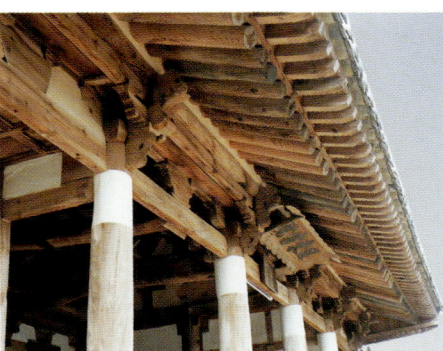

Foundation platform of Jungjeongdang, detail

Foundation platform of Jungjeongdang

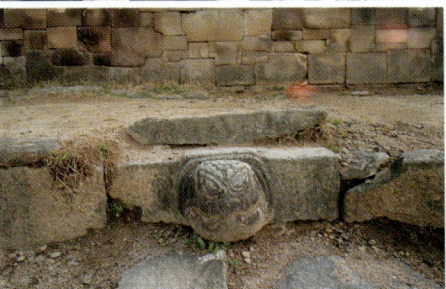

Foundation platform of Jungjeongdang, detail

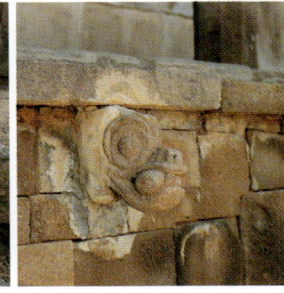

Examples of *seowon* architecture 137

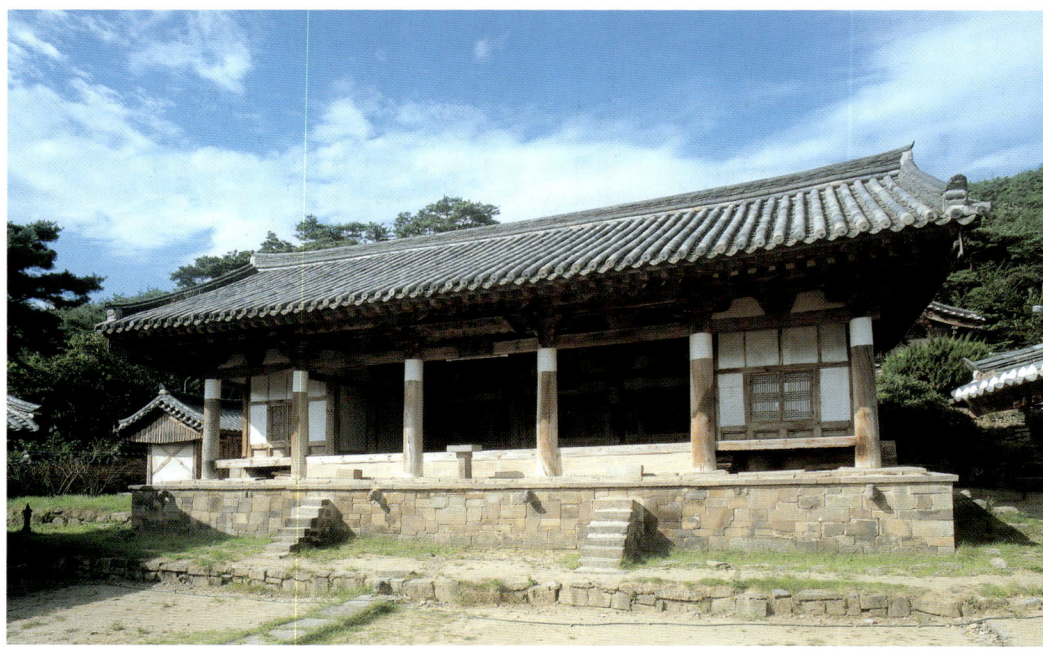

View of Jungjeongdang

passed the civil service examination at the age of 26, but during the literati purge of 1498 he was condemned for belonging to Kim Jong-jik's faction and exiled to Huicheon in Pyeongan-do province. Later he was transferred to Suncheon in Jeolla-do province, where he was forced to take poison during the literati purge of 1504. He was posthumously exonerated at the time of Jungjong's restoration, after which his reputation started to grow.

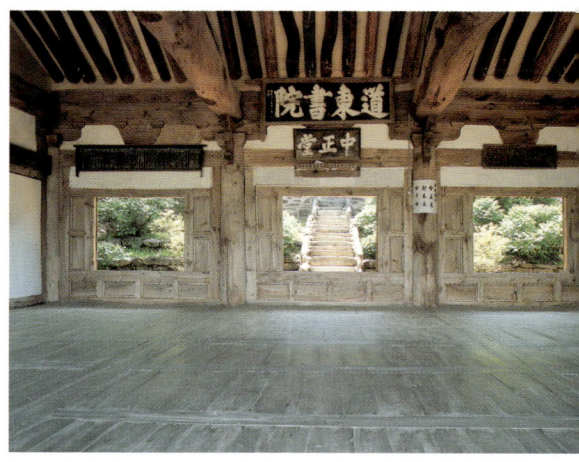

The main wood-floored hall of Jungjeongdang, Dodong seowon's lecture hall

Dodong seowon faces north, and is located at the foot of a northwest offshoot of Mt. Daenisan. In front of the academy flows the Nakdonggang river, and on the other side of the river a wide expanse of fields stretches out across neighboring Gaejin-

138 THE ARCHITECTURE OF KOREA'S PRIVATE ACADEMIES

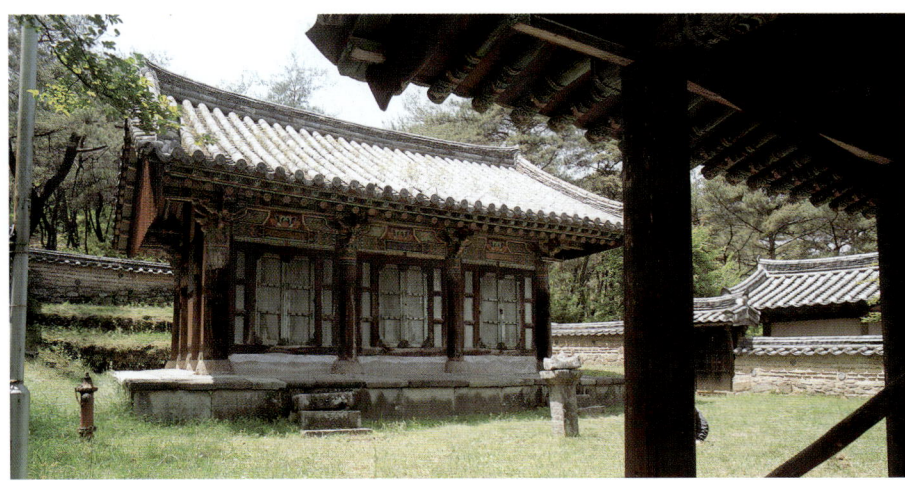

Shrine, Dodong seowon

myeon, Goryeong-gun county. An old gingko tree, which has now been protected as a designated natural treasure, stands in front of the academy, which itself is built on a fairly steeply rising incline.

The academy's buildings are laid out evenly along a central axis, from Suwollu to Hwanjumun, Jungjeongdang, Naesammun, and the shrine. To make this alignment even more explicit, pathways and stairs are built to accentuate the central axis. This is thought to be a manifestation of what the Neo-Confucian systematizer Zhu Xi called the "pivotal knot," the axis and centrality of all things. In its architectural composition and layout, Dodong seowon is therefore the most normative and typical example of the architecture of private academies in Korea, and is unsurpassed in the perfection of its buildings

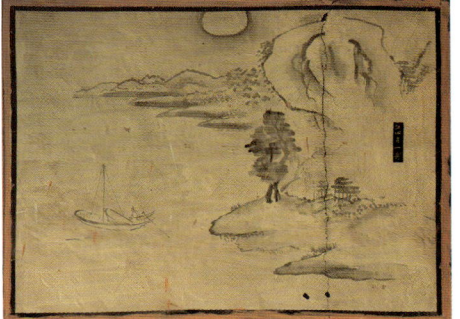

Boat on a moonlit river, painted on the southern wall inside the shrine of Dodong seowon

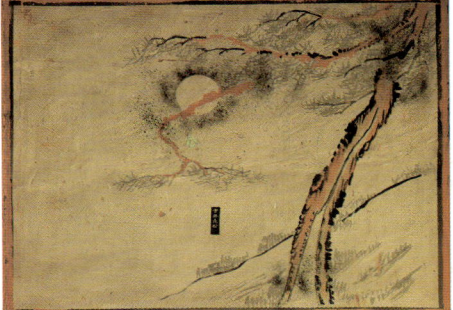

Pine tree along a snowy road, painted on the northern wall inside the shrine of Dodong seowon

Examples of *seowon* architecture 139

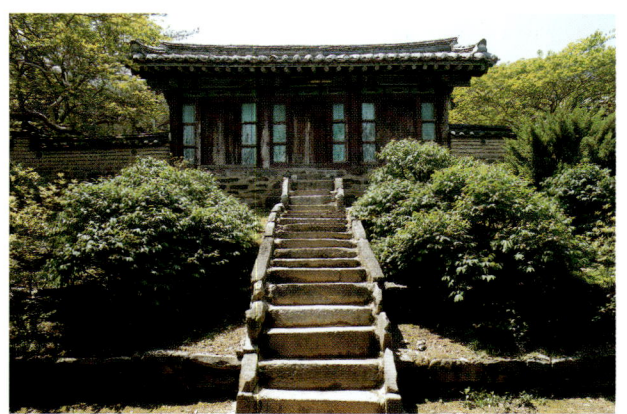

Steps leading to the spirit gate of Dodong seowon's shrine

and its spatial arrangement. Especially the lecture hall and shrine, built in the 1600s, are splendid examples of the construction technique of academies and shrines of the time, while the wall surrounding the academy and its stonework are also exquisite.

The Suwollu gate pavilion was used by students to release stress and unwind. The original building burned down in 1888 and was only replaced in 1973. Suwollu, a name which evokes the image of students reading by the light of the moon reflected in the water, is architecturally less accomplished than the other buildings, but when you climb up to the open veranda lined with a balustrade, and see the blue water of the river surging past and the surrounding landscape, it becomes clear that its purpose was to take in this scenery.

The main gate of the academy, called Hwanjumun, is a small gate with a square roof, and stands in the middle of a stone wall. The small stairway leading up from Suwollu to Hwanjumun is so narrow that only one person at a time can pass, and is meant to impress on students the fact that scholars should always ground themselves in propriety when studying, so that they would eventually reach a broadness of mind, neither shrinking back from nor feeling ashamed of anything.

Jungjeongdang serves as a lecture hall. It is built on a foundation platform using stones of different colors, which are assembled so neatly that there is not the slightest space between them, thus achieving a sense of harmony. Dragon heads are inserted in this foundation, and a row of different-sized pairs of blossoms have been carved on its upper part. In each pair one blossom represents the sun rising in the east and

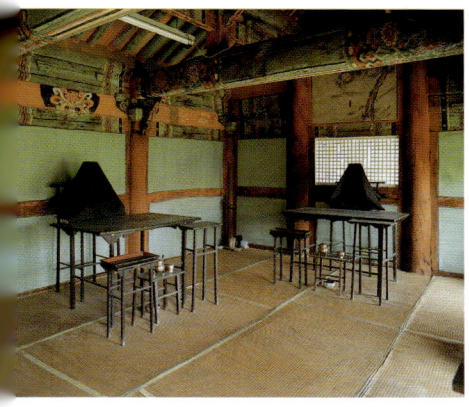

Interior of the Dodong seowon shrine

another one the moon rising in the west. The sun on the right rises high, its rays representing the Yang force, while the moon on the left, which reflects the sun's rays, represents Yin. Yin and Yang, the opposing forces that give rise to all things, are here symbolized by pairs of flowers.

To the left and right in front of the lecture hall the dormitory buildings face each other in perfect symmetry. When you stand in the yard between these two buildings, you can feel both the spaciousness of the landscape unfolding outside the Suwollu, and the enclosedness of the space surrounded by buildings and walls. The study compound is thus a space where you simultaneously receive the teaching of previous sages and awaken to the principles ruling nature.

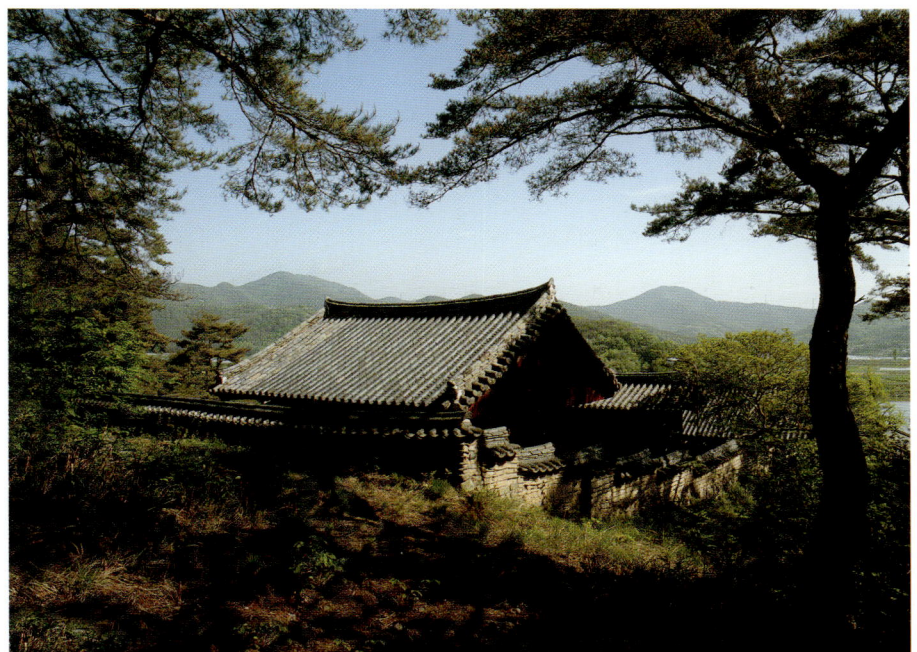

View from behind the shrine of Dodong seowon

Examples of *seowon* architecture 141

Left from the lecture hall is the altar for inspecting sacrifices (*saengdan*). On the day before a memorial service, ritual officiants would inspect the animals to be used in the sacrifice here. Climbing a steep stairway behind the lecture hall, you reach the Naesammun, which gives access to an enclosure where the shrine stands. In the shrine itself, Kim Goeng-pil's spirit tablet is enshrined against the central wall, together with the tablet of Jeong Gu (pen name Hangang, 1543-1620), flanked by two wall paintings, expressing Kim Goeng-pil's desire to return to nature and become one with it. Although the *mangnyewi*, the place where the eulogy is burnt after the memorial rite, is usually made of stone and placed on the ground, in Dodong seowon a little niche has been carved in the wall west of the shrine to bury the eulogy.

6) Donam seowon

Donam seowon was founded in 1634 to commemorate Kim Jang-saeng (pen name Sagye, 1548-1631) and continue his philosophy. It was chartered in 1660, receiving its present name, at that time.

"Donam" is the name of a rock at the edge of a forest at the foot of a mountain in Haim-ni, Yeonsan-myeon, Nonsan, Chungcheongnam-do province, where the academy was originally located. The academy is

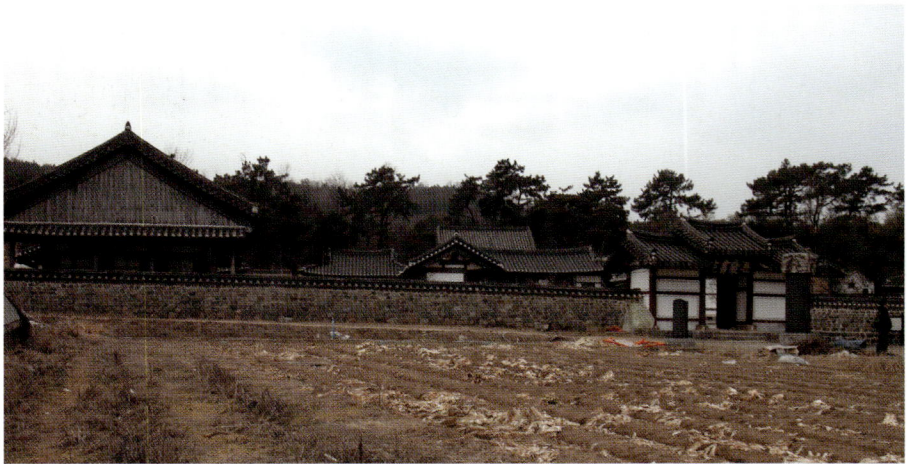

General view of Donam seowon

now located about 1.5 kilometers northwest of this spot. It was moved to 74 Im-ni, Yeonsan-myeon, in 1880 because its original location was too low, making it impossible to protect it from flooding.

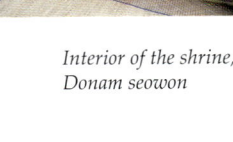

Kim Jang-saeng studied Neo-Confucianism with Song Ik-pil (pen name Gubong, 1534-1599) and Yulgok Yi I, and was a crucial figure in the development of ritual studies commensurate with the climate of the 17th century and the dominance of the *sarim*. He

Interior of the shrine, Donam seowon

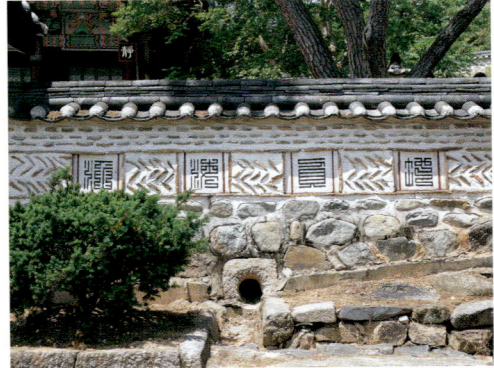

was interested in ritual because he thought that "in order for people to live together and help each other with a wise and righteous mind, we need norms that define specifically the behavior of each individual." It was precisely these norms that he considered to be ritual (or ritual propriety). As an academy dedicated to the man who made ritual studies florish, Donam seowon not only exemplifies the ritual studies movement of the later Joseon period, but is also the product of this new trend.

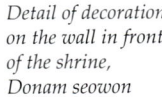

Detail of decoration on the wall in front of the shrine, Donam seowon

Before Donam seowon was built, in 1557 Kim Jang-saeng's father Kim Gye-hwi (1526-1581) had already built Jeonghoedang in the grounds of Gounsa temple, near Mt. Daedunsan in Yeonsan, where he devoted himself to training disciples and educating

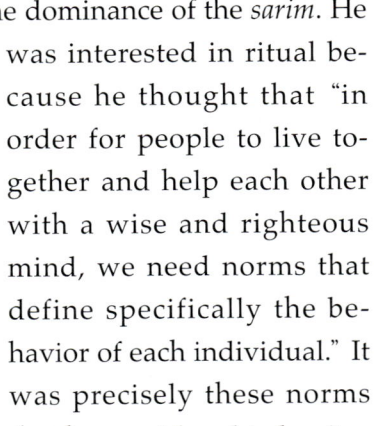

Yard of the shrine compound, Donam seowon

The lecture hall, Cheongjeonldang, seen from Hwagyeollu

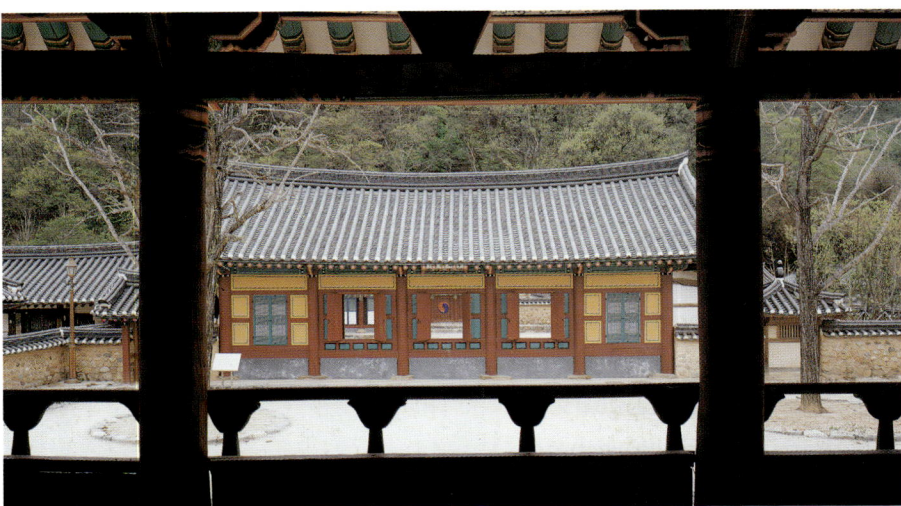

Memorial service at Piram seowon

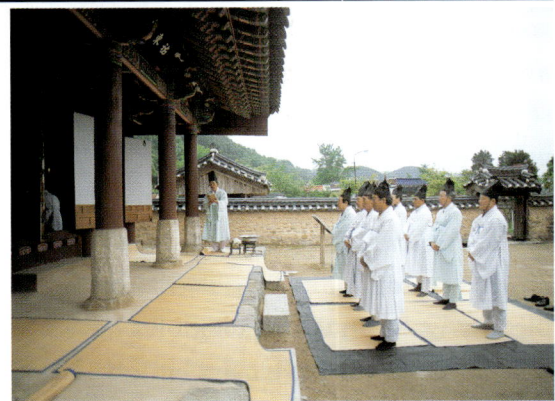

external space, a building arrangement emerges in which the lecture hall faces the shrine, and thus the spirit tablet enshrined therein. Within the Udongsa shrine, Kim In-hu's spirit tablet occupies the central position, and that of Yang Ja-jing (pen name Goam, 1523-1594) the eastern wall to the left. Yang Ja-jing, the son of Yang San-bo (1503-1557), learned to write from Kim In-hu, who had nothing but praise for his student and eventually betrothed him to his daughter.

8) Byeongsan seowon

Byeongsan seowon is located in Byeongsan-ri, Pungcheon-myeon, Andong, Gyeongsangbuk-do province. It has its origins in the Pungak private school, which was founded in nearby Pungsan-eup.

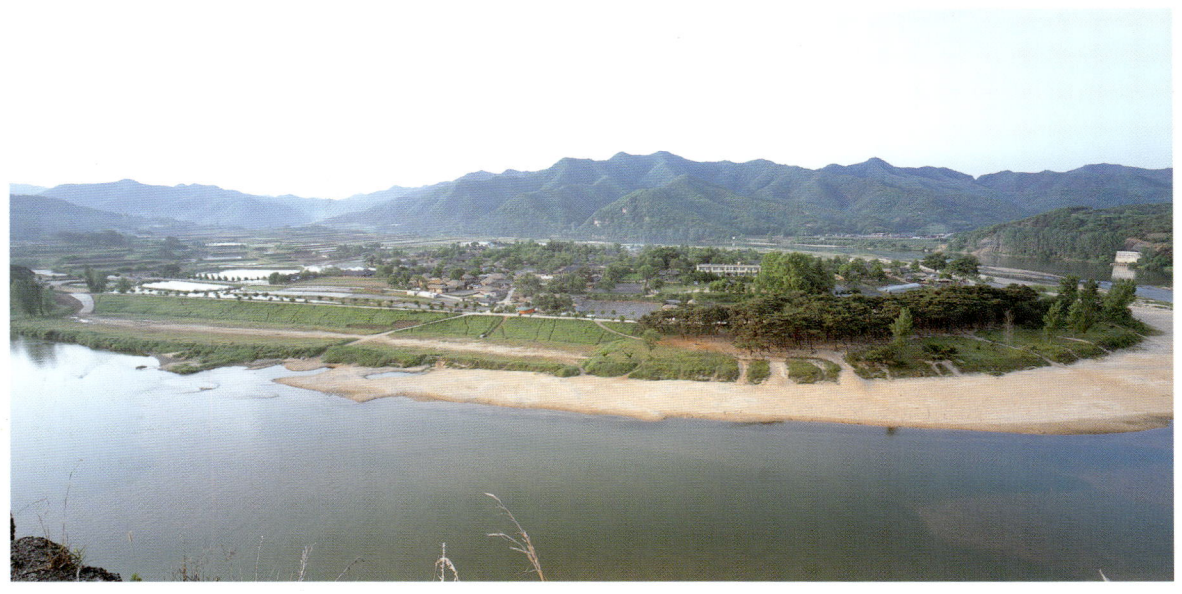

View of Hahoe village

Since it was located near a noisy thoroughfare, it was not a suitable place for study, and so Yu Seong-nyong (pen name Seoae, 1542-1607) decided to move the school, founded by his ancestors, to the present location in 1572. Pungak seodang was destroyed during the Hideyoshi invasions of 1592-1598 and rebuilt in 1607. In 1614, through the construction of a shrine dedicated to Yu Seong-nyong, it was transformed into a private academy. In 1863 it was chartered as Byeongsan seowon and thereby escaped the large-scale destruction of *seowon* by the Daewongun. It is now one of the 47 remaining original private academies.

Yu Seong-nyong, who had studied with Toegye, was prime minister during the Hideyoshi invasions and contributed greatly to saving the country from this disaster. In 1598, he retired from all government positions and retreated to his hometown of Hahoe. There, in the Ogyeon jeongsa cloister at the foot of Mt. Buyongdae, on the other side of the Nakdonggang river that flows around Hahoe, he reflected on what he had learned and compiled the "Record of Warnings and Cautions" (*Jingbirok*). The *Jingbirok* reflects on the seven years of military strife between 1592 and 1598. Its title is derived from a verse in the *Book*

Building Arrangement, Byeongsan seowon

1. main gate (Bongnyemun)
2. pond (Gwangyeongji)
3. pavilion (Mandaeru)
4. eastern dormitory
5. western dormitory
6. lecture hall (Ipgyodang)
7. storehouse for printing blocks (jangpangak)
8. spirit gate (naesammun)
9. stone lantern (jeongnyodae)
10. shrine (Jondeoksa)
11. building for preparing offerings (jeonsacheong)
12. stewards' house (gojiksa)
13. toilet

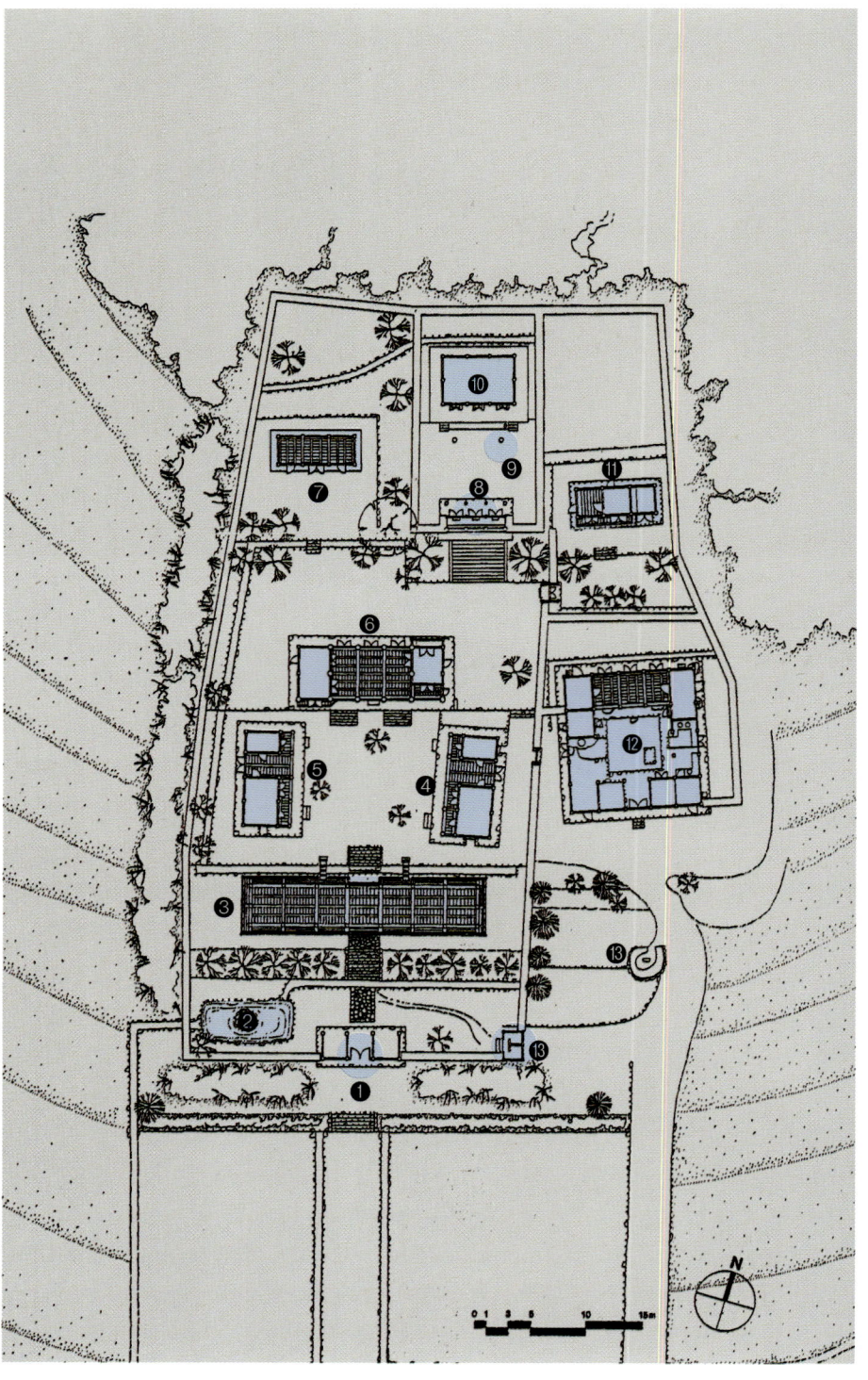

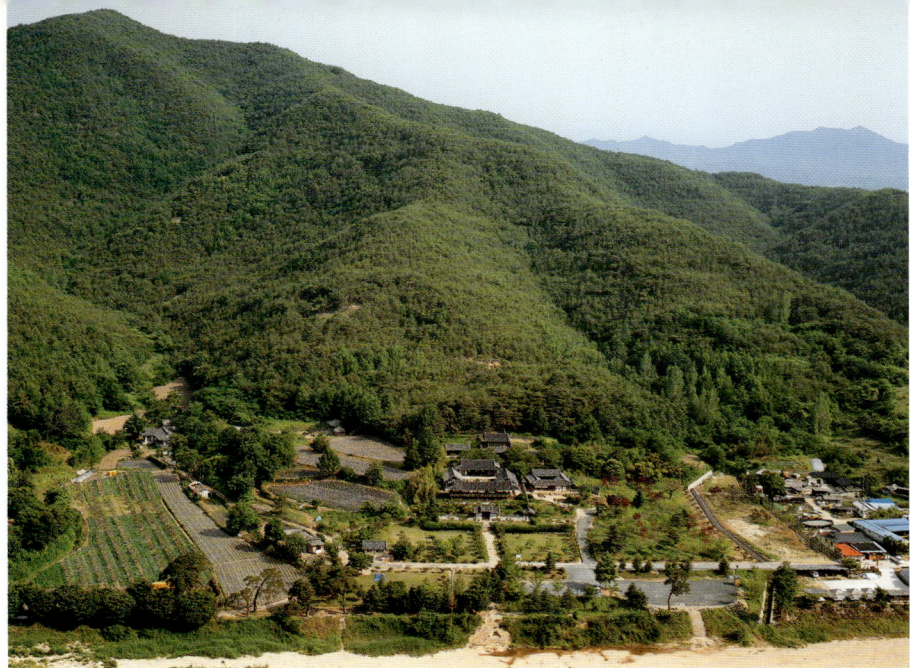

View of Byeongsan seowon

of Odes, which reads: "One should take past events as a warning so as to be prepared for them in the future." Consequently, the work was intended as a warning to future generations not to let a calamity like the Hideyoshi invasions happen again.

Byeongsan seowon is separated from Hahoe village by Mt. Hwasan: The academy is located at the eastern foot of Mt. Hwasan, and the village on the other side of the mountain. On the other side of the academy, across the river, is its namesake, Mt. Byeongsan. This mountain meets the Nakdonggang river at a spot where the river, coming from a mountainous region in Gangwon-do province, opens up widely, forcing the current to speed up and pushing the river back so that it makes a loop in the shape of a jar; the mountain, standing beside the river like a screen, is thus aptly named "Screen Mountain" (Byeongsan). The academy looks out over a superb view of the mountain's shadow falling far over the river that flows beneath its cliffs.

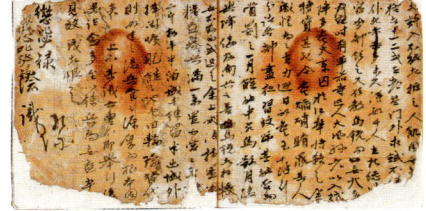

Jingbirok (Record of Warnings and Cautions) by Yu Seong-nyong

It is commonly argued that a chief characteristic of Korean architecture is its achievement of harmony with the natural environment.

Examples of *seowon* architecture

Entrance to Byeongsan seowon

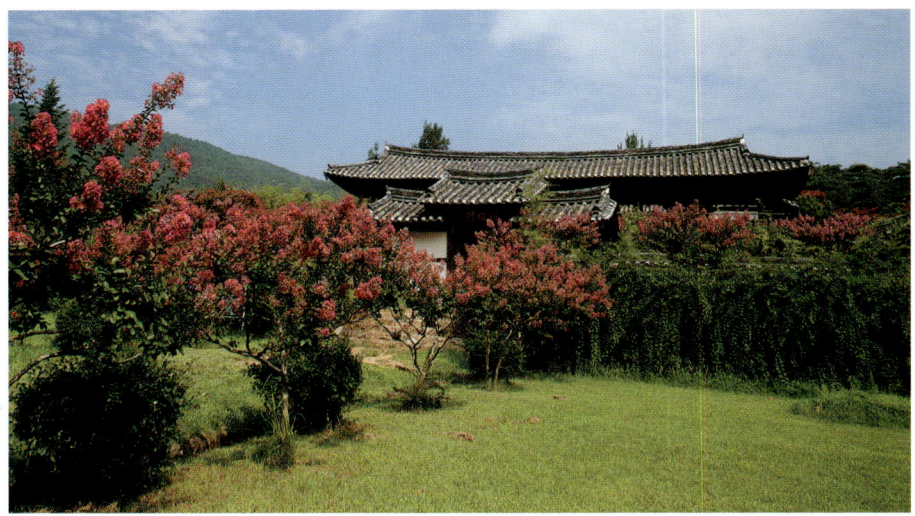

Achieving such harmony depends on correctly assessing the landscape so that buildings can be arranged in agreement with it. As far as its buildings are concerned, Byeongsan seowon is not very different from other private academies, as it consists of a shrine where memorial rites are performed, a lecture hall for academic study and training of the mind, dormitories, and other buildings. Although Byeongsan seowon is thus made up of buildings grounded in Neo-Confucian principles, these buildings also form an outstanding spatial arrangement that achieves unity with nature.

Upper story of Mandaeru, Byeongsan seowon

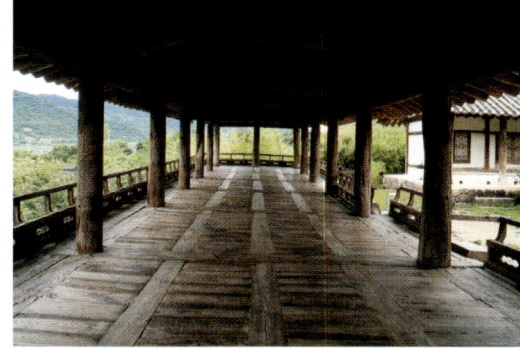

Lower story of Mandaeru, Byeongsan seowon

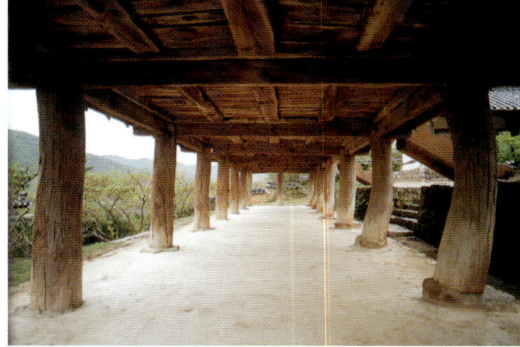

Passing through Bongnyemun, the main gate, you will see a pond to the left and on a higher

158 THE ARCHITECTURE OF KOREA'S PRIVATE ACADEMIES

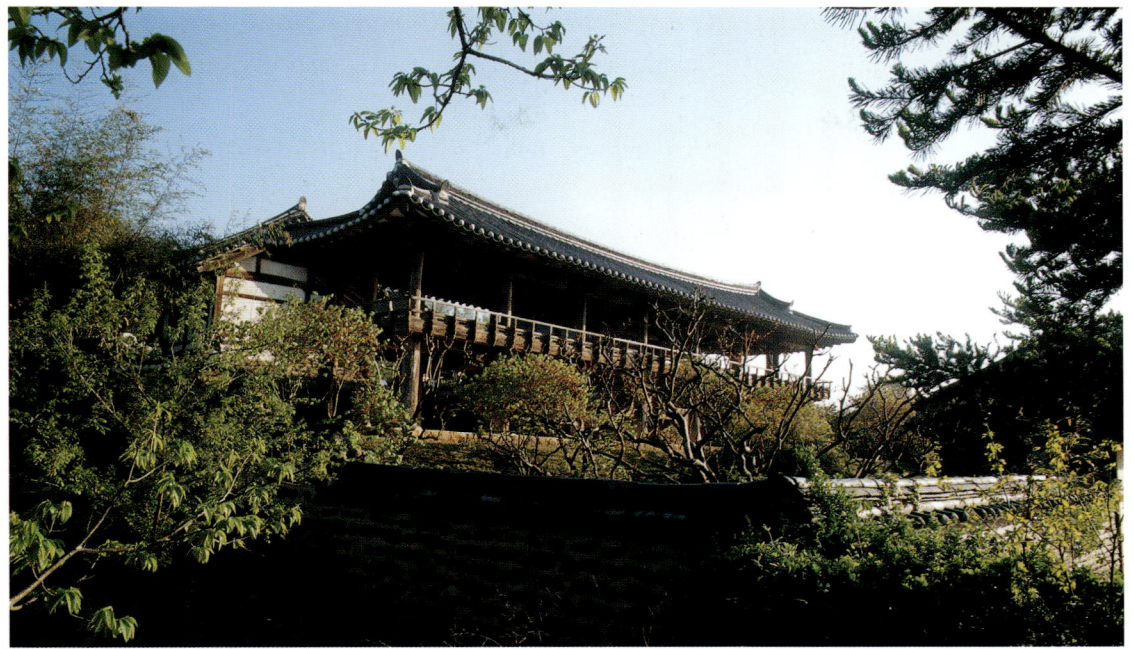

Mandaeru, Byeongsan seowon

level in front a two-story pavilion called Mandaeru, stretching out widely to one side at the end of a steep flight of stairs. Mandaeru is a seven-by-two-*kan* building topped by a hipped and gabled roof, its second-story loft supported by rows of twisted and bent wooden pillars, reflecting the natural shapes of the trees used to make them. Passing under this pavilion, you enter the academy via the forecourt of the lecture hall.

    In contrast to the ground floor which uses unworked pillars, the loft itself is constructed with straight, smoothed pillars, as if the building unites in these two different floors the Neo-Confucian view of nature and the rigid and puritanical tradition of Korean Confucianism. Standing in this upper floor, it is possible to take in at a glance the unfolding scenery of Mt. Byeongsan and the Nakdonggang river on one side, and the whole of the academy complex on the other. The name Mandaeru was inspired by the Tang poet Du Fu's poem "The White Emperor's Tower" (*Baidi chenglou*), which contains the passage "The emerald-green screen should be faced late in the day" (*chwibyeong i man-*

Examples of *seowon* architecture 159

dae); here the "emerald-green screen" can be identified with Byeongsan, and the phrase "facing late" (*mandae*) was thus adopted for the pavilion.

In the courtyard you reach after passing underneath Mandaeru, to the right and left you will see the eastern and western dormitory, respectively, and the Ipgyodang lecture hall in front. The lecture hall measures five by two *kan* and has a hipped and gabled roof. The three *kan* at the center of the building form the main wood-floored hall, with a one-

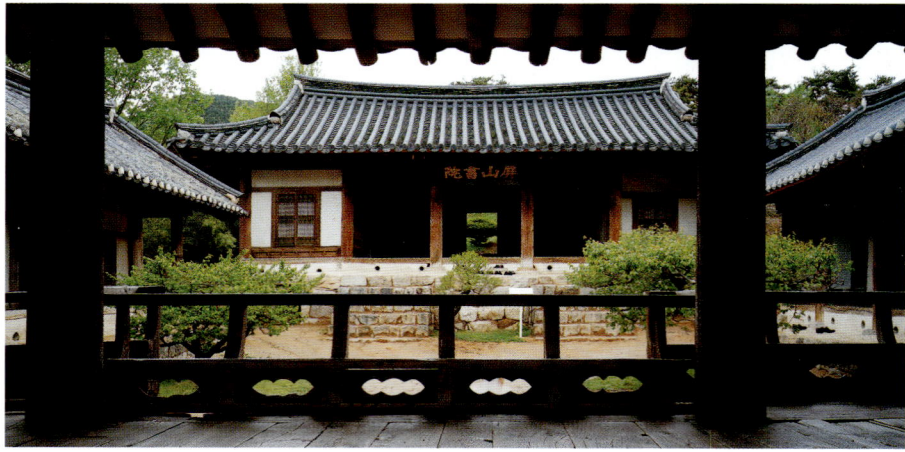

Ipgyodang, Byeongsan seowon's lecture hall, seen from Mandaeru

kan ondol room on each side. The eastern *ondol* room was the president's residence, from which every part of the academy can be seen. The western *ondol* room was used by the resident Confucian scholars.

Sitting inside the main floored hall and looking outside towards the Mandaeru pavilion, the academy's scenery appears in a whole new light. Between the pillars of the second-story loft, the river, the mountain opposite and the sky turn into a folding screen with seven scenes as if they are part of a painting. This creates a dramatic spatial effect in which it is not clear whether you are inside or outside, conveying a feeling of being immersed in nature. To the left and right of the yard in front of the lecture hall were the eastern and western dormitories, where students slept and studied.

Turning around the eastern side of the lecture hall, a staircase appears, leading to the shrine on top of a hill planted with beautiful

View of Mandaeru and the surrounding landscape from Ipgyodang

crape myrtle trees. Within the Jondeoksa shrine Yu Seong-nyong is enshrined in the middle of the northern wall, and Yu Jin (1582-1635) is enshrined additionally on the eastern wall. Like the lecture hall, the shrine faces Mt. Byeongsan, but rather than being directed towards its peak, these buildings face a place where the ridge splits in seven parts. This kind of arrangement, in which buildings and nature become one, is typical of Korean architecture.

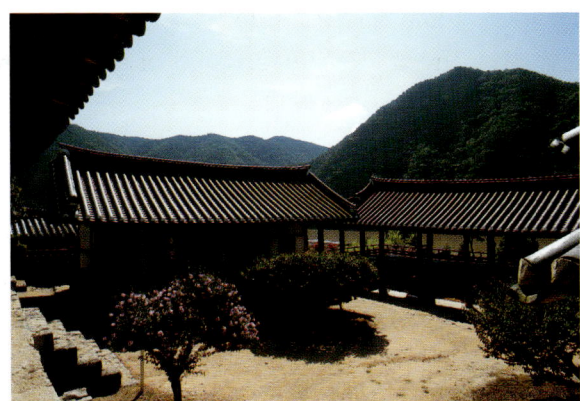

Study compound, Byeongsan seowon

Examples of *seowon* architecture 161

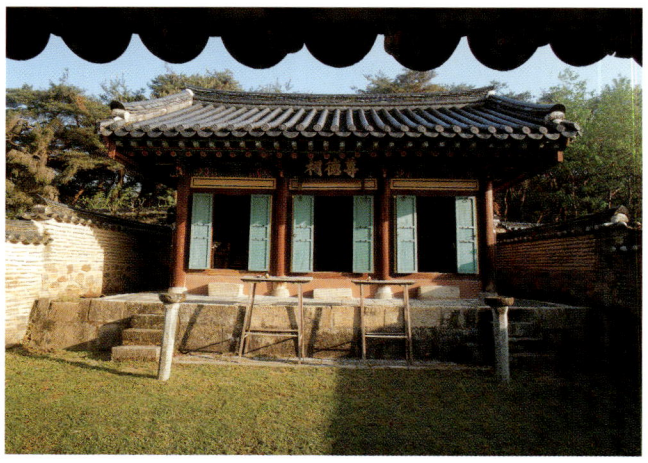

Jondeoksa, the shrine of Byeongsan seowon

Memorial rites at Byeongsan seowon

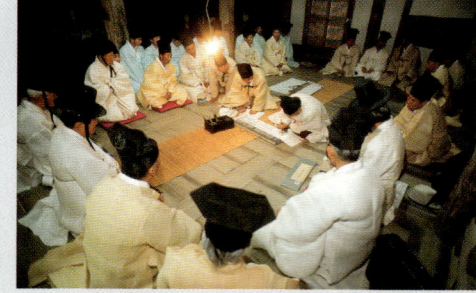
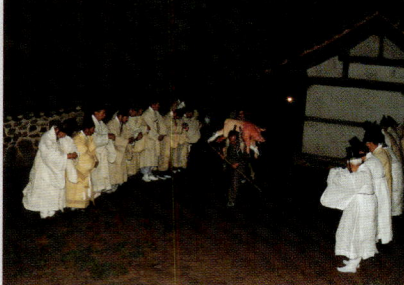
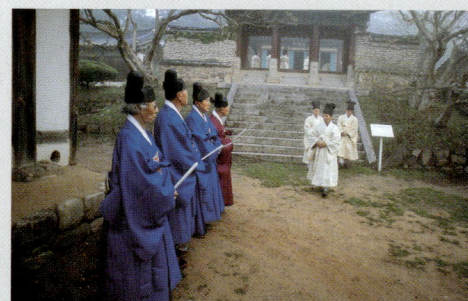
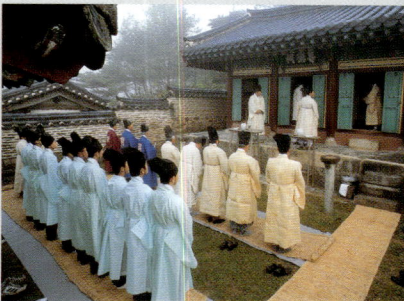
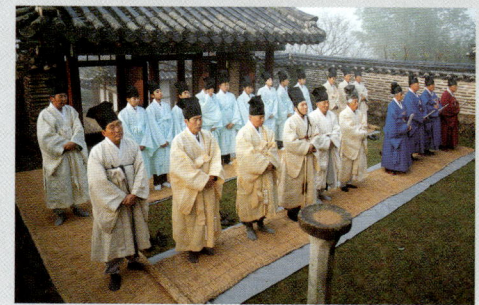
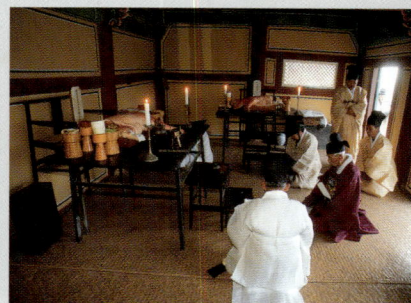

❶ ❷
❸ ❹
❺ ❻

❶ Memorial offerings to Yu Seong-nyong's spirit take place in the spring and autumn. Three days before the event the participating Confucian scholars come to the academy. They gather in the main wood-floored hall of Ipgyodang, the lecture hall, to decide on the main officiant, the eulogy, and the master of ceremonies.

❷ The pig to be used in the sacrifice must be approved at a ceremony held in the morning before the ritual.

❸❹❺❻ The ritual takes place around two o'clock in the morning and lasts for about an hour.

162 THE ARCHITECTURE OF KOREA'S PRIVATE ACADEMIES

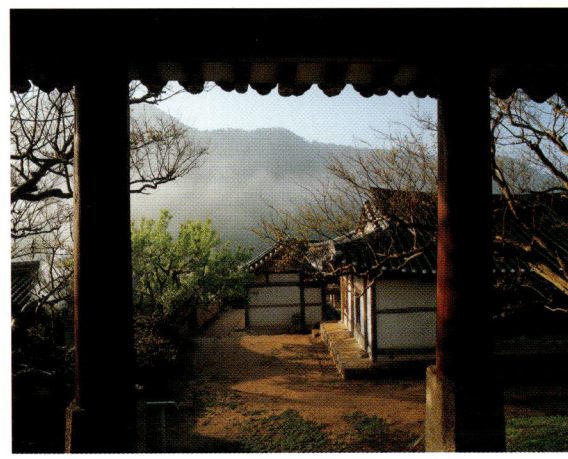

View from the spirit gate towards the front

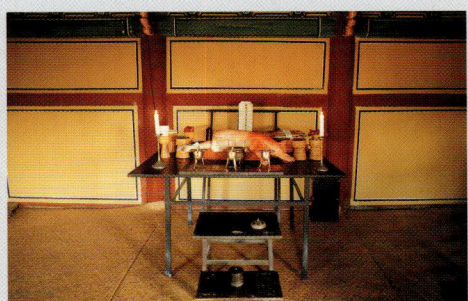

❼ Sacrificial foods offered to the spirit tablet of Yu Seong-nyong.

❽❾ After the ritual is finished, the main officiant burns and then buries the eulogy.

❿ When the ritual offering is over, all the participants take part in the *eumbongnye*, in which they partake of the sacrificial food and drink.

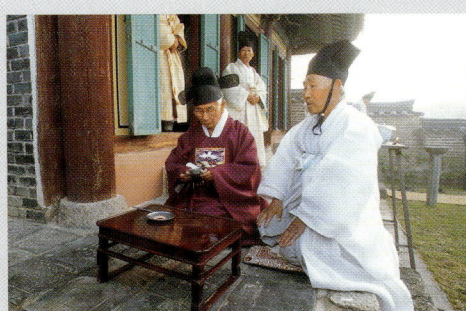
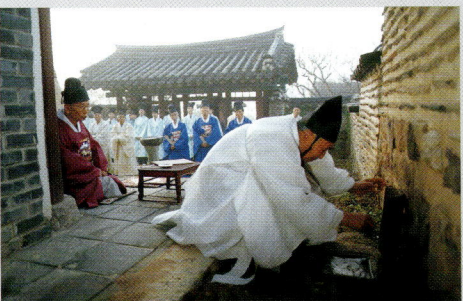
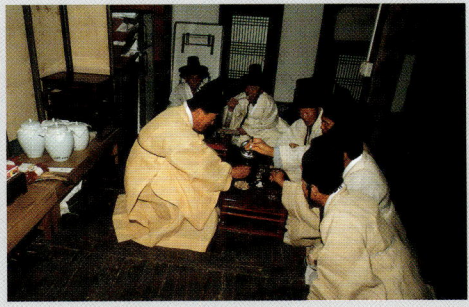

Examples of *seowon* architecture 163

5. Hallmarks of *seowon* architecture

Unlike county schools, the official educational institutions of the Joseon dynasty, private academies were established far away from cities and villages in quiet and beautiful places. Amidst the hustle and bustle of town life, the county schools offered a less-than-ideal environment for study. The literati of the Joseon period established private academies in the midst of nature, close to valleys with flowing brooks and mountains with beautiful scenery, to immerse themselves in study and nurture their students. Thus the pavilion, the most suitable type of building for bringing people into close proximity with nature, was reclaimed by private academies and used for ardent debates, poetry meetings, and engaging with nature. These pavilions were usually placed close to the entrance of academies.

Also, because academies were places where students lived and studied together, dormitories to house the students were built around an artificial court, and although they appear closed because they turn their backs on the surrounding environment, from this inner court the space is arranged in such a way that the eye is always drawn towards the outside. By being completely immersed in nature and at the same time separated from it, an abstract space was created geared exclusively towards study and self-cultivation. However, through the arrangement of buildings and the management of space, it is always possible to see the "front mountain" when seated in the lecture hall, the center of the academy or the pavilion, a factor which contributed to the further cultivation of the students' minds and aspirations. The spirit of the earth thus helped to produce people of outstanding ability. This philosophy is enunciated in Yi Jung-hwan's (1690-1756) *Primer for Choosing Settlements* (*Taengniji*): "If there are no mountains and streams, emotions cannot be good and people will be coarse. If mountains and rivers are engaged from afar, people will harbor ambition, but if they are engaged closely people's minds will be pure and their spirits joyful."

The shrine, located behind the lecture hall, was encircled by its own wall, and access was regulated by the spirit gate, also known as the *naesammun*, because the shrine was the most solemn part of the academy. In the backyard between the lecture hall and the shrine a stone-reinforced wall or flower terraces were usually constructed, and a few trees or shrubs planted so that the changing of the seasons could be witnessed; in front of the lecture hall a lotus pond was sometimes dug, its flowers and water providing the resident scholars with a chance to appreciate nature and explore the changes of the universe. Moreover, not only the buildings, but also the surrounding trees, rocks, water and mountains were given names that reflected Neo-Confucian thinking, enhancing their existential quality and allowing the students to interact with nature in a varied way and experience its influence.

Seowon architecture was thus arranged in a stern and orderly way in accordance with Neo-Confucian teachings, and the appearance of the buildings themselves, modest and simple rather than adorned and majestic, was a condensation and sublimation of the Neo-Confucian worldview in architecture. Although one would expect that those who managed the academies, the *sarim*, through their elite status would muster material and labor so as to construct the finest buildings, in fact the scale of the academies was not so big, and the buildings were plain and simple.

Unlike the religious architecture of Buddhist temples, which displays features of a decorative, popular style, the nature of *seowon* architecture is based on a sparse and abstract aesthetic. Also, the architecture of private academies is restricted by the rules and norms of a ritual system more than that of Buddhist temples. Thus the arrangement of the Confucian private academies is not as free as the layout of Buddhist temples: It is an arrangement which pursues changes within the boundaries of certain rules, thus achieving a more structured whole within a more confined space. In a nutshell, *seowon* architecture is a material manifestation of the Neo-Confucian value system, worldview and view of nature.

In *seowon* architecture, the modest and refined architectural forms and the regulated order, as well as the spatial management and building arrangement, all reflect conscious efforts to integrate nature and man-made construction; this is a clear manifestation of Confucian ideals. These ideals underlie the virtues of modesty and clarity pursued by the literati, who sought to put Confucian ritual elements into practice.

In its organization of space, layout and location, the architecture of private academies thus betrays some common characteristics. Summarizing, we can say that the private academies were located in beautiful places far away from the city to avoid worldly interference, that their arrangement of buildings and the ensuing spatial organization contains a hierarchical system, and that this hierarchy is reinforced by multiplying external spaces demarcated by buildings and walls. As a result, the academies employ an arrangement that achieves harmony with nature, and while expressing clearly the mutual relations between buildings they also produce various spatial forms. Although the buildings are basically arranged symmetrically, it is not a geometric symmetry, but an arrangement that is principally artificial yet completely conversant with naturalness. Thus the study compound is a lively and dynamic space, the shrine compound is a solemn and quiet space, and through the *seowon* complex as a whole a spatial system is achieved in which forceful tension and relaxation alternate.

These defining characteristics of the Korean *seowon* are closely tied to the Neo-Confucian worldview of the literati who were behind them. The location of academies in or near beautiful landscapes is related to the ideology of "Unity of Heaven and Man," and the consolidation of the centrality, hierarchy and compartmentalization in their spatial arrangement, together with the differentiation between principal and subordinate, reflects an unseen, logical realization and development of Neo-Confucian ideology through architecture. Constructed on the basis of this Neo-Confucian worldview, the architecture of private academies is endowed with its own system of order and meaning.

Map of *seowon* sites

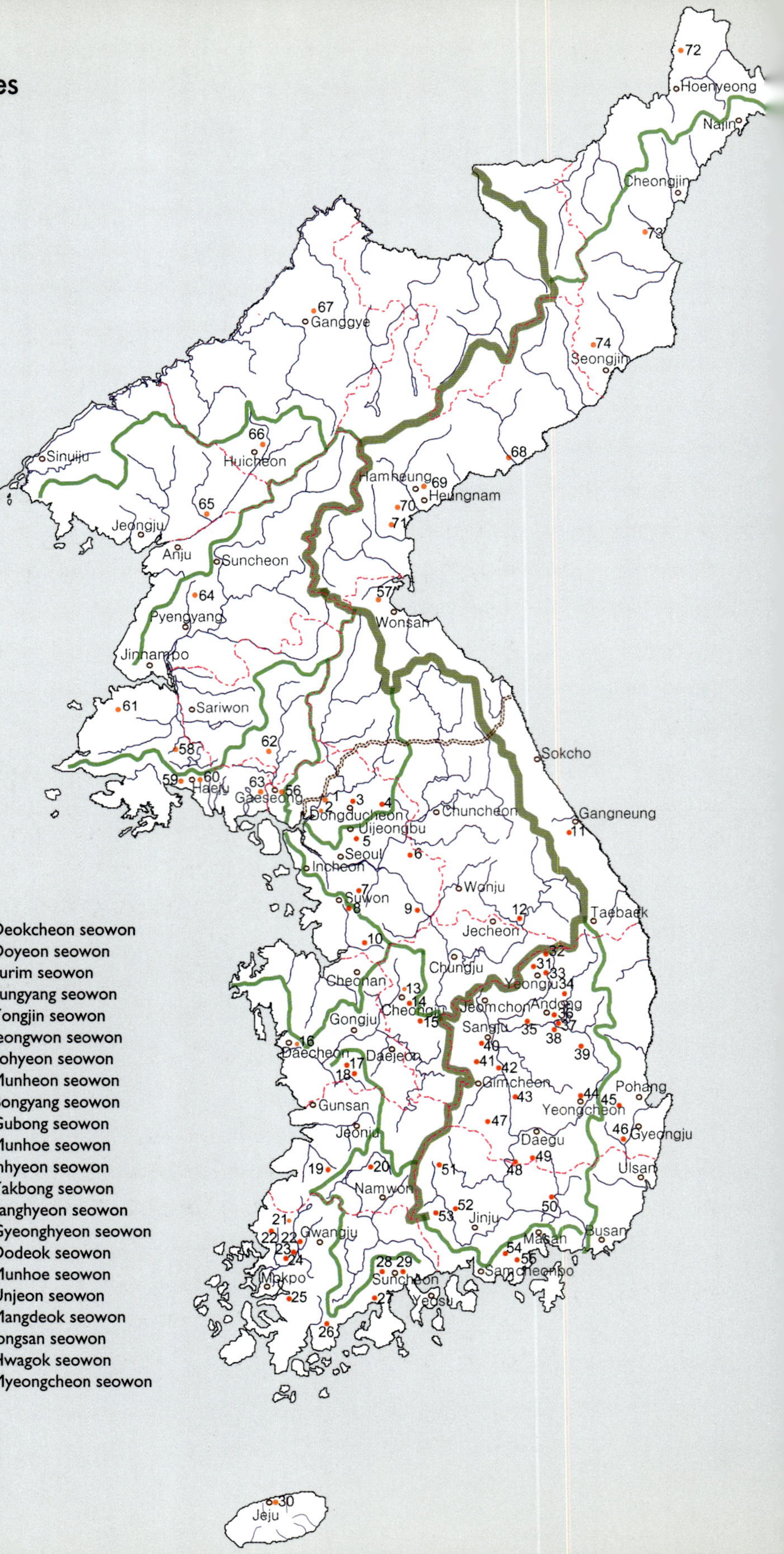

01 Pasan seowon
02 Jaun seowon
03 Yongyeon seowon
04 Hwasan seowon
05 Nogang seowon
06 Ungye seowon
07 Chungnyeol seowon
08 Simgok seowon
09 Ganghansa
10 Deokbong seowon
11 Obong seowon
12 Changjeol seowon
13 Sinhang seowon
14 Hwayang seowon
15 Sanghyeon seowon
16 Hwaam seowon
17 Nogang seowon
18 Donam seowon
19 Museong seowon
20 Sinan seowon
21 Piram seowon
22 Naesan seowon
23 Gyeonghyeon seowon
24 Micheon seowon
25 Jukjeong seowon
26 Yoengok seowon
27 Jaedong seowon
28 Okcheon seowon
29 Okgye seowon
30 Gyulrim seowon
31 Sosu seowon
32 Samgye seowon
33 Isan seowon
34 Dosan seowon
35 Byeongsan seowon
36 Imcheon seowon
37 Yeokdong seowon
38 Hogye seowon
39 Mukgye seowon
40 Heungam seowon
41 Okdong seowon
42 Geumo seowon
43 Dongrak seowon
44 Imgo seowon
45 Oksan seowon
46 Seoak seowon
47 Hoeyeon seowon
48 Dodong seowon
49 Jagye seowon
50 Yerim seowon
51 Namgye seowon
52 Docheon seowon
53 Deokcheon seowon
54 Doyeon seowon
55 Surim seowon
56 Sungyang seowon
57 Yongjin seowon
58 Jeongwon seowon
59 Sohyeon seowon
60 Munheon seowon
61 Bongyang seowon
62 Gubong seowon
63 Munhoe seowon
64 Inhyeon seowon
65 Yakbong seowon
66 Sanghyeon seowon
67 Gyeonghyeon seowon
68 Dodeok seowon
69 Munhoe seowon
70 Unjeon seowon
71 Mangdeok seowon
72 Jongsan seowon
73 Hwagok seowon
74 Myeongcheon seowon

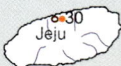

References

Primary sources

Dongguk wonurok (Record of Korean academies and shrines)
Seowon deungnok (Records on the *seowon*)
Yeoreup wonu sajeok (Materials on academies and shrines of all the towns)
Jeongo daebang (Almanac of important events from history)
Jodurok (Records of sacrificial halls)
Hakkyo go, Jeungbo munheon bigo ("On schools," Enlarged and annotated collection of documents)
Joseon wangjo sillok (Annals of the Joseon dynasty)

Articles

Choe Wan-gi. "Joseonjo seowon seongnip ui jemunje" (Unresolved problems regarding the founding of *seowon* in the Joseon dynasty). Guksa pyeonchan wiwonhoe ed., *Hanguk saron* 8 (1981): 1-24.

Guksa pyeonchan wiwonhoe ed. "Joseon jeongi seowon gwa hyangyak" (*Seowon* in the early Joseon period and the community compact). *Hanguk saron* 8 (1981): 25-57.

Jeong Man-jo. "17-18 segi ui seowon – sau e daehan siron" (On the *seowon* and shrines in 17th and 18th-century Korea). Guksa pyeonchan wiwonhoe ed., *Hanguk saron* 2 (1975): 212-280.

Jeong Man-jo. "Joseon seowon ui seongnip gwajeong" (The founding process of *seowon* in the Joseon period). Guksa pyeonchan wiwonhoe ed., *Hanguk saron* 8 (1981): 25-57.

Lee Sang-hae. "Toegye ui seowon geonchukgwan mit Dosan seowon geonchuk e banyeong doen joyeong sasang" (Toegye's views on the construction of *seowon* and the construction philosophy reflected in Dosan seowon). In *Dosan seowon*. Hangilsa, 2001, pp. 293-321.

Seong Dae-gyeong. "Daewongun ui seowon hwecheol" (The destruction of *seowon* by the Daewongun). In *Cheon Gwang-u seonsaeng hwallyeok ginyeom Hanguk sahak nonchong*, 1985, pp. 745-770.

Yi Hae-jun. "Joseon hugi munjung seowon yeongu" (A study on the lineage *seowon* in the late Joseon period). Ph.D. dissertation, Kookmin University, 1993.

Yi Seong-mu. "Joseon ui Seonggyungwan gwa seowon" (The National Confucian Academy and *seowon* in the Joseon period). *Hanguksa simin gangjwa* 18 (1996): 45-71.

Yi Su-hwan. "Seowon geollip hwaldong" (The founding of *seowon*). In Guksa pyeonchan wiwonhoe ed., *Hanguksa* 28 (1996): 278-306.

Yi Tae-jin. "Sarim gwa seowon" (The s*arim* and *seowon*). Guksa pyeonchan wiwonhoe ed., *Hanguksa* 12 (1984): 115-163.

Yi U-seong. "Yi Toegye wa seowon changseol undong" (Toegye and the *seowon*-founding movement). In *Hanguk ui yeoksasang*, Changjak gwa pipyeongsa, 1982, pp. 282-285.

Books in Korean Language

Andong Univ. Andong munhwa yeonguso. *Seowon, Hanguk sasang ui sumgyeol eul chajaseo* (*Seowon*: In search of the life force of Korean thought). Yemun seowon, 2000.

Choe Wan-gi. *Hanguk ui seowon* (Korea's *seowon*). Daewonsa, 1991.

Gyeonggi Univ. Soseong Haksul Yeonguwon. *Hanguk ui seowon gwa hangmaek yeongu* (Korean *seowon* in relation to their academic lineages). Gukhak jaryowon, 2002.

Hanguk hyangtosa yeongu jeonguk hyeobuihoe, ed. *Hwecheol seowon josa bogo* (Survey report on destroyed *seowon*). 1993.

Jeong Man-jo. *Joseon sidae seowon yeongu* (Studies on the *seowon* of the Joseon period). Jimmundang, 1997.

Jeong Sun-mok. *Hanguk seowon gyoyuk jedosa yeongu* (Studies on the history of the educational system of Korea's *seowon*). Yeongnam daehakkyo chulpanbu, 1979.

Ji Du-hwan. *Joseon jeongi uirye yeongu* (Studies on the rituals of the early Joseon period). Seoul daehakkyo chulpanbu, 1994.

Kim Bong-nyeol. *Seowon geonchuk* (The architecture of *seowon*). Daewonsa, 1998.

Kim Byeong-gu. *Hoeheon An Hyang seonsaeng ui saengae wa sajeok* (The life and achievements of An Hyang). Sinji seowon, 1996 (1993).

Kim Eun-jung. *Hanguk ui seowon geonchuk* (The architecture of Korea's *seowon*). Munudang, 1994.

Kim Ji-min. *Hanguk ui yugyo geonchuk* (Confucian architecture of Korea). Bareon, 1996.

Lee Sang-hae. *Seowon*. Yeorhwadang, 1998.

Min Byeong-ha. *Hanguk jungse gyoyuk jedosa yeongu* (Studies in the history of the education system in medieval Korea). Seonggyungwan daehakkyo chulpanbu, 1992.

Mokpo Univ. Museum. *Jeonnam ui seowon - sau I, II* (*Seowon* and shrines of Jeollanam-do province I, II). 1988, 1989.

Yi Chun-hui. *Joseonjo ui gyoyuk mungo e gwanhan yeongu* (Studies on the educational archives of the Joseon dynasty). Gyeongin munhwasa, 1984.

Yi Su-hwan. *Joseon hugi seowon yeongu* (Studies on the *seowon* of the late Joseon period). Iljogak, 2001.

Yi Tae-jin. *Joseon yugyo sahoesa ron* (On the history of Confucianism and society in the Joseon period). Jisik saneopsa, 1989.

Yu Hong-yeol. *Joseon sahoe sasangsa rongo* (Studies in the history of Joseon society and ideology). Iljogak, 1980.

Books in Chinese

Deng Hongbo. *Zhongguo shuyuanshi (History of Chinese Private academies)*, Shanghai, China: Dongfang chuban zhongxin, 2004.

Yang Shenchu, *Zhongguo shuyuan wenhua yujianzhu (Private academy culture and buildings of China)*. Wuhan, China: Hubei jiaoyu chubanshe, 2002.

Yang Shenchu, Cai Daoxin, Cai Ling. *Shuyuanjianzhu (Private academy architecture)*, Beijing, China: Zhongguo jianzhu gongye chubanshe, 2001.

Zhu Hanmin, Deng Hongbo, Chen He. *Zhongguo shuyuan (Chinese Private academies)*. Shanghai, China: Shanghai Educational Publishing House, 2002.

Books in Western Languages

De Bary, Wm. Theodore and JaHyun Kim Haboush eds. *The Rise of Neo-Confucianism in Korea*. New York: Columbia University Press, 1985.

Palmer, Spencer J. *Confucian Rituals in Korea*. Berkeley: Asian Humanities Press, Seoul: Po Chin Chai Ltd., 1992 (1984).

Smith, Jr. Warren W. *16th Century Seowon: The Rise of Private Neo-Confucian Education in Korea*. Suwon, Korea: Sosung Institute of Advanced Studies, Kyonggi University, 2003.

Glossary
용어 설명

aheongwan / 아헌관 / 亞獻官 / second wine officiant   22

Ailian shuo / 아이리앤슈어 (애련설) / 愛蓮說 / On Loving Lotuses   93

ak / 악 / 樂 / music   89

amyeon jasu / 암연자수 / 闇然自修 / "cultivate oneself in tranquility"   93

ansan / 안산 / 案山 / front mountain (geomantic term)   28

bangmun yangnye / 박문약례 / 博文約禮 / "broaden your learning, hold on to ritual"   93

beopdang / 법당 / 法堂 / Dharma hall, main hall of Buddhist temple   77

bo / 보 / 簠 / brass container for rice and millet   82

bongnye / 복례 / 復禮 / "restoring rituals"   95

bunhyang / 분향 / 焚香 / offering of incense   19

buyusa / 부유사 / 副有司 / vice-administrator   25

Byeogong / 벽옹 / 辟雍 / Ceremonial Hall, built outside the capital seat as an expression of the ruler's civilizing power   65

byeolseo / 별서 / 別墅 / cottage in rural area   54, 59, 60, 61, 62

byeon / 변 / 籩 / implements made of bamboo for serving dry offerings such as fruits and dried foods   83

chanja / 찬자 / 贊者 / hymnodist   19

Chengzi jiaxun / 청즈 쟈순 (정자가훈) / 程子家訓 / *Family Instructions of Master Cheng*   91

cheolli / 천리 / 天理 / principle of Heaven   52, 53

cheondo / 천도 / 天道 / Way of Heaven   52

cheonin gameung seol / 천인감응설 / 天人感應說 / theory of the mutual correspondence and affection between Heaven and Man   50

cheonin habil / 천인합일 / 天人合一 / unity of Heaven and Man   31, 49

cheonin hapdeok / 천인합덕 / 天人合德 / Heaven and Man unite in virtue   52

cheonin sanggwan seol / 천인상관설 / 天人相關說 / theory of the interconnectedness of Heaven and Man   50

cheonseok gohwang / 천석고황 / 泉石膏肓 / "a heart for sources and stones"   59

choheongwan / 초헌관 / 初獻官 / first wine officiant   22

choya usaeng / 초야우생 / 草野愚生 / "a foolish student in the wilderness"   59 chuk / 축 / 祝 / eulogy 19

chukgwan / 축관 / 祝官 / eulogist 19

chuksi / 축시 / 丑時 / hour of the ox 21

Chunchu / 춘추 / 春秋 / *Spring and Autumn Annals* 24

chung / 충 / 充 / adequate 20, 85

Daehak / 대학 / 大學 / *Great Learning* 24

dancheong / 단청 / 丹靑 / lit. "red and blue", decorative painting style 132, 134

danggan jiju / 당간지주 / 幢竿支柱 / stone flagpole props 99

darak / 다락 / loft, attic 74

deok / 덕 / 德 / pure virtue 52, 90

do / 도 / 道 / way 89, 135

dohak / 도학 / 道學 / learning of the Way 7, 13

dohak jeongchi / 도학 정치 / 道學 政治 / moral government 13

dol / 돌 / 腯 / lit. "fat", adequate for sacrifice 20, 85

dongbang ohyeon / 동방오현 / 東方五賢 / five sages of Joseon 14

Dongguk wonurok / 동국원우록 / 東國院宇錄 / *Record of Korean Academies and Shrines* 169

dongjae / 동재 / 東齋 / eastern dormitory 67, 68, 74, 77

dongmu / 동무 / 東廡 / eastern chamber or detached wing where the spirit tablets of Chinese and Korean Confucian sages were formerly placed 67

Dosan jabyeong / 도산잡영 / 陶山雜詠 / *Hymns to Dosan, Miscellaneous Poems on Dosan* 33, 112

Dosan sibi gok / 도산십이곡 / 陶山十二曲 / *Twelve Songs of Dosan* 32, 58

dotong / 도통 / 道通 / transmission of the Way through student-teacher lineages 65

doyusa / 도유사 / 都有司 / general administrator 25

du / 두 / 豆 / wooden implements for serving moist or liquid offerings such as meat and broth 83

eumbongnye / 음복례 / 飮福禮 / partaking of the sacrificial food and drink 21, 163

gangdang / 강당 / 講堂 / lecture hall 41, 74, 77

gangjang / 강장 / 講長 / head instructor 25

gasa / 가사 / 歌詞 / linked verse, a traditional form of Korean poetry in the vernacular   32

geogyeong gungni / 거경궁리 / 居敬窮理 / residing in reverence to attain the utmost principle   60, 91

geoin / 거인 / 居仁 / residing in benevolence   93

geoui / 거의 / 居義 / residing in righteousness   93

geumdang / 금당 / 金堂 / golden hall; originally the main building in Buddhist temples   77

geun / 근 / 斤 / traditional unit of weight, about 1.3 lbs.   22

gi / 기 / 氣 / material force; in Neo-Confucian philosophy, the energy, manifested either as positive (Yang) or negative (Eum/Yin), that gives shape to things   11

gojiksa / 고직사 / 庫直舍 / stewards' house, custodians' house   84, 99, 109, 118, 122, 130, 144, 150, 156

gongnon / 공론 / 公論 / official position   27

gue / 궤 / 簋 / brass container for putting in Chinese millet   82

gugok / 구곡 / 九曲 / lit. "Nine bends", a landscape feature inspired by Wuyishan in China   56, 58

gugok do / 구곡도 / 九曲圖 / paintings of the Nine bends   56, 57

guin / 구인 / 求仁 / "pursuing benevolence"   90

gwanbun / 관분 / 盥盆 / washbasin   86

gwansewi / 관세위 / 盥洗位 / stand to wash one's hands before a ritual   86, 130, 144

gwon / 권 / 卷 / the smallest bound unit of a book, and hence a traditional subdivision of a book   23

gyeol / 결 / 結 / traditional unit of area, which varied according to the agricultural yield of the land (one *gyeol* = approx. 1 ha.)   26

gyeong / 경 / 敬 / reverence   91, 103, 104

gyeongmul chiji / 격물치지 / 格物致知 / "investigation of things to establish knowledge"   53, 60

gyeongui / 경의 / 敬義 / reverence and righteousness   92

gyeongui haerip / 경의해립 / 敬義偕立 / "approach everyone and everything with reverence and righteousness"   92

gyesaengbi / 계생비 / 繫牲碑 / stele to which sacrificial animals are tied   86, 150

| Gyogu / 교구 / 郊丘 / suburban altar to Heaven and Earth | 65 |

hakgu / 학구 / 學求 / "pursuit of scholarship" 92

hamaseok / 하마석 / 下馬石 / dismounting stone 72, 73, 130, 144, 150

hangnyeong / 학령 / 學令 / official educational instruction 23

heongwan / 헌관 / 獻官 / main officiant 19

hogo mini guji / 호고민이구지 / 好古敏以求之 / in pursuing benevolence you should be agile 93

holgi / 홀기 / 笏記 / ceremonial tablet 19

hongsalmun / 홍살문 / red-arrow gate; symbolic gate, consisting of two poles and a crossbar comprising two horizontal bars supporting a row of vertical red arrows 71, 72, 73, 130, 144, 146, 150, 152

hongeui / 홍의 / 弘毅 / "broaden your mind and be resolute" 93

hungupa / 훈구파 / 勳舊派 / faction of the meritorious and conservative 10

hunjang / 훈장 / 訓長 / head tutor 25

hwagyeon / 확연 / 廓然 / "vast and just" 94, 152

hwanju / 환주 / 喚主 / "calling forth the root that can be the master of one's mind" 94

Hwayang mukpae / 화양묵패 / 華陽墨牌 / Hwayang ink plaques, distributed to forcibly raise money for Hwayang seowon 45

hyanggyo / 향교 / 鄕校 / county school, a traditional school belonging to the local Confucian shrine 8

hyangni / 향리 / 鄕吏 / local village clerks during the Goryeo dynasty 12

hyangsa / 향사 / 享祀 / sacrificial food offering during ancestor ritual 19

hyangyak / 향약 / 鄕約 / community compact 27, 75

i / 이 / 理 / principle; in Neo-Confucian philosophy, the noumen of things 11

igi / 이기 / 理氣 / principle-material force 52

ilsin / 일신 / 日新 / "renew every day" 92

in / 인 / 仁 / benevolence 90

indo / 인도 / 人道 / Way of Man 52

iu boin / 이우보인 / 以友輔仁 / "achieving benevolence with friends" 92

jadeuk gyoyuk / 자득교육 / 自得教育 / "learning through one's own efforts" 23

jaejang / 재장 / 齋長 / dormitory inspector 25
jaesa / 재사 / 齋舍 / dormitory 41, 77
jagi naejaehwa / 자기내재화 / 自己內在化 / internalization [of the Way of Heaven] in oneself 53
jak / 작 / 爵 / brass goblet 83
jangpangak / 장판각 / 藏板閣 / storehouse for printing blocks (woodblocks used for printing) 78, 109, 118, 130, 136, 144, 146, 150, 156
jangseogak / 장서각 / 藏書閣 / library 71, 79, 99, 107, 150
jangui / 장의 / 掌議 / chief council 25
jegigo / 제기고 / 祭器庫 / storage for ritual vessels 85, 109, 119, 120
jeong / 정 / 丁 / fourth of the ten Heavenly Stems in the East Asian traditional system of dating, thus a *jeong* day is either the fourth, fourteenth, or twenty-fourth; days were counted according to the sixty-day cycle of Heavenly Stems and Earthly Branches 19
jeongja / 정자 / 亭子 / pavilion 54
jeongnyodae / 정료대 / 庭燎臺 / alternative name for stone lantern (*seokdeung*) 87, 109, 122, 156
Jeongo daebang / 전고대방 / 典故大方 / *Almanac of Important Events from History* 169
jeongsa / 정사 / 精舍 / cloister 54, 57, 62
jeonsacheong / 전사청 / 典祀廳 / building for preparing offerings 77, 79, 84, 85, 99, 107, 119, 122, 130, 132, 136, 144, 150, 156
Jeungbo munheon bigo / 증보문헌비고 / 增補文獻備考 / *Enlarged and Annotated Collection of Documents* 169
jibeui isaeng / 집의이생 / 集義以生 / "gathering righteousness to live" 91
jigil / 직일 / 直日 / steward for the day 25
jigwol / 직월 / 直月 / steward for the month 25
jikbang / 직방 / 直方 / make your inner mind honest and your outward actions straight 92
jinsa / 진사 / 進士 / literary licentiate who had passed the sogwa or "lower course" government service examination of literature 24
jipchanja / 집찬자 / 執饌者 / attendant for the ritual 19
jipgang / 집강 / 執綱 / drill master 25
Jiphyeonjeon / 집현전 / 集賢殿 / Hall of Worthies 11

jipsa / 집사 / 執事 / ceremonial attendant 19
jirak / 지락 / 至樂 / "studying harder brings joy" 92
Jodurok / 조두록 / 俎豆錄 / *Records of Sacrificial Halls* 169
jongheongwan / 종헌관 / 終獻官 / third wine officiant 22
Jongmyo / 종묘 / 宗廟 / Royal Ancestral Shrine 11, 65
Joseon wangjo sillok / 조선왕조실록 / 朝鮮王朝實錄 / *Annals of the
    Joseon Dynasty* 169
Jukgyeji / 죽계지 / 竹溪誌 / *The Records of Jukgye Stream* 101
jungjeong / 중정 / 中正 / "exactly right" 90, 119
Jungyong / 중용 / 中庸 / The *Doctrine of the Mean* 24, 90
kan / 칸 (간) / 間 / bays, the rectangular space delineated by four
    columns, a traditional unit for measuring the size of
    houses 62, 63, 69, 73, 76, 78, 80, 81, 82, 105, 106,
    110, 112, 113, 117, 118, 120, 125, 133, 134, 146, 147,
    148, 159, 160
Maengja / 맹자 / 孟子 / *The Works of Mencius* 24
mangnyewi / 망례위 / 望瘞位 / place to bury the eulogy after a sacrifice 86,
    87, 142, 150
mangnyowi / 망료위 / 望燎位 / place to burn the eulogy after a sacrifice
    87
maru / 마루 / wooden floor, or a room which has a wooden floor 62
mongi yangjeong / 몽이양정 / 蒙以養正 / "to foster a work to make it
    correct" 92
Munmyo / 문묘 / 文廟 / Shrine for Confucius 14, 66, 101
myeong / 명 / 明 / brightness 90, 91
myeongdang / 명당 / 明堂 / bright hall 65
Myeongnyun-dang / 명륜당 / 明倫堂 / Hall of Bright Ethics; name of the
    lecture hall in the National Confucian Academy and
    other county schools 37, 67, 69, 77, 99, 104, 105
myeongseong / 명성 / 明誠 / "brightness and sincerity" 92, 133
naemun / 내문 / 內門 / inner gate, leading to the shrine 41, 80
naesammun / 내삼문 / 內三門 / inner triple gate, another name for the
    naemun 80, 109, 136, 139, 142, 144, 146, 147, 150,
    156, 165
nobi / 노비 / 奴婢 / a class of indentured people, similar to slaves in

			other societies	26, 36, 38, 148
Noneo	/ 논어	/ 論語 /	*Analects of Confucius*	24
Noron	/ 노론	/ 老論 /	Old Doctrine, name of one of the dominant factions of the seventeenth and eighteenth centuries	44, 45, 46
nu	/ 누	/ 樓 /	pavilion	74
nujeong	/ 누정	/ 樓亭 /	pavilion; building characterized by openness to nature, usually incorporating a loft which is open on all four sides	54
numaru	/ 누마루	/ 樓 마루 /	elevated veranda, open on four sides	63, 125
numun	/ 누문	/ 樓門 /	pavilion-gate	67, 74
oemun	/ 외문	/ 外門 /	outer gate; main gate and entrance to the private academy	41, 73
oesammun	/ 외삼문	/ 外三門 /	outer triple gate, another name for the main gate	73, 146
ohyeon	/ 오현	/ 五賢 /	the five sages of Joseon (Kim Goeng-pil, Jeong Yeo-chang, Jo Gwang-jo, Yi Eon-jeok, Yi Hwang)	14
okgyu	/ 옥규	/ 玉圭 /	jade mace	100
ondol	/ 온돌	/	hypocaust; system of underground heating, channeling hot air through a system of ducts under the floor	63, 76, 105, 106, 111, 113, 117, 118, 120, 125, 127, 133, 134, 147, 160
pungsu	/ 풍수	/ 風水 /	the art of choosing an auspicious site, geomancy, *fengshui* in Chinese	31, 66
pungwol mubyeon	/ 풍월무변	/ 風月無邊 /	"nature has no borders"	94
li	/ 리	/ 里 /	1 li is about 393 meters	33
saaek	/ 사액	/ 賜額 /	royal warrant, government approval by conferring an official name	36
saaek seowon	/ 사액서원	/ 賜額書院 /	chartered academy on which, together with a name plaque, the king bestowed books, land and *nobi*	36
sadaebu	/ 사대부	/ 士大夫 /	the ruling elites of Joseon who were obliged, in accordance with Confucian teaching, to perfect themselves morally first before ruling the people through moral persuasion	6, 7
sadang	/ 사당	/ 祠堂 /	shrine	18, 41, 80, 130, 136

| saekjang / 색장 / 色掌 / amanuensis | 25 |

saengdan / 생단 / 牲壇 / stone dais or altar for inspecting the sacrificial animal   85, 86, 99, 130, 136, 142

saengganpum / 생간품 / 牲看品 / ceremonial inspection and assessment of the sacrificial animal   85

saengwon / 생원 / 生員 / classics licentiate who had passed the *sogwa* or "lower-course" government service examination of classics   24

sahak / 사학 / 四學 / four schools in the capital   66

Sajikdan / 사직단 / 社稷壇 / Altar for the Earth and Grain Gods   65

sajungwan / 사준관 / 司罇官 / master of the jar   19

samasi / 사마시 / 司馬試 / examinations held at the Confucian academy   24

sammun / 삼문 / 三門 / triple gate   69

sarangchae / 사랑채 / men's quarters   84, 129

sarim / 사림 / 士林 / landed scholars; members of the local elite, usually landowners with small or medium-sized landholdings, steeped in Confucian morality and philosophy, usually without office   1, 2, 7, 9, 10, 11, 12, 13, 14, 15 ,25, 27, 31, 39, 40 42, 54, 67, 69, 129, 143, 165, 170

saron / 사론 / 士論 / factional positions   27

seodang / 서당 / 書堂 / private school   12

Seogyeong / 서경 / 書經 / The *Book of Documents (or The Book of History)*   24

seojae / 서재 / 西齋 / western dormitory   67, 68, 74, 77

seokdeung / 석등 / 石燈 / stone lantern   87, 136, 150

seokgasan / 석가산 / 石假山 / artificial mountain   129

seomu / 서무 /西廡 / western chamber or detached wing where the spirit tablets of Chinese and Korean Confucian sages were formerly placed   67

seong / 성 / 誠 / sincerity   90, 91

Seonggyungwan / 성균관 / 成均館 / National Confucian Academy   11, 66

seong jeuk i / 성즉리 / 性卽理 / "human nature is nothing but principle"; the orthodox Neo-Confucian view on human nature as an expression of the deeper truth underlying all beings   52

seong-myeong / 성명 / 性命 / nature-mandate   52

seonhyeon / 선현 / 先賢 / former sage, Confucian patron saint 8
seowon / 서원 / 書院 / private academy   1, 2, 3, 7, 9, 16, 24, 29, 36, 46, 47, 54, 68, 69, 70, 90, 134, 155, 165, 166
Seowon deungnok / 서원등록 / 書院謄錄 / *Records on the Seowon* 169
seowongi / 서원기 / 書院記 / private academy record; also *wongi* (院記) 39
Sigyeong / 시경 / 詩經 / *The Book of Odes* (or *The Book of Songs*) 24
sinju / 신주 / 神主 / spirit tablet 18
sinmun / 신문 / 神門 / spirit gate; another name for the *naemun*, the entrance gate to the shrine compound   41, 79, 99, 129
Sohak / 소학 / 小學 / *Elementary Learning* 24
ssijok burak / 씨족부락 / 氏族部落 / single-surname villages 27
sugi chiin / 수기지인 / 修己治人 / "cultivating the self and ruling others" 6
Taengniji / 택리지 / 擇里志 / *Primer for Choosing Settlements* 164
toetkan / 툇칸 / 退間 / outer bay, extra space with added columns, created outside a building 82
ui / 의 / 義 / righteousness 91
wigi ji hak / 위기지학 / 爲己之學 / "learning for oneself" 40
wijeong cheoksa ron / 위정척사론 / 衛政斥邪論 / defending orthodoxy and rejecting heterodoxy 46
wongi / 원기 / 院記 / private academy's record 77
wongyu / 원규 / 院規 / private academy rules 26
won-i / 원이 / 院貳 / vice-president 25
won-im / 원임 / 院任 / chancellor 25
wonjang / 원장 / 院長 / president 25
wonjung yurim / 원중유림 / 院中儒林 / resident scholars of private academy 25
Wuyi jiuqu / 무이구곡 / 武夷九曲 / The Nine Bends of Wuyishan, China (see *gugok*) 57
ye / 예 / 禮 / ritual; ritualized behavior, propriety 49, 65, 89
Yebu / 예부 / 禮部 / Board of Rites 65
yehak / 예학 / 禮學 / ritual studies 42
yeje / 예제 / 禮制 / ritual codes, ritual system 65, 148

yeje geonchuk	예제건축	禮制建築	ritual architecture	65
Yeokkyeong	역경	易經	The *Book of Changes*	89
Yeoreup wonu sajeok	열읍원우사적	列邑院宇事蹟	*Materials on Academies and Shrines of all the Towns*	169
yogeoseok	요거석	燎炬石	alternative name for stone lantern (*seokdeung*)	87
yuhoe	유회	儒會	meeting of all the private academy's Confucian scholars	25
yurim	유림	儒林	generic term for Confucian scholars	25
yusa	유사	有司	administrators	25
Zhongyong	(see *Jungyong*)			90

Index

English/한글/漢字

aeryeon / 애련 / 愛蓮		134
Aeryeonheon / 애련헌 / 愛蓮軒		92, 93, 134
Agye / 아계 / 鵝溪		127
aheongwan / 아헌관 / 亞獻官		22
Ailian shuo / 아이리앤슈어 (애련설) / 愛蓮說		93
ak / 악 / 樂		89
Amseoheon / 암서헌 / 巖棲軒		113, 115
Amseojae / 암서재 / 巖棲齋		63
Amsujae / 암수재 / 闇修齋		93, 122
amyeon jasu / 암연자수 / 闇然自修		93
An Bo / 안보 / 安輔		107
An Chuk / 안축 / 安軸		107
Andong / 안동 / 安東		29, 30, 35, 58, 115, 116, 119, 128, 154
Angang / 안강 / 安康		61
Angang-eup / 안강읍 / 安康邑		121
An Hyang / 안향 / 安珦		8, 29, 36, 66, 81 98, 100, 101, 102, 103, 107, 171
ansan / 안산 / 案山		28
An Sang / 안상 / 安瑺		40
Baegamsan / 백암산 / 白巖山		132
Baegokdong / 백옥동 / 白玉洞		88
Baegundong / 백운동 / 白雲洞		31, 32, 36, 38, 66, 68, 101, 104, 105,
Baegundong seowon / 백운동서원 / 白雲洞書院		8, 10, 14, 22, 31, 39, 41, 98, 101, 102, 110
Bagyakjae / 박약재 / 博約齋		93, 109, 117
Baidi chenglou / 바이디청로우 (백제성루) / 白帝城樓		159
Bailudong / 바이루동 (백록동) / 白鹿洞		23, 33, 57, 75, 76
Bailudong shuyuan / 바이루동슈유앤 (백록동서원) / 白鹿洞書院		103
bangmun yangnye / 박문약례 / 博文約禮		93
beopdang / 법당 / 法堂		77
Biseulsan / 비슬산 / 琵瑟山		135
bo / 보 / 簠		82
Boinjae / 보인재 / 輔仁齋		92, 130, 133, 134
Bongam seowon / 봉암서원 / 鳳巖書院		71, 75
bongnye / 복례 / 復禮		95
Bongnyemun / 복례문 / 復禮門		94, 157, 158
Borodong seowon / 보로동서원 / 甫老洞書院		135
Buncheon / 분천 / 汾川		115

bunhyang	분향	焚香	19
Buyongdae	부용대	芙蓉臺	155
buyusa	부유사	副有司	25
Byeogong	벽옹	辟雍	65
byeolsa	별사	別祠	81
byeolseo	별서	別墅	54, 59, 60, 61, 62
byeon	변	邊	83
Byeongsan	병산	屛山	35, 88, 95, 157, 159, 161
Byeongsan-ri	병산리	屛山里	154
Byeongsan seowon	병산서원	屛山書院	28, 35, 69, 73, 74, 75, 85, 88, 91, 94, 154, 155, 156, 157, 158, 159, 160, 161, 162
Changdeokgung palace	창덕궁	昌德宮	45
chanja	찬자	贊者	19
che	체	體	90
Cheinmun	체인문	體仁門	122, 127
Cheinmyo	체인묘	體仁廟	90, 122, 126, 127, 128
Cheng Hao	청하오 (정호)	程顥	49, 89
Cheng Yi	청이 (정이)	程頤	49, 52, 89, 94, 131, 152
Chengzi jiaxun	청즈 쟈순 (정자가훈)	程子家訓	91
Cheoljong	철종	哲宗	43, 44
cheolli	천리	天理	52, 53
cheondo	천도	天道	52
Cheongbungak	청분각	淸芬閣	122
Cheonggye sewon	청계서원	靑溪書院	24
Cheongjeoldang	청절당	淸節堂	76, 150, 152, 154
Cheongju	청주	淸州	30, 44, 58, 63
Cheongnyangsan	청량산	淸凉山	33
Cheongok seowon	천곡서원	川谷書院	39
cheonin gameung seol	천인감응설	天人感應說	50
cheonin habil	천인합일	天人合一	31, 49
cheonin hapdeok	천인합덕	天人合德	52
cheonin sanggwan seol	천인상관설	天人相關說	50
cheonseok gohwang	천석고황	泉石膏肓	59
Cheonyeondae	천연대	天淵臺	114, 115
Choe Chi-won	최치원	崔致遠	31, 89
Choe Ik-hyeon	최익현	崔益鉉	46
Choe San-du	최산두	崔山斗	149
choheongwan	초헌관	初獻官	22
choya usaeng	초야우생	草野愚生	59
chuk	축	祝	19

chukgwan	/ 축관	/ 祝官	19
chuksi	/ 축시	/ 丑時	21
Chunchu	/ 춘추	/ 春秋	24
chung	/ 충	/ 充	20, 85
Chungan	/ 충안 (숭안)	/ 崇安	56
Chungcheongbuk-do	/ 충청북도	/ 忠淸北道	63
Chungcheong-do	/ 충청도	/ 忠淸道	44, 84
Chungcheongnam-do	/ 충청남도	/ 忠淸南道	142
chunghyo	/ 충효	/ 忠孝	107
Chungnyeol seowon	/ 충렬서원	/ 忠烈書院	31
Chusa	/ 추사	/ 秋史	127
chwibyeong i mandae	/ 취병이만대	/ 翠屛宜晚對	159
Chwihandae	/ 취한대	/ 翠寒臺	99, 104
Daedunsan	/ 대둔산	/ 大芚山	143
Daegu	/ 대구	/ 大邱	39, 135
Daehak	/ 대학	/ 大學	24
Daenisan	/ 대니산	/ 戴尼山	137, 138
Daeseongjeon	/ 대성전	/ 大成殿	14, 67
Daewongun	/ 대원군	/ 大院君	27, 43, 44, 45, 46, 47, 155, 170
Dalseonggun	/ 달성군	/ 達城郡	135
dancheong	/ 단청	/ 丹靑	132, 134
dang	/ 당	/ 堂	76
Danyang	/ 단양	/ 丹陽	108
dao	/ 다오 (도)	/ 道	89
darak	/ 다락		74
Deogyusan	/ 덕유산	/ 德裕山	132
deok	/ 덕	/ 德	52, 90
Deokbong seowon	/ 덕봉서원	/ 德峰書院	71
Deokcheon	/ 덕천	/ 德川	88
Deokcheon seowon	/ 덕천서원	/ 德川書院	30, 42, 69, 71, 88, 91
Deokseong seowon	/ 덕성서원		41
do	/ 도	/ 道	89, 135
Dodong gok	/ 도동곡	/ 道東曲	100
Dodong seowon	/ 도동서원	/ 道東書院	28, 29, 34, 41, 69, 74, 76, 81, 85, 86, 87, 89, 90, 91, 93, 94, 95, 135, 136, 137, 138, 139, 140, 141, 142
dohak	/ 도학	/ 道學	7, 13
dohak jeongchi	/ 도학정치	/ 道學政治	13
dol	/ 돌	/ 腯	20, 85
Donam	/ 돈암	/ 遯巖	88, 142

Donam seowon	돈암서원	遯巖書院	7, 29, 30, 34, 72, 87, 88, 142, 144, 145, 146, 147
dong	동	東	89, 135, 152
dongbang ohyeon	동방오현	東方五賢	14
Dongchundang	동춘당	同春堂	146
Dongchwibyeong	동취병	東翠屏	33
Dongguk wonurok	동국원우록	東國院宇錄	169
Dong Gwangmyeongsil	동광명실	東光明室	109, 117, 118
dongjae	동재	東齋	67, 68, 74, 77
dongmu	동무	東廡	67
Dongnakdang	독락당	獨樂堂	60, 61, 121, 123
Dongnak seowon	동락서원	東洛書院	89
Dong Zhongshu	동종슈 (동중서)	董仲舒	50, 51
Dosan	도산	陶山	32, 33, 58, 59, 61, 88, 107, 108, 111, 112, 116
Dosan jabyeong	도산잡영	陶山雜詠	33, 112
Dosan jabyeong byeonggi	도산잡영병기	陶山雜詠幷記	58
Dosan seodang	도산서당	陶山書堂	62, 108, 109, 110, 111, 112, 113, 114, 115, 116
Dosan seowon do	도산서원도	陶山書院圖	62
Dosan seowon	도산서원	陶山書院	16, 19, 20, 28, 30, 33, 34, 40, 41, 42, 69, 75, 78, 80, 81, 84, 85, 88, 90, 93, 94, 107, 108, 109, 112, 114, 115, 116, 117, 119, 120, 153, 170
Dosan sibi gok	도산십이곡	陶山十二曲	32, 58
dotong	도통	道通	65
doyusa	도유사	都有司	25
du	두	豆	83
Du Fu	두푸 (두보)	杜甫	159
eumbongnye	음복례	飮福禮	21, 163
Eunbyeong	은병	隱屏	58
Eungdodang	응도당	凝道堂	144, 145, 146, 147
fengshui	펑슈이 (풍수)	風水	28, 31
Fujian	푸지앤 (복건)	福建	56
Gaepyeong-ni	개평리	介平里	129
gam	감	坎	136
gangdang	강당	講堂	41, 74, 77
Gang Ik	강익	姜翼	132
gangjang	강장	講長	25
Gangneung	강릉	江陵	39, 82
gangwon	강원	講院	77

Gangwon-do	/ 강원도	/ 江原道	157
gasa	/ 가사	/ 歌詞	32
geogyeong gungni	/ 거경궁리	/ 居敬窮理	60, 91
Geogyeongjae	/ 거경재	/ 居敬齋	91, 136, 144
geoin	/ 거인	/ 居仁	93
Geoinjae	/ 거인재	/ 居仁齋	93, 136
Geonjisan	/ 건지산	/ 搴芝山	108
geoui	/ 거의	/ 居義	93
Geouijae	/ 거의재	/ 居義齋	93
geumdang	/ 금당	/ 金堂	77
Geumo seowon	/ 금오서원	/ 金烏書院	29, 41, 42, 69, 88
Geumsadam	/ 금사담	/ 金沙潭	63
geun	/ 근	/ 斤	22
gi	/ 기	/ 氣	11
Giho	/ 기호	/ 畿湖	18
Gil Jae	/ 길재	/ 吉再	13, 29, 42
Gimpo	/ 김포	/ 金浦	29
Gimyo sahwa	/ 기묘사화	/ 己卯士禍	10
Gisan	/ 기산	/ 岐山	88
Gisan-ri	/ 기산리	/ 岐山里	148
Goam	/ 고암	/ 鼓巖	154
Gogun gugok	/ 곡운구곡	/ 谷雲九曲	58
Goheung	/ 고흥	/ 高興	82
gojik	/ 고직	/ 庫直	118
gojiksa	/ 고직사	/ 庫直舍	84, 99, 109, 118, 122, 130, 144, 150, 156
Gojong	/ 고종	/ 高宗	27, 43, 44, 82
Gokguam	/ 곡구암	/ 谷口巖	115
gon	/ 곤	/ 坤	91
gongnon	/ 공론	/ 公論	27
Goryeo	/ 고려	/ 高麗	6, 8, 10, 11, 12, 13, 15, 29, 36, 77, 98
Gosan	/ 고산	/ 高山	58
Gosan gugok ga	/ 고산구곡가	/ 高山九曲歌	58
Gosan seowon	/ 고산서원	/ 高山書院	34
Gounsa	/ 고운사	/ 孤雲寺	143
gu	/ 구	/ 求	90
Gubong	/ 구봉	/ 龜峯	143
gwe	/ 궤		82
gugok	/ 구곡	/ 九曲	56, 58
gugok do	/ 구곡도	/ 九曲圖	56, 57

guin	구인	求仁	90
Guindang	구인당	求仁堂	76, 90, 91, 122, 124, 125, 127, 128
Guji-myeon	구지면	求智面	135
Gusan seowon	구산서원	丘山書院	39
Gwak	곽	郭	137
gwanbun	관분	盥盆	86
Gwanghaegun	광해군	光海君	14, 42, 43, 44
Gwangyeongji	광영지	光影池	156
gwansewi	관세위	盥洗位	86, 130, 144
gwon	권	卷	23
Gwon Sang-ha	권상하	權尙夏	45
Gyedang	계당	溪堂	111
Gyejeong	계정	溪亭	61, 121, 123
gyeol	결	結	26
Gyeomjae	겸재	謙齋	62
gyeong	경	敬	91, 103, 104
Gyeongbonggak	경봉각	敬奉閣	45
gyeonggak	경각	經閣	122, 127
gyeongja	경자	敬字	103
Gyeongjanggak	경장각	敬藏閣	149, 150, 151
gyeongja rock	경자암	敬字岩	99, 103, 104
Gyeongjong	경종	景宗	43, 44
Gyeongju	경주	慶州	30, 39, 42, 61, 121
gyeongmul chiji	격물치지	格物致知	53, 60
Gyeongnyeomjeong	경렴정	景濂亭	99, 102, 103
Gyeongsangbuk-do	경상북도	慶尙北道	98, 154
Gyeongsang-do	경상도	慶尙道	8, 13, 37, 41. 42, 46, 84, 102
gyeongui	경의	敬義	92
Gyeonguidang	경의당	敬義堂	91
gyeongui haerip	경의해립	敬義偕立	92
gyesaengbi	계생비	繫牲碑	86, 150
Gyesang	계상	溪上	61, 62
Gyesang jeonggeo do	계상정거도	溪上靜居圖	62
Gyesang seodang	계상서당	溪上書堂	62, 108, 111
Gyogu	교구	郊丘	65
Haeju	해주	海州	58, 128
Haeripjae	해립재	偕立齋	91, 92
Hahoe	하회	河回	35, 155, 157
Haim-ni	하임리	下林里	88, 142
hakgu	학구	學求	92

Hakgujae	학구재	學求齋	92, 99, 106
hamabi	하마비	下馬碑	72
hamaseok	하마석	下馬石	72, 73, 130, 144, 150
Hamyang	함양	咸陽	29, 39, 128, 129, 137
Hamyang-gun	함양군	咸陽郡	128
Han	한	漢	50, 51
Hangang	한강	寒岡	142
hangnyeong	학령	學令	23
Hanhwondang	한훤당	寒暄堂	135, 137
Hanjangsa	한장사	汗丈舍	150
Hanjonjae	한존재	閑存齋	117
Hanquan jingshe	한츄앤징셔 (한천정사)	寒泉精舍	57
Hanseoam	한서암	寒棲庵	110, 111
Han Seok-bong	한석봉	韓石峰	117, 127
Hanyang	한양	漢陽	18, 128
Hapcheon-gun	합천군	陜川郡	137
Haseo	하서	河西	148
Heo Mok	허목	許穆	29
heongwan	헌관	獻官	19
Heonjong	헌종	憲宗	43, 44
Heungam seowon	흥암서원	興巖書院	71, 75
Hoeam	회암	晦庵	121
Hoejae	회재	晦齋	120
Hoeyeon seowon	회연서원	檜淵書院	30
hogo mini guji	호고민이구지	好古敏以求之	93
holgi	홀기	笏記	19
hongui	홍의	弘毅	93
Honguijae	홍의재	弘毅齋	78, 93, 109, 117
hongsalmun	홍살문	紅箭門	71, 72, 73, 130, 144, 146, 150, 152
Huicheon	희천	熙川	138
Huiyan	휘야	晦庵	121
hungupa	훈구파	勳舊派	10
hunjang	훈장	訓長	25
Hwaam seowon	화암서원	畵巖書院	39
Hwacheon	화천	華川	58
hwagyeon	확연	廓然	94, 152
Hwagyeollu	확연루	廓然樓	74, 94, 150, 152, 154
Hwanghae-do	황해도	黃海道	58
Hwang Heui	황희	黃喜	88
Hwangnyong-myeon	황룡면	黃龍面	148

hwanju	환주	喚主	94
Hwanjumun	환주문	喚主門	94, 95, 136, 139, 140
Hwarim gugok	화림구곡	花林九曲	132
Hwasan	화산	花山	31, 35, 157
Hwasan seowon	화산서원	花山書院	31
Hwayang	화양	華陽	46, 58, 63
Hwayang-dong	화양동	華陽洞	45, 63
Hwayang mukpae	화양묵패	華陽墨牌	45
Hwayang seowon	화양서원	華陽書院	30, 45, 46
hyanggyo	향교	鄕校	8
hyangni	향리	鄕吏	12
hyangsa	향사	享祀	19
hyangyak	향약	鄕約	27, 75
hyeommun	협문	夾門	84
Hyeongaru	현가루	絃歌樓	74, 94
Hyeonjong	현종	顯宗	43, 44, 69
Hyeonpung	현풍	玄風	42, 135, 137
Hyojong	효종	孝宗	14, 42, 43, 44
i	이	理	11
i	이	履	114
Ibdeokmun	입덕문	入德門	144
igi	이기	理氣	52
Ildu	일두	一蠹	128, 131
ilsin	일신	日新	92
Ilsinjae	일신재	日新齋	92, 99, 105,
Imcheon seowon	임천서원	臨川書院	29
Imgo seowon	임고서원	臨皐書院	14, 29, 39, 41, 88
Im-ni	임리	林里	143
in	인	仁	90
indo	인도	人道	52
Injo	인조	仁祖	14, 42, 43, 44
Ipgyodang	입교당	立敎堂	36, 91, 156, 160, 161, 162
Isan seowon	이산서원	伊山書院	24, 39, 40
Isan seowon wongyu	이산서원원규	伊山書院院規	40
iu boin	이우보인	以友輔仁	92
jadeuk gyoyuk	자득교육	自得敎育	23
Jaedong seowon	재동서원	齋洞書院	82
jaejang	재장	齋長	25
jaesa	재사	齋舍	41, 77
jagi naejaehwa	자기내재화	自己內在化	53

Jagye	자계	紫溪	122
Jagye seowon	자계서원	紫溪書院	85
jak	작	爵	83
jangui	장의	掌議	25
Jang Hyeongwang	장현광	張顯光	89
jangpangak	장판각	藏板閣	78, 109, 118, 130, 136, 144, 146, 150, 156
jangseogak	장서각	藏書閣	71, 79, 99, 107, 150
Jangseong	장성	長城	30
Jangseong-gun	장성군	長城郡	148
Jaoksan	자옥산	紫玉山	88, 124
Jaun seowon	자운서원	紫雲書院	31
jegigo	제기고	祭器庫	85, 109, 119, 120
Jeolla-do	전라도	全羅道	84, 138
Jeollanam-do	전라남도	全羅南道	148
jeong	정	丁	19
Jeongeuijae	정의재	精義齋	144
Jeongeup	정읍	井邑	30
Jeong Gu	정구	鄭逑	30, 142
Jeonghoedang	정회당	靜會堂	143, 144
jeongja	정자	亭子	54
Jeongjo	정조	正祖	43, 44, 151
Jeong Mong-ju	정몽주	鄭夢周	13, 14, 29, 31, 81, 137
jeongnyodae	정료대	庭燎臺	87, 109, 122, 156
Jeongo daebang	전고대방	典故大方	169
Jeong On	정온	鄭蘊	132
jeongsa	정사	精舍	54, 57, 62
Jeong Seon	정선	鄭敾	62
Jeongudang	정우당	淨友塘	109, 113
Jeong Yeo-chang	정여창	鄭汝昌	14, 29, 88, 92, 121, 128, 129, 132, 133, 134
Jeongyodang	전교당	典教堂	20, 109, 117, 118
jeonsacheong	전사청	典祀廳	71, 79, 84, 85, 99, 107, 119, 122, 130, 132, 136, 144, 150, 156
Jeorusa	절우사	節友社	113, 115
Jeungbanso	증반소	蒸飯所	136
Jeungbo munheon bigo	증보문헌비고	增補文獻備考	169
jibui isaeng	집의이생	集義以生	91
Jibuijae	집의재	集義齋	91
jigil	직일	直日	25

Jigok-myeon	지곡면	池谷面	129
jigwol	직월	直月	25
jikbang	직방	直方	92
Jikbangjae	직방재	直方齋	92, 99, 105
Jindeokjae	진덕재	進德齋	150
Jindomun	진도문	進道門	93, 94, 109, 116, 118
Jingbirok	징비록	懲毖錄	155
jingshe	징셔 (정사)	精舍	57
jinsa	진사	進士	24
jipchanja	집찬자	執饌者	19
jipgang	집강	執綱	25
Jiphyeonjeon	집현전	集賢殿	11
jipsa	집사	執事	19
jirak	지락	至樂	92
Jirakjae	지락재	至樂齋	92, 99, 106
jiuqu	쥬추 (구곡)	九曲	56
Jodurok	조두록	俎豆錄	169
Jo Gwang-jo	조광조	趙光祖	10, 13, 14, 31, 121
Jo Heon	조헌	趙憲	29
Jo Mok	조목	趙穆	119
Jondeoksa	존덕사	尊德祠	156, 161, 162
jongheongwan	종헌관	終獻官	22
Jongmyo	종묘	宗廟	11, 65
Jongseong	종성	鐘城	129
Joseon	조선	朝鮮	1, 6, 7, 8, 9, 10, 11, 12, 13, 14, 15, 18, 22, 25, 31, 35, 36, 37, 39, 40, 41, 42, 45, 47, 48, 56, 57, 66, 74, 78, 79, 81, 107, 108, 114, 129, 131, 143, 164, 169, 170, 171
Joseon wangjo sillok	조선왕조실록	朝鮮王朝實錄	169
Jo Sik	조식	曺植	30, 42
jucheong	주청	酒廳	109, 119, 120
Jukgyeji	죽계지	竹溪誌	101
Jukgyesa	죽계사	竹溪辭	100
Jukgye seowon	죽계서원	竹溪書院	39
Jukgyesu	죽계수	竹溪水	32, 99, 100, 101, 102, 103
Jundomun	준도문	遵道門	130
jungjeong	중정	中正	90, 119
Jungjeongdang	중정당	中正堂	90, 91, 135, 136, 137, 138, 139, 140
Jungjong	중종	中宗	10, 43, 44, 120, 138
Jungnim seowon	죽림서원	竹林書院	145

Jungyong	중용	中庸	24, 90
Ju Se-bung	주세붕	周世鵬	8, 22, 32, 36, 98, 100, 101, 102, 104, 107
kan	칸(간)	間	62, 63, 69, 73, 76, 78, 80, 81, 82, 105, 106, 110, 112, 113, 117, 118, 119, 120, 125, 133, 134, 147, 148, 159, 160
Kim Goeng-pil	김굉필	金宏弼	13, 14, 31, 42, 89, 121, 129, 135, 137, 142, 146
Kim Gye-hwi	김계휘	金繼輝	145
Kim In-hu	김인후	金麟厚	30, 94, 149, 151, 152, 153, 154
Kim Jang-saeng	김장생	金長生	30, 142, 143, 145, 147, 148
Kim Jeong-hui	김정희	金正喜	127
Kim Jip	김집	金集	146
Kim Jong-jik	김종직	金宗直	13, 29, 41, 129, 137, 138
Kim Mun-jeong	김문정	金文鼎	98
Kim Seong-il	김성일	金誠一	29
Kim Su-jeung	김수증	金壽增	58
Kim Suk-ja	김숙자	金叔滋	13
kkotdam	꽃담		146
Li Bo	리보 (이발)	李渤	103
Loyang	로양 (낙양)	洛陽	89
Lu	루 (노)	魯	89
Lushan	루샨 (여산)	廬山	32, 103
Lushan Guoxue	루샨구어슈에 (여산국학)	廬山國學	103
Lushan Guozijian	루샨구어쯔지앤 (여산국자감)	廬山國子監	103
Maengja	맹자	孟子	24
mandae	만대	晚對	159
Mandaeru	만대루	晚對樓	36, 73, 74, 157, 158, 159, 160, 161
Mandongmyo	만동묘	萬東廟	44, 45, 46, 47
mangnyewi	망례위	望瘞位	86, 87, 142, 150
mangnyowi	망료위	望燎位	87
Mangyeongdae	만경대	晚景臺	45
maru	마루		62
Micheon seowon	미천서원	眉泉書院	29
Ming	밍 (명)	明	45
Mingujae	민구재	敏求齋	93, 122
Miryang	밀양	密陽	29, 41
Mongcheon	몽천	蒙泉	113
mongi yangjeong	몽이양정	蒙以養正	92
Mubyeollu	무변루	無邊樓	74, 94, 122, 123, 124, 125, 126,

	127, 128
Muhaksan / 무학산 / 舞鶴山	29, 124
Munheon seowon / 문헌서원 / 文憲書院	41, 78, 128
munjip / 문집 / 文集	118, 127
Munmyo / 문묘 / 文廟	14, 66, 101
Munseonggongmyo / 문성공묘 / 文成公廟	36, 37, 99, 106, 107
Muo sahwa / 무오사화 / 戊午士禍	10
Museong seowon / 무성서원 / 武城書院	24, 30, 74, 80, 89, 94
myeong / 명 / 明	90, 91
myeongdang / 명당 / 明堂	65
myeongdangsu / 명당수 / 明堂水	122, 123, 125
Myeongjong / 명종 / 明宗	14, 37, 39, 41, 42, 43, 44, 69, 102, 105
Myeongnyundang / 명륜당 / 明倫堂	37, 67, 69, 77, 99, 104, 105
myeongseong / 명성 / 明誠	92, 133
Myeongseongdang / 명성당 / 明誠堂	76, 90, 91, 130, 133
Naejuk-ri / 내죽리 / 內竹里	98
naemun / 내문 / 內門	41, 80
naesammun / 내삼문 / 內三門	80, 109, 136, 139, 142, 144, 146, 147, 150, 156, 165
Nagyang / 낙양 / 洛陽	89
Naju / 나주 / 羅州	29
Nakcheon / 낙천 / 洛川	34
Nakdonggang / 낙동강 / 洛東江	29, 35, 113, 114, 115, 116, 128, 135, 138, 155, 157, 159
Namgye seowon / 남계서원 / 灆溪書院	14, 29, 34, 39, 41, 69, 74, 75, 76, 78, 81, 84, 85, 88, 90, 91, 92, 128, 129, 130, 131, 132, 133
nobi / 노비 / 奴婢	26, 36, 38, 148
Noneo / 논어 / 論語	24
Nogang seowon / 노강서원 / 魯岡書院	30, 69
Nongun jeongsa / 농운정사 / 隴雲精舍	109, 110, 111
Nonsan / 논산 / 論山	30, 69, 142
Noron / 노론 / 老論	44, 45, 46
nu / 누 / 樓	74
nujeong / 누정 / 樓亭	54
numaru / 누마루	63, 125
numun / 누문 / 樓門	67, 74
Nupan go / 누판고 / 鏤板考	23
Obong seowon / 오봉서원 / 五峯書院	82
oemun / 외문 / 外門	41, 73

oesammun / 외삼문 / 外三門		73, 146
Ogyeon jeongsa / 옥연정사 / 玉淵精舍		155
ohyeon / 오현 / 五賢		14
Okcheon seowon / 옥천서원 / 玉川書院		31
Okdong seowon / 옥동서원 / 玉洞書院		88
okgyu / 옥규 / 玉圭		100
Okjingak / 옥진각 / 玉振閣		109, 120
Oksan seowon / 옥산서원 / 玉山書院		7, 29, 30, 34, 41, 42, 69, 72, 74, 75, 76, 87, 88, 90, 91, 93, 120, 121, 122, 123, 124, 126, 127, 128, 153
ondol / 온돌		63, 76, 77, 105, 106, 111, 113, 117, 118, 120, 125, 127, 133, 134, 147, 160
Paju / 파주 / 坡州		29, 31
Pasan seowon / 파산서원 / 坡山書院		29
Piram / 필암 / 筆巖		88
Piram seowon / 필암서원 / 筆巖書院		28, 30, 31, 70, 71, 74, 75, 76, 85, 86, 87, 88, 94, 148, 149, 150, 151, 152, 153, 154
Pocheon / 포천 / 抱川		31
Pungak seodang / 풍악서당 / 豊岳書堂		155
Pungcheon-myeon / 풍천면 / 豊川面		154
Punggi / 풍기 / 豊基		8, 29, 36, 39, 41, 98, 102, 104, 110, 128
pungsu / 풍수 / 風水		31, 66
pungwol mubyeon / 풍월무변 / 風月無邊		94
Pungyeongnu / 풍영루 / 風咏樓		74, 130, 134
Pyeongan-do / 평안도 / 平安道		138
Qin / 친 (진) / 秦		49
li / 리 / 里		33
saaek / 사액 / 賜額		36
saaek seowon / 사액서원 / 賜額書院		36
sadaebu / 사대부 / 士大夫		6, 7
sadang / 사당 / 祠堂		18, 41, 80, 130, 136
saekjang / 색장 / 色掌		25
saengdan / 생단 / 牲檀		85, 86, 99, 130, 136, 142
saengganpum / 생간품 / 牲看品		85
saengwon / 생원 / 生員		24
Sagye / 사계 / 沙溪		142
sahak / 사학 / 四學		66
Sajik / 사직 / 社稷		65
Sajikdan / 사직단 / 社稷壇		11
sajungwan / 사준관 / 司罇官		19

samasi / 사마시 / 司馬試		24
sammun / 삼문 / 三門		69
Sancheong / 산청 / 山淸		30, 42
Sancheonjae / 산천재 / 山天齋		30
sang / 상 / 尙		90
Sangdeoksa / 상덕사 / 尙德祠		20, 81, 90, 109, 119
Sanggye / 상계 / 上溪		110
Sangju / 상주 / 尙州		88
sarangchae / 사랑채		84, 129
sarim / 사림 / 士林		1, 2, 7, 9, 10, 11, 12, 13, 14, 15, 25, 27, 31, 39, 40, 42, 54, 67, 69, 129, 143, 165, 170
saron / 사론 / 士論		27
Sejo / 세조 / 世祖		11
Seoae / 서애 / 西厓		154
Seoak seowon / 서악서원 / 西岳書院		39, 41, 69, 85
Seochwibyeong / 서취병 / 西翠屛		33
seodang / 서당 / 書堂		12
Seo Gwangmyeongsil / 서광명실 / 西光明室		109, 117, 118
Seogyeong / 서경 / 書經		24
Seogye seowon / 서계서원 / 西溪書院		69
seojae / 서재 / 西齋		67, 68, 74, 77
seokdeung / 석등 / 石燈		87, 136, 150
seokgasan / 석가산 / 石假山		129
Seomhakjeon / 섬학전 / 贍學錢		98
seomu / 서무 / 西廡		67
seong / 성 / 誠		90, 91
Seonggyungwan / 성균관 / 成均館		11, 66
seong jeuk i / 성즉리 / 性卽理		52
Seongjong / 성종 / 成宗		9, 13
Seongju / 성주 / 星州		30, 39
seongmyeong / 성명 / 性命		52
seongsaengdan / 성생단 / 省牲壇		103
Seong Su-chim / 성수침 / 成守琛		29
seonhyeon / 선현 / 先賢		8
Seonjo / 선조 / 宣祖		14, 41, 42, 43, 44, 69, 116
Seonsan / 선산 / 善山		29, 42
seowon / 서원 / 書院		1, 2, 3, 7, 9, 16, 24, 27, 29, 36, 46, 47, 54, 68, 69, 70, 90, 134, 155, 165, 166, 169, 170, 171
Seowon deungnok / 서원등록 / 書院謄錄		169
seowongi / 서원기 / 書院記		39

Seo Yu-gu	서유구	徐有榘	23
Sesimdae	세심대	洗心臺	122, 123, 124
Shao Yong	샤오용 (소옹)	邵雍	49
Shenzong	션종 (신종)	神宗	45
Sigyeong	시경	詩經	24
Silla	신라	新羅	77
Simgok seowon	심곡서원	深谷書院	31, 71, 72
Sim Tong-won	심통원	沈通原	38, 102
sindobigak	신도비각	神道碑閣	122, 126, 127
Sindokjae	신독재	愼獨齋	146
Sin Gwang-han	신광한	申光漢	102
Sinjae	신재	新齋	149
sinju	신주	神主	18
sinmun	신문	神門	41, 79, 99, 129
Sobaek	소백	小白	100
sochuk	소축	小畜	90
Sohak	소학	小學	24
Sollye	솔례		137
Song	송	宋	6, 10, 39, 49, 51, 93, 103
Song Ik-pil	송익필	宋翼弼	143
Song Jun-gil	송준길	宋浚吉	146
Song Si-yeol	송시열	宋時烈	30, 42, 45, 58, 63, 94, 146, 152
Sosu seowon	소수서원	紹修書院	9, 14, 16, 22, 24, 29, 32, 36, 37, 39, 41, 68, 69, 81, 82, 89, 92, 98, 99, 100, 102, 103, 104, 105, 107, 128, 131
Ssanggye seowon	쌍계서원	雙溪書院	42
ssijok burak	씨족부락	氏族部落	27
Sudong-myeon	수동면	水東面	128
sugi chiin	수기치인	修己治人	6
Sukjong	숙종	肅宗	24, 26, 43, 44, 70
Suksusa	숙수사	宿水寺	101, 102
Suncheon	순천	順天	31, 138
Sungnyesa	숭례사	崇禮祠	144, 145
Sunguijae	숭의재	崇義齋	150
Sunheung	순흥	順興	8, 32, 36, 101
Sunheung-myeon	순흥면	順興面	98
Sunjo	순조	純祖	43, 44
Suwollu	수월루	水月樓	74, 94, 136, 137, 139, 140, 141
Taengniji	택리지	擇里志	164
Taesan	태산	泰山	30, 31

Tang / 탕 (당) / 唐		51, 103, 159
Toegye / 퇴계 / 退溪		14, 18, 19, 20, 25, 30, 31, 32, 33, 34, 36, 37, 38, 39, 40, 42, 54, 57, 58, 59, 61, 62, 69, 81, 90, 102, 104, 105, 107, 108, 110, 111, 112, 113, 114, 115, 116, 118, 119, 120, 121, 129, 135, 149, 155, 170
toetkan / 툇칸 / 退間		82
toenmaru / 툇마루		107
Togye / 토계 / 兎溪		108
u / 우 / 祐		152
Uam / 우암 / 尤庵		146
Udongsa / 우동사 / 祐東祠		87, 150, 151, 152, 154
ui / 의 / 義		91
Ujeo seowon / 우저서원 / 牛渚書院		29
umul / 우물		106, 119
U Tak / 우탁 / 禹倬		89
Wallakjae / 완락재 / 玩樂齋		113, 114
wigi jihak / 위기지학 / 爲己之學		40
wijeong cheoksa ron / 위정척사론 / 爲政斥邪論		46
Wolbong seowon / 월봉서원 / 月峯書院		22
Wolcheon / 월천 / 月川趙穆		119
wongi / 원기 / 院記		77
wongyu / 원규 / 院規		26
won-i / 원이 / 院貳		25
won-im / 원임 / 院任		25
wonjang / 원장 / 院長		25
wonjung yurim / 원중유림 / 院中儒林		25
Wonpyeong-ni / 원평리 / 院坪里		128
Wuyi / 우이 (무이) / 武夷		56, 57, 58, 63
Wuyi jingshe / 우이징셔 (무이정사) / 武夷精舍		56, 57
Wuyi jingshe zayong bingji / 우이징셔자용빙지 (무이정사잡용병기) / 武夷精舍雜詠幷記		58
Wuyi jiuqu / 우이쥬추 (무이구곡) / 武夷九曲		57
Wuyishan / 우이샨 (무이산) / 武夷山		55, 56, 57
Wuyishan zhi / 우이샨쯔 (무이산지) / 武夷山志		56
Wuyi zhaoge / 우이자오거 (무이도가) / 武夷櫂歌		57
yang / 양 / 陽		90, 141
yangban / 양반 / 兩班		121, 129
Yangdong / 양동 / 良洞		121
Yang Ja-jing / 양자징 / 梁子澂		154
Yangjeongjae / 양정재 / 養正齋		92, 130, 133, 134

Yangjinam	양진암	養眞庵	108
Yangjinjae	양진재	兩進齋	91
Yang San-bo	양산보	梁山甫	154
Yangseongdang	양성당	養性堂	144, 145, 146, 147
Yaro	야로	野老	137
ye	예 (례)	禮	49, 65, 89
ye	예 (례)	瘞	87
Yean	예안	禮安	39, 42, 61, 108, 115
yebu	예부	禮部	65
yehak	예학	禮學	42
yeje	예제	禮制	65, 148
yeje geonchuk	예제건축	禮制建築	65
Yeokdong seowon	역동서원	易東書院	39, 41, 89, 118
Yeokkyeong	역경	易經	89
Yeoljeong	열정	洌井	20, 109, 115
Yeongbong seowon	영봉서원	迎鳳書院	39, 40
Yeongcheon	영천	永川, 榮川	29, 39, 88
Yeongjeonggak	영정각	影幀閣	99, 107
Yeongjisan	영지산	靈芝山	33
Yeongjo	영조	英祖	43, 44, 70
yeongmae	영매	咏梅	134
Yeongmaeheon	영매헌	咏梅軒	92, 93, 134
Yeongnangmun	역락문	亦樂門	93, 122, 123, 125
Yeongnak seojae	역락서재	亦樂書齋	109
Yeongnam	영남	嶺南	18
Yeongyeong seowon	연경서원	研經書院	39, 40
Yeonhwasan	연화산	蓮花山	132
Yeonsan	연산	連山	143, 145, 146
Yeonsangun	연산군	燕山君	10, 11
Yeonsan-myeon	연산면	連山面	88, 142, 143
Yeoreup wonu sajeok	열읍원우사적	列邑院宇事蹟	169
Yerim seowon	예림서원	禮林書院	29, 41, 69, 75, 86
Yi Eon-jeok	이언적	李彦迪	14, 30, 42, 61, 120, 121, 123
Yi Ha-eung	이하응	李昰應	43
Yi Hang-bok	이항복	李恒福	31
Yi Hwang	이황	李滉	14, 19, 31, 34, 38, 90, 102, 129
Yi I	이이	李珥	14, 18, 31, 43, 58, 143
Yijing	이징	易經	89
Yi Jung-hwan	이중환	李重煥	164
yin	인 (음)	陰	90, 141

Yi San-hae / 이산해 / 李山海   127
Yizong / 이종 (의종) / 毅宗   45
yo / 요 (료) / 燎   87
yogeoseok / 요거석 / 燎炬石   87
Yongchu / 용추 / 龍湫   124
Yongin / 용인 / 龍仁   31
Yuan / 유앤 (원) / 元   6, 89, 98
Yuelu / 유에루 (악록) / 岳麓   57
yuhoe / 유회 / 儒會   25
Yujeongmun / 유정문 / 幽貞門   109, 114, 115
Yu Jin / 유진 / 柳袗   161
Yulgok / 율곡 / 栗谷   14, 18, 42, 58, 143
Yungu / 윤구 (운곡) / 雲谷   63
Yun Hwang / 윤황 / 尹煌   30
yurim / 유림 / 儒林   25
yusa / 유사 / 有司   25
Yu Seong-nyong / 유성룡 / 柳成龍   35, 155, 157, 160, 162, 163

Zhang Zai / 쟝자이 (장재) / 張載   49
Zhongyong / 종용 (중용) / 中庸   90
Zhou Dunyi / 조우둔이 (주돈이) / 周敦   49, 93, 94, 134
Zhulin jingshe / 주린징셔(죽림정사) / 竹林精舍   57
Zhu Xi / 주시 (주희) / 朱熹   6, 15, 23, 32, 46, 49, 52, 56, 57, 58, 63, 66, 93, 98, 103, 120, 121, 139